Spectatorship

EDITED BY
ROXANNE SAMER
AND WILLIAM
WHITTINGTON

Spectatorship

Shifting Theories of Gender, Sexuality, and Media

University of Texas Press
Austin

Printed in the United States of America
First edition, 2017

Requests for permission to reproduce material from this work should be sent to:

Permissions
University of Texas Press
PO Box 7819
Austin, TX 78713-7819
utpress.utexas.edu/rp-form

♾ The paper used in this book meets the minimum requirements of ANSI/NISO Z39.48-1992 (R1997) (Permanence of Paper).

Library of Congress Cataloging-in-Publication Data

Names: Samer, Roxanne, 1986– editor. | Whittington, William (William Brian), editor.
Title: Spectatorship : shifting theories of gender, sexuality, and media / edited by Roxanne Samer and William Whittington.
Description: First edition. | Austin : University of Texas Press, 2017. | Includes bibliographical references and index.
Identifiers: LCCN 2016053411 | ISBN 978-1-4773-1349-7 (cloth : alk. paper) | ISBN 978-1-4773-1376-3 (pbk. : alk. paper) | ISBN 978-1-4773-1377-0 (library e-book) | ISBN 978-1-4773-1378-7 (non-library e-book)
Subjects: LCSH: Spectator (Los Angeles, Calif.) | Gender identity in mass media—History. | Sex role in mass media—History. | Film criticism. | Motion picture literature—History and criticism—Periodicals.
Classification: LCC P96.G44 S66 2017 | DDC 302.23081—dc23
LC record available at https://lccn.loc.gov/2016053411

doi:10.7560/313497

List of articles in the volume and year of first appearance

Benshoff, Harry M. "Resurrection of the Vampire and the Creation of Alternative Life: An Introduction to *Dark Shadows* Fan Culture." *Spectator* 13, no. 3 (1993): 50–61.

Bonomo, Elena. "The Rumors Are True!: *Gossip Girl* and the Cooptation of the Cult Fan." *Spectator* 30, no. 1 (2010): 35–38.

DeClue, Jennifer. "Lesbian Cop, Queer Killer: Leveraging Black Queer Women's Sexuality on HBO's *The Wire*." *Spectator* 31, no. 2 (2011): 53–62.

Everett, Anna. "'You Don't Know What It Is to Look White and Be Black': The Black Press Mediates Race in the Classic Hollywood Studio System, 1930–1940." Published under the original title: "'I Want the Same Things Other People Enjoy': The Black Press and the Classic Hollywood Studio System, 1930–40." *Spectator* 17, no. 1 (1996): 40–53.

Freedman, Eric. "From Excess to Access: Televising the Subculture." *Spectator* 14, no. 1 (1994): 44–55.

Griffin, Hollis. "Soap Slash: Gay Men Rewrite the World of Daytime Television Drama." *Spectator* 25, no. 1 (2005): 23–33.

Griffin, Sean. "Pronoun Trouble: The 'Queerness' of Animation." *Spectator* 15, no. 1 (1994): 94–109.

Kearney, Mary Celeste. "Of Fleiss and Men: The Transgressions and Containment of a Hollywood Madam." *Spectator* 15, no. 2 (1995): 8–21.

———. "Riot Grrrl: It's Not Just Music, It's Not Just Punk." *Spectator* 16, no. 1 (1995): 82–95.

Lawrence, Amy. "Feminine Discourse in *Blackmail*." *Spectator* 3, no. 2 (1984): 3–4.

Milliken, Christie. "The Articulation of Body and Space in *Speak Body*." *Spectator* 8, no. 1 (1987): 9–11.

Paulin, Scott D. "Unheard Sexualities?: Queer Theory and the Soundtrack." *Spectator* 17, no. 2 (1997): 37–49.

Sarkissian, Raffi. "Out on Stage: LGBT Politics of Entertainment Award Shows." *Spectator* 34, no. 1 (2014): 25–27, 29–31.

Scott, Suzanne. "The Trouble with Transmediation: Fandom's Negotiation of Transmedia Storytelling Systems." *Spectator* 30, no. 1 (2010): 30–34.
Studlar, Gaylyn. "Venus in Furs: Masoch, Deleuze, and the Films of von Sternberg." *Spectator* 4, no. 1 (1983): 7–8.
Tropiano, Stephen. "Joe Dallesandro—A 'Him' to the Gaze: *Flesh*, *Heat*, and *Trash*." *Spectator* 10, no. 1 (1989): 47–55.
Williams, Melissa. "'I Kinda Prefer to Be a Human Being': Roseanne Barr and Defining Working-Class Feminism and Authorship." *Spectator* 25, no. 2 (2005): 26–38.

Dedicated to Marsha Kinder

Contents

Acknowledgments

The editors wish to thank all the contributors to this volume for their generosity in allowing us to revisit their contributions to *Spectator—The University of Southern California Journal of Film and Television Criticism*. We are also indebted to Eleanor Huntington for her enthusiastic support in preparing the various articles for publication. Thanks also to Marsha Kinder and Kara Keeling for their insight and advice. The production of this collection was made possible by the School of Cinematic Arts at the University of Southern California. Finally, thanks to our editor Jim Burr for his assistance in the peer review and publication process.

Spectatorship

INTRODUCTION

Gender, Sexuality, and Media

Audience and Spectatorship

ROXANNE SAMER AND WILLIAM WHITTINGTON

The first issue of *Spectator* appeared in the spring of 1982 in newsprint form and was distributed widely to students, staff, and faculty at the University of Southern California (USC). The cover story profiled a visit by director Orson Welles (*Citizen Kane, Touch of Evil*) to one of the popular film courses in Norris Theater, and the cover image featured Steven Spielberg and George Lucas at the long-awaited groundbreaking for the first of two new cinema buildings on campus. Together these events signaled a commitment by USC to establishing the new School of Cinema-Television as an academic center to facilitate film and television production as well as film and television scholarship. In her brief mission statement for *Spectator*'s premier issue, founding editor Professor Marsha Kinder described the aims of the journal as threefold: "to provide a vehicle for our students' writing, to document and reflect on the diverse range of exciting film and television events that occur at USC, and to present our perspectives on the state of the art and the state of film and television discourse."[1] Not surprisingly for a journal called *Spectator*, issues of spectatorship would soon become central to the biannual publication.

During this same period, feminist film theory exerted incredible influence over the fledgling field of film studies and became part of the core curriculum of the Critical Studies Division at USC and other research institutions.[2] Early theories of film spectatorship, first articulated by Christian Metz, Raymond Bellour, Jean-Louis Baudry, and Stephen Heath, were fast being revised to consider questions of sexual difference and gendered desire.[3] By the start of the 1980s, British feminist film theorists Pam Cook, Claire Johnston, and Laura Mulvey had been publishing on cinema and the unconscious mechanisms of sexual difference for nearly a decade. Perhaps the most notable contribution came in 1975, when Mulvey published her canonical essay "Visual Pleasure and Narrative Cinema" in *Screen*. In the essay, Mulvey introduced a critical evaluation of the "male gaze" which she identified as central to cinematic codes in Hollywood cinema, and in the course of her argument, she called for a feminist avant-garde countercinema that would challenge this tradition.[4] Two years prior, Johnston had published a *Screen* pamphlet, entitled *Notes on Women's Cinema*, in which she claimed that in cinema the characterization of "woman as woman is largely absent," having been replaced by a sign merely constitutive of male power.[5] Rather than calling for the representation of real women on-screen, which was a goal of many 1970s feminist documentary filmmakers, of whom she was skeptical, Johnston advocated for the repurposing of cinematic signifiers. In a series of case studies, she analyzed the films of Dorothy Arzner and Ida Lupino, identifying them as exemplary models for such work. This scholarship called for not only new approaches to filmmaking but also new approaches to the study of spectatorship in order to consider issues of gendered desire, identification, and power within cinema.

Both Mulvey's and Johnston's essays would direct much of feminist film studies for the coming decades, encouraging scholars to reconsider film form, style, and ideology through feminist critiques of classical Hollywood cinema and giving filmmakers a chance to foster feminist alternatives to film practice, from script development to the direction of performers (and by extension film's labor practices). Although many foundational articles were first published in the United Kingdom, their concerns soon circulated throughout the United States and Australia, inspiring the establishment of new feminist film journals, conferences, and academic courses.[6] In varying ways, journals like *Jump Cut* (1974–present), *Camera Obscura* (1976–present), and the *Australian Journal of Screen Theory* (1976–1983) continued the work initiated in *Screen*. However, they also introduced new methodologies and critical models for their case studies. *Jump Cut* centralized issues of class and later race and sexuality to offer a socialist feminist approach to cinema, while the *Australian Journal of Screen Theory* detailed the traditions of Australian feminist films, which took a much different approach to sexism and female sexuality than the films that Johnston and Mulvey advocated.

USC's new journal soon joined the critical conversation, often challenging and complicating the arguments of early feminist film studies. In its third issue, *Spectator* published its first article on feminist film theory, Gaylyn Studlar's "Venus in Furs: Masoch, Deleuze, and the Films of von Sternberg" (reprinted in this volume). The essay reconsidered hierarchies of power and expanded our understanding of cinematic pleasure. Like other scholars engaging with Mulvey's and Johnston's work, Studlar and her peers submitted essays on classical Hollywood cinema and its representation of women, but frequently, as was the case for Studlar, they returned to the films central to early feminist film theory in order to complicate the theorists' often-stark characterizations of gendered forms of viewing. In other cases, *Spectator* published works, such as Amy Lawrence's essay on Hitchcock's *Blackmail* (also reprinted in this volume), that considered the lesser-studied examples of classical Hollywood filmmakers as a means of investigating unexplored formal and thematic elements as they related to gender. For Lawrence, spectatorship was not simply about the power of the image but also about the power of soundtrack to contain the female voice. Why, she asked, were all the Hollywood narrative voice-overs performed by men? And what impact did this have on the control of the narrative and the ability of women to tell their stories in their own voices? Before long the journal's contributors were interweaving the fields of psychoanalysis, semiotics, and audience studies to further expand contemporary understandings of spectatorship. They were also quick to challenge the centrality of sexual difference to feminist theoretical paradigms, analyzing how the structures of mainstream and avant-garde media represented, appealed to, and addressed queer people and people of color.

Given its proximity to Hollywood, USC's School of Cinematic Arts (renamed in 2006) could have relied solely on presenting students with the voices of directors, producers, and writers from within the industry; however, the faculty and graduate students in the Critical Studies Division (many of whom served as editors and writers for *Spectator*) demanded that the voices from alternative media be heard in classes and at special screening events, particularly the newly created venue known as Cinematheque108, established by Professor Michael Renov and Professor David E. James. As a result, the third issue of the journal also presented a retrospective on three female filmmakers (Donna Deitch, director of *Woman to Woman* and, later, the lesbian classic *Desert Hearts*; Stephanie

Rothman, *The Working Girls*; and Jane Weinstock, *Sigmund Freud's Dora*), all of whom were working outside the mainstream Hollywood system at the time in order to "interrogate the representation of women in American narrative cinema, while simultaneously offering new possibilities of survival for women in society."[7] These three filmmakers visited Professor and Chair Beverle Houston's graduate seminar in "Women and Film," and after screening their films, they discussed with Houston's students their varied approaches to directing and producing, new representational possibilities for women, and alternative forms of pleasure for women in cinema.[8] The death of Beverle Houston in 1988 from cancer was a great loss to the school and the journal, but her legacy endured through a scholarship fund for graduate conference travel and the dedication of the division's main seminar room, where similar courses on gender, sexuality, and race are still taught today. Around this same time in 1988, the journal switched from newsprint to a bound journal and became known as *The University of Southern California Journal of Film and Television Criticism—Spectator.* Its issues grew in length, and its editors began to expand the journal's breadth by including longer reviews and articles on a variety of screen cultures, most notably television and new media.

While most of the essays published in *Spectator* have been contributions from current PhD and MA students within USC's School of Cinematic Arts, the journal has also benefited from a number of collaborations with outside scholars. Over the years, *Spectator* has published dozens of papers presented at film festivals and international conferences as well as conferences organized by USC students and faculty, such as Todd Gitlin's 1988 keynote on popular culture and political unrest in 1968.[9]

In addition, the conference "Border Crossings: Mexican and Chicano Cinema," an *encuentro* programmed by USC's Cristina Venegas and Marsha Kinder in 1991, was documented in a special issue guest-edited by UCLA's Chon Noriega.[10] The journal has also solicited a number of contributions from students in other USC departments. Jennifer DeClue's essay on black queer female sexuality and *The Wire* (featured here) came out of the Department of American Studies and Ethnicity. Raffi Sarkissian received his master's from the Cinema School and has since continued his PhD work at USC's Annenberg School for Communication and Journalism, where he wrote his essay on the LGBT politics of award shows. This interdisciplinary exchange of ideas across the USC campus is in large part indebted to the professors of the Division of Cinema and Media Studies, including Marsha Kinder (now emeritus), Kara Keeling, Henry Jenkins, Ellen

Seiter, and Tara McPherson, whose courses on gender, sexuality, race, and media attract graduate students from a great variety of graduate programs in the humanities and social sciences at USC. Furthermore, every other issue of *Spectator* is edited by a USC postdoctoral fellow, according to their research interests, thus ensuring the continued commitment to young scholars and their innovative scholarship with issues on topics ranging from "Post-Identity" (edited by Janani Subramanian) to "Race, Sexuality, and Television" (edited by Julia Himberg). *Spectator*'s calls for papers solicit contributions from scholars at other institutions as well. Scott D. Paulin's essay on queer theory and the soundtrack and Melissa Williams's essay on Roseanne Barr's working-class feminism, both republished here, are two such examples.

Early feminist film scholarship was primarily concerned with the cinematic representation of women and the voyeuristic gaze, sadistic narratives, and broader suturing processes through which film connects with its spectators. Since then, *Spectator* has sought to keep pace with the rapidly changing media landscape, and as a result, essays on television, games, ephemera, and social media now appear more regularly in the publication.[11] Historically, the reach of spectatorship has expanded well beyond theatrical venues to include home theaters and new platforms such as podcasts and webisodes, yet concerns about hierarchy, representation, and inequity remain no less pressing. Unfortunately, public discourse too often breaks down these concerns into sound bites, tweets, posts (reposts), and a cascade of polarizing "viewpoints" that are designed to clash rather than consider the depth of these concerns. Conversely within the academy, a new relational awareness of issues of race, class, gender, and sexuality has brought foundational arguments to even the most specialized areas of media design, such as the ones and zeros of computer coding. Rather than taking for granted that things are the same online as they are offline, or accepting narratives about women and people of color being technologically inferior, cyberfeminists and scholars studying digital diasporas ask: "How wide is the digital divide?" and "What communities of practice and production shape and are in turn shaped by the Internet and associated technological environments?"[12] These lines of inquiry reveal robust online communities where identity constructions can be routinely transformed and rendered fluid. Furthermore, as media platforms like virtual reality (VR) are developed, varied points of view could soon commonly become replicated for spectators in an unprecedentedly immersive way. The Sundance Film Festival's virtual reality exhibit in 2016 demonstrated the potential gendered repercussions of this platform when spectators became immersed in the point of view of a pregnant woman confronted by picketers as she walked into a women's clinic. Cases such as these reveal that theories of gender, sexuality, and media cannot be viewed as monolithic or static. Instead, they should be developed dynamically both in print and in the classroom.

This collected volume of essays from the *Spectator* journal allows the reader to revisit the foundational concerns of the study of gender, sexuality, and media, while offering nuanced models of analysis that can be applied to forms of media and spectatorship in transition. We have organized the volume into five parts that are attentive to both the history of the study of film, TV, and media spectatorship and its rapid transformation with the introduction of new media forms. Part 1 assembles essays from the 1980s and 1990s that, in addressing various modes of spectatorship in classical Hollywood film, reconsider the canonical arguments of feminism as related to form, spectatorship, and pleasure. These essays revisit the foundations of feminism, but also reveal hidden histories as they consider less studied works and areas of scholarly emphasis, like racially and sexually marginalized spectators. The second part focuses on an oft-neglected element of media—sound and music. These articles do not, however, simply explore the materiality of sound or the soundtrack, but consider the nature of feminist voices as they relate to discourse and the social and culture mechanisms that attempt to stifle or mute these voices. In part 3, the contributors acknowledge the past theoretical foundations of the field and turn to the ways in which traditional formats—soap operas, public access TV, animation—have been queered by gay and lesbian audiences. In turn, these works explore how feminist theory served as a model for a new avenue of critical inquiry related to marginalized sexual groups. In part 4, the essays examine the ways in which media producers have attempted to contain unruly female and queer bodies, often in response to such transgressive audience practices. Social policing and political backlash are located in this tension. The collection concludes by looking to the future with essays that consider fan cultures in the transmedia age and their gendered negotiations of power.

With the rapid changes in media, producers and spectators are more closely aligned, but unfortunately some of the same issues of the past still arise in representations of gender and sexuality. This underscores the need for renewed considerations of how contemporary approaches to media are connected to the critical conversations of the past. The issues raised by

Johnston and Mulvey in their canonical essays and further explored in the pages of *Spectator*—namely, how to navigate media's complex power structures and create alternative media cultures—have not disappeared. Instead, they continue to grow and mature as media platforms and their attendant forms of spectatorship change. This change belies the stakes and importance of this ongoing work in both theory and practice. Without these discursive inquiries and their influence on a new generation of media makers on platforms like YouTube, would the mainstream media have considered so fully the issues of gay marriage and women's continued economic inequality? And would the related labor practices of Hollywood, with its propensity to shut out women and people of color from the production process, be challenged by a new wave of media makers now producing work for on-demand Internet streaming providers, such as Amazon Prime (*Transparent*, 2014–present) and Netflix (*Luke Cage*, 2016–present; *Orange Is the New Black*, 2013–present)? Much work remains to be done as hierarchies and points of view shift, and we believe that this collected volume of *Spectator*, intended for scholars and students in the field, is well situated to contribute to these conversations.

Part 1: Revisiting Film Subjects and the Pleasures of Cinema

The essays in part 1 revisit some of feminist film theory's primary lines of inquiry into the study of gendered subjectivity in cinema. They return to some of the most written-about films and filmmakers in film studies and extend early feminist analyses of their representations and receptions to other formal components, cinematic pleasures, and marginalized audiences. Amy Lawrence's essay "Feminine Discourse in *Blackmail*" (1984) explores the use of sound in the first British sound film, Hitchcock's *Blackmail* (1929), and its reinforcement of gendered dynamics of speech as they relate to power and control. Laura Mulvey looked to visual pleasure and how it delimited gendered representations and ways of looking in classical cinema, considering Hitchcock's films as exemplar; Lawrence analyzes instead the limited means of articulation available for an earlier Hitchcock heroine when it comes to voice. In the next essay, "Venus in Furs: Masoch, Deleuze, and the Films of von Sternberg" (1983), Gaylyn Studlar returns to the oeuvre of Josef von Sternberg, which was second only to Hitchcock's in its centrality to 1970s feminist film theory. Studlar's Deleuzian model, which she would later develop in her book *In the Realm of Pleasure: Von Sternberg, Dietrich, and the Masochistic Aesthetic* (1988), keeps precarious hierarchies of power across sexual differences in spectatorship in tension, revealing a breadth to cinematic pleasure previously unacknowledged by feminist film theory.[13]

The last two essays in part 1 shift away from feminist film theory's preoccupation with white heterosexuality to focus on the cinematic desires of racially and sexually marginalized spectators. In her essay "'You Don't Know What It Is to Look White and Be Black': The Black Press Mediates Race in the Classic Hollywood Studio System, 1930–1940" (1996), Anna Everett offers a history of black film critics' engagement with the technical, social, and artistic controversies of the studio era. She looks closely at the black press's reception of the 1934 Universal Pictures adaptation of Fannie Hurst's novel *Imitation of Life*. Everett foregrounds the range of opinions in the black community about cinematic depictions of blackness during the interwar years, demarcating the racialized limits of spectatorial film theory to that date and disproving the possibility of a monolithic theoretical framework for black spectatorship. In "Joe Dallesandro—A 'Him' to the Gaze: *Flesh*, *Heat*, and *Trash*" (1989), Stephen Tropiano analyzes three films produced by Andy Warhol and directed by Paul Morrissey in the late 1960s and early 1970s to show how their appropriation of gay male pornography codes offered a much-needed intimacy and eroticism in the face of Hollywood disavowal of all things queer. Tropiano does not merely celebrate the liberatory over the repressive. Even Warhol and Morrissey played to their period, he points out, and included elements to make Dallesandro less threatening. However, he does argue that the study of early gay cinema reveals unique, historically situated spectatorial strategies for gazing at the male body regardless of authorial intentionality.

Together, these essays broaden the methodological scope of the feminist study of film spectatorship. They incorporate additional bodies of theory and turn to previously unexplored archives, privileging historically specific considerations of cinematic subjects and their pleasures in watching films. Their analysis, in turn, expands our knowledge of spectators beyond feminist film theory's distinctions between, as Mulvey put it, "active/male and passive/female."

Part 2: Speaking Up and Sounding Out

While feminist film theory has made the gendered stakes of cinema's visual pleasure apparent, substantially less attention has been paid over the years to the film soundtrack. As Lawrence's early essay on the subject in part 1 demonstrates, however, it is crucial to understand how various subjects are made to speak and what they are allowed to speak about. Similarly, as Everett's essay shows, extratextual discourse has become an increasingly important area of study. The essays in part 2 listen on both of these registers. Their authors demonstrate that listening is itself a form of spectatorship, located in specific bodies and tied to different subject positions. Furthermore, they share a politicized commitment to letting their subjects of study speak up and speak out so that they in turn may be heard by media studies.

The first two essays in part 2 examine sonic elements of films and their unruly political functions. In "Unheard Sexualities?: Queer Theory and the Soundtrack" (1997), Scott D. Paulin argues that music participates in the construction of onscreen representations of desire and more often than not does so in a fashion that encourages the audience to identify with heterosexuality and its consumption. In his analyses of *Rebel Without a Cause* and *Sunday Bloody Sunday*, both of which center on a bisexual love triangle, Paulin shows just how much work goes into the construction of heterosexuality through music. Drawing on D. A. Miller's seminal essay on the gay signifiers of Hitchcock's *Rope*, Paulin claims that a different kind of queer work, located more in the bodies and fantasies of viewers, is identifiable in all three films. As a result, even heterosexism's most valiant efforts are doomed to partial failure from the start.

The next essay, Christie Milliken's "The Articulation of Body and Space in *Speak Body*" (1987), looks to an explicitly feminist film and examines the discursive, rather than sonic, work that it performs. *Speak Body* was a rare women's movement film in that it centralized the discussion of abortion in its narrative. Milliken argues for the desirability of women speaking between discourses on the topic, noting in her analysis that the film provides space for various perspectives, while refusing to declare one such perspective as the "right" one. In the third essay in part 2, Melissa Williams's "'I Kinda Prefer to Be a Human Being': Roseanne Barr and Defining Working-Class Feminism and Authorship" (2005), the feminist discourse up for debate is that of academic feminism itself. Williams argues that academic feminists need to learn to talk about working-class women as people with ideas as well as bodies. Working-class women are not merely feminist mascots, but feminist authors in their own right. Williams models how such a body of scholarship might proceed with an analysis of Barr's authorship of working-class feminism in the writer's room and studio as well as in publicity and press materials. Williams thus links working-class women's marginalization in academia and mass media and articulates a politics for rethinking the parameters and language of feminist media studies.

The final essay in part 2 returns to the analysis of music, but within a similar feminist discursive framework. In "Riot Grrrl: It's Not Just Music, It's Not Just Punk" (1995), Mary Celeste Kearney critiques the mainstream media's overwhelming tendency to discuss riot grrrl music either in relation to the more masculine punk genre or as just another iteration of silly girl fan cultures—both of which serve to contain and trivialize it—by contextualizing its feminism. Her analysis makes space for female youth in both the fight to end gender discrimination and the fight to end age-based discrimination. In discussing arguments for separatism, alternative institutions, and autonomous "womyn's culture," Kearney draws a number of important connections between riot grrrl and lesbian feminism of the 1970s. Although riot grrrl may share some of the more problematic elements of this past politics—namely essentialism—Kearney points out that it also reveals a unique ability to incorporate the strengths of other cultural and political movements.

In this part of the book, the study of media expands to consider its work on sonic and discursive fronts, thus delineating feminism and queerness as discourses sounding across media.

Part 3: Queering Media

In part 3, each of the authors takes up a different form of media—specifically, daytime soaps, public access television, and animation, all of which have had underexplored ties to queerness and sexual representation. For much of film and television history, queer spectators have had to make do with creative readings of beloved texts—Susan Sontag noted this tendency in her canonical article "Notes on 'Camp'" as she explored rereadings of older films.[14] Not surprisingly, early gay and lesbian film studies were largely devoted to these analyses of exaggerated seriousness and other connotative strategies with long histories in queer cultures that can be traced in identity constructions and performance in queer communities. The three scholars represented in part 3 contributed to the proliferation of queer media studies methodologies in the 1990s as they theorized alternative forms of queer media spectatorship.

Building on the rich body of scholarship devoted to heterosexual women "slashing" traditionally male television genres by writing male characters, such as Kirk and Spock, as romantic lovers in fanzines, in "Soap Slash: Gay Men Rewrite the World of Daytime Television Drama" (2005), Hollis Griffin turns to gay male soap opera spectators' similar practices online. While in Kirk/Spock (or K/S) fan fiction the male characters' sexual identities were of little concern, their attraction and love being written more as cosmic destiny, Griffin argues that, with the long history of gay male under- and misrepresentation in television programming, gay men's slashing of soap opera is an act of identity politics as well as sexual pleasure. Griffin offers a brief history of gay male representation on soap operas, which have relegated queerness to the margins, when it has been dealt with at all. With their slash-writing, then, gay television spectators rewrite the genre of soap, appropriating its characters, story lines, and conventions, while also shifting its queerness from the level of connotation to denotation. In showing examples of how this translation happens, and drawing on these same fans' disclaimers for why they wrote these stories, Griffin claims this body of work as a necessary and important liberatory practice.

In "From Excess to Access: Televising the Subculture" (1994), Eric Freedman contends that queer people must take control of their own desires by inserting themselves into its flow of representations. One place where production of such representations might be most possible and reception most easily accessible by queer audiences, he writes, is localized and specialized public access television. Drawing on past scholarship on camp and mass media theory, Freeman analyzes both the queer activist media common to public access TV—such as AIDS documentaries—and the queer entertainment fare also available, locating the platform's subversive potential in its unapologetically "cheap" aesthetics as well as its propensity for drag performance. Public access TV, in offering relatively easy access to production facilities and targeted distribution systems, provides a vibrant space for creating queer community through conjoined self-representation and reception.

In "Pronoun Trouble: The 'Queerness' of Animation" (1994), Sean Griffin provides a history of the queerness of animation and offers a model for reconciling historical media studies approaches with the relatively ahistorical methods developing in queer theory. Like the two previous contributors, Griffin looks to both the workings of the genre itself, whose formal properties are permeated by queerness, and viewers' engagements with it. He draws on Eve Sedgwick and Judith Butler's theories of gender performativity and queer theory's methods of textual analyses, but supplements these with contextual analyses of the gay historians George

Chauncey and John D'Emilio. Through three case studies from across animation history—*Snow White* (1933), *Rabbit Fire* (1951), and *The Lion King* (1994)—Griffin outlines the attempts of animated films to draw boundaries between heterosexuality and its other, according to contemporary conceptions. He finds references to Harlem drag balls, 1950s homosexual paranoia, and, in *The Lion King*, appeals to gay consumers that still nonetheless ring with the white heteronormativity of the earlier films. Finally and significantly, Griffin's analysis reveals that such films' homophobias are so inflected with contemporary racisms that they cannot be thought about separately.

With these essays, we witness gay and lesbian spectators refusing to remain just that. In the face of underrepresentation, they create their own representations as a counterpublic, using the technology most easily accessible. They have queered media, and in turn popular culture has become less and less straight. These essays support Alexander Doty's influential claim that "queer readings aren't 'alternative' readings, wishful or willful misreadings, or 'reading too much into things' readings." Instead, "they result from the recognition and articulation of the complex range of queerness that has been in popular texts and their audiences all along."[15] Even as such queer readings continue, adapting to contemporary media environments, they face challenges. As the last essay proves, there are complications when queer readings become mainstream. Queer media scholars, these essays suggest, need to continue to interrogate why we get the representations we do, what queer subjects are appropriate on-screen, and which remain absent, become cloaked in evil, or are eroticized for others.

Part 4: Containment and Its Critiques

Scholarship as critical resistance has been one of the driving aims and strengths of academic inquiry in the study of gender and sexuality in media. In the 1970s, feminist film theorists were part of a larger counterpublic of women, people of color, and gays and lesbians resisting structures of oppression. Each of these groups used media in unprecedented ways to tell their stories and reveal a point of view that did not mimic the dominant traditions, and they did so in conversation with scholars, who were studying how such media typically represented such groups. When one speaks truth to power, however, power often speaks back, and just as activists' methods developed, so too did those of patriarchy, heteronormativity, and structural racism. The essays in part 4 identify and challenge the adherence of popular media to historical patterns of containment through recurrent representations, such as stereotypes and surveillance. In this way, the work toward a more inclusive (and less ideologically rigid) media landscape continues, with critical theory functioning as both an instrument of resistance and a means by which to foster alternative voices and subjectivities that reach beyond the mainstream.

Scandals and their containment seem to cycle ever more rapidly now with online news platforms. In her essay "Of Fleiss and Men: The Transgressions and Containment of a Hollywood Madam" (1995), Mary Celeste Kearney explores a case from the early 1990s that is now long forgotten in cultural memory but that still provides fruitful insights into how journalism polices women's sexualities, especially when racialized or sexualized as other. Kearney studies the entanglement of the tabloid press and "legitimate" journalism in the reporting on the arrest and trial of Hollywood madam Heidi Fleiss. She reveals how these various media worked together to code Fleiss as deviant in a way that exemplified broader narratives of Jewish and queer women's transgression and necessary containment. In the coverage of Fleiss's arrest, trial, and sentencing, her "flamboyant" lifestyle—rumored to include providing call girls to male Hollywood executives and their wives as well as lesbian relations of her own—became the center of media attention. While the media indulged its audiences' curiosities, Kearney argues, it ultimately contained such unruly sexual acts through panoptic surveillance and rehabilitation. Interestingly, despite newspapers' many attempts at self-reflexive coverage of the case's sensationalism, rhetorical differences between "legitimate" and "illegitimate" media failed to hold, signaling an already changing media landscape. Reading Kearney's essay today leads us to questions about the continuing surveillance of women's and queer bodies in the social media era.

In "Out on Stage: LGBT Politics of Entertainment Award Shows" (2014), Raffi Sarkissian compares how the Oscars and the Emmys valuate LGBT diversity through wins and nominations and argues that the acting categories of these award shows reinforce the stereotypes and gendered binaries that have shaped film and television for decades. Beginning in the 1990s, LGBT content on film and television gained greater prominence with the emergence of an identifiable gay market. In turn, the awards given to actors in each medium echoed broader ideologies about not just gays and lesbians but film and television as gendered institutions with varying cultural capital. Actors nominated for Oscars for playing gay or transgender characters, Sarkissian points out, are lauded for being able to make those characters likable or relatable. Furthermore, they are dramatic roles, and most of these characters die, tragically, by the end of the film. Meanwhile, the actors nominated for Emmys for the gay roles they play on television disproportionately appear in comedic sitcoms in stereotypically "queenie" roles. At the podium, Tom Hanks and Sean Penn could at least allude briefly to contemporary LGBT politics, reinforcing film's self-image of high cultural seriousness, but television actors playing gay have regularly downplayed politics in their acceptance speeches, a trend at least partially attributable to networks' dependency on advertising revenue. Sarkissian reveals how queerness is thus invariably contained, even as it emerges in mainstream media, and how this containment itself has a history.

In the final essay of this section, "Lesbian Cop, Queer Killer: Leveraging Black Queer Women's Sexuality on HBO's *The Wire*" (2011), Jennifer DeClue argues that *The Wire* both complicates and exploits black queer sexuality to produce provocative quality TV. Like Sarkissian, DeClue draws on scholarship on the "gay nineties" as she contends that the expanded representations of black sexualities in popular media have been tempered by the use of black sexual taboo to produce an aesthetic of quality TV. Black sexuality has always been constructed as existing outside of heterosexuality, writes DeClue, and *The Wire* relies on this pathology to create quality TV that is scintillating for its liberal, affluent viewers. Although quality TV's desire for both controversial subject matter and "realism" often coalesces into a greater demand for black queer sexuality, this very realism does not extend to its representation of black queer women. By making black queer women characters visible but refusing to represent their masculine sexualities, *The Wire* reinscribes the indelibility of masculinity within white male bodies. Put simply, the spectator addressed and appeased is not the black queer spectator.

Kearney, Sarkissian, and DeClue thus contribute to the study of gender, sexuality, and media by showing how representations of queer and transgender subjects often serve to stereotype and surveil. In the popular media, more often than not this is done by and for the benefit of others. Containment, these scholars demonstrate, need not mean erasure. Instead, it too adapts to changing times, and as long as white cisgender heterosexuality remains the norm, capital and culture remain content.

Part 5: Fandom and Transmedia

The shifting of the media landscape has led to a reassessment of hierarchy, spectatorship, and power with regard to the audience, specifically in terms of the audience's influence on media publicity, distribution, casting, and meaning production. Fan communities' increasing visibility is inseparable from fan studies' development in the 1990s, when scholars like Henry Jenkins, Constance Penley, and Camille Bacon-Smith began creating a space within media studies for the analysis of fan community formation through fanzines, fan fiction, slide shows, filking, and vidding.[16] Since then, fan studies has considered the reach of media "universes" (the Marvel Universe and the Star Wars Universe are recent examples) and content development across media platforms, specifically addressing these "transmedia" connections in regard to narrative and community building. New pathways between fans and media producers have resulted, and fans have even sought to reinscribe and address gaps in mainstream media's representations in regard to gender and sexuality. After the release of *Star Wars: The Force Awakens* (2015), for example, it was only a matter of weeks before fans' speculations about the possibility of a future romance between the two new male leads garnered public attention and discussion.[17] In this final part of this volume, gender, sexuality, and audience are explored through three case studies that chart the movement of fan activities from subculture to mainstream.

Harry M. Benshoff's "Resurrection of the Vampire and the Creation of Alternative Life: An Introduction to *Dark Shadows* Fan Culture" (1993) is an early example of queer fan studies. In this essay, Benshoff offers an ethnography of the fans of the fantastical daytime soap *Dark Shadows* (which ran from 1966 to 1971 before spawning a number of spin-offs and remakes in TV, film, and novel formats). Drawing on surveys of *Dark Shadow* fans that he circulated and analyses of *DS* fan activities, such as fan clubs, conventions, filking, and music videos, Benshoff finds that *DS* fans have created and sustained an elaborate alternative community. Importantly, its diverse individuals have not come together merely to celebrate their shared text, and the desires they explore together could not be met by just more canon material. Instead, together they have founded an ancillary space in which to discuss issues of gender and sexuality, from sexual desire to gay aesthetics, only first hinted at in the original text.

Elena Bonomo's "The Rumors Are True!: *Gossip Girl* and the Cooptation of the Cult Fan" (2010), an example of twenty-first-century fan studies, examines the "mainstream" appropriation by media producers of "cult" fan practices, such as those Benshoff studied, through their use of transmedia storytelling, which spreads media content across platforms. For Bonomo, *Gossip Girl* is exemplary of how, through transmedia storytelling, dominant representations come to co-opt spaces previously carved out for minoritarian subjects. Although Bonomo focuses on this as a popular trend in contemporary television, citing the similar transmedia work done by the producers of *Dawson's Creek*, *Lost*, and *Heroes*, she also notes the unique ways in which *Gossip Girl* features notions of convergence as part of the narrative itself, the "gossip" of the series' title circulating largely through digital media platforms. Convergence culture may often be as central to the lives of actual teenagers as it is to the series' characters, but Bonomo concludes, with a twist of her own, that female fans may not actually always want multimedia experiences. Although *Gossip Girl* fans are encouraged to build on their identifications with characters and narrativize their own lives online accordingly, they are not in control of the outlets created for them to do this, and as a result elements of their desires get lost in translation.

In "The Trouble with Transmediation: Fandom's Negotiation of Transmedia Storytelling Systems" (2010), Suzanne Scott makes an even stronger critique of the commercial imperative often underlying the creation of transmedia stories today.[18] She does so by analyzing how "official" ancillary content, such as podcasts and webisodes, reinforces the textual authority of the few, rather than allowing for many interpretations to flourish and meet, as fan-authored content frequently did in fan subcultures. Often this authority, Scott points out, is that of "fanboy author-gods," such as J. J. Abrams, Ron Moore, and George Lucas. In this convergence culture, the boundaries between "official" and "unofficial" narrative expansion are reinforced and the female fans and queer reading practices that inspired transmedia storytelling become delegitimized. While issuing a clear call for reconsidering these sexist and homophobic practices, Scott concludes her essay by commending those artists who remain artists in their own right.

These final essays chart a history of media that in all likelihood will only continue to be transformed, in ways that we have not yet imagined. The essays collected in this volume draw attention to the fact that despite the innovations of the present, the latest forms and trends in media often reproduce some of the same problems of the past when it comes to gender and sexuality. As the feminist blogosphere has been quick to point out, this is often a matter of not representing the varied interests of women, which include not just the tropes of romance but also friendship, professional endeavors, and creative projects that do not center on men.[19] Similarly, in popular discourse, sexuality in media has often been reduced to a game of numbers—simply counting up how many of a particular category appear or don't appear in certain formats. Today media producers are constructing diverse dynamics between these media and their spectators—through fan websites, mobile apps, print media, gaming, and, very soon, VR. As this collection demonstrates, however, even the most cunning producers can never totally contain spectators and their discourse. Social media campaigns regular "go wrong" when spectators take them over and rewrite their meaning or question their underlying assumptions. Although it is often a struggle to keep up with changing technologies, we can be reassured in knowing that an archive of forty years of gender, sexuality, and media studies scholarship is available to assist us in our thinking about contemporary media, audiences, and spectatorship.

Notes

1. Marsha Kinder, "Editorial," *Spectator* 1, no. 1 (Spring 1982): 11.

2. Before Laura Mulvey's article appeared (see note 4), it is important to note that Marsha Kinder and Beverly Houston had collaborated on numerous essays for *Sight and Sound*, *Women and Film* (America's first feminist film journal), and *Film Quarterly* that considered feminism and gender in the context of cinema. When they began working at USC in 1980 and 1982, respectively, they consciously introduced feminist and other theoretical discourses (Marxist, psychoanalytic, phenomenological, and semiotic) into the curriculum, departing from its former insularity and almost exclusive identification with Hollywood. This was a move toward a stronger engagement with the international field and its theoretical debates, especially those on gender and sexuality.

3. Christian Metz, *The Imaginary Signifier: Psychoanalysis and the Cinema*, translated by Celia Britton, Annwyl Williams, Ben Brewster, and Alfred Guzzetti (Bloomington: Indiana University Press, 1982); Jean-Louis Baudry, "Ideological Effects of the Basic Cinematographic Apparatus," translated by Alan Williams, *Film Quarterly* 28, no. 2 (1974–1975): 39–47; Raymond Bellour, "Hitchcock, the Enunciator," translated by Bertrand Augst and Hilary Radner, *Camera Obscura*, no. 2 (1977): 66–92; and Stephen Heath, *Questions of Cinema* (Bloomington: Indiana University Press, 1981).

4. Laura Mulvey, "Visual Pleasure and Narrative Cinema," *Screen* 16, no. 3 (Autumn 1975): 6–18.

5. Claire Johnston, *Notes on Women's Cinema* (London: Society for Education in Film and Television, 1973).

6. For a very interesting recent account of British feminist film theory's influ-

ence on Australian feminists working across a variety of media and disciplines, see Kyla McFarlane, ed., *A Different Temporality: Aspects of Australian Feminist Art Practice 1975–1985* (Victoria, Australia: Monash University Museum of Art, 2011).

7. Ben Vanaman, "The Positioning of Women in Film," *Spectator* 2, no. 2 (Spring 1983): 8.

8. Ibid.

9. The conference "May '68: 20 Years Later" was curated by Lili Berko in 1988. Todd Gitlin, "1968: The Two Popular Cultures," *Spectator* 8, no. 2 (Spring 1988): 8–17.

10. *Spectator* 13, no. 1 (1992).

11. For more on suture, see Kaja Silverman, *The Subject of Semiotics* (New York: Oxford University Press, 1983).

12. Anna Everett, *Digital Diaspora: A Race for Cyberspace* (Albany: State University of New York Press, 2009), 9–48; and Radhika Gajjala, *Cyber Selves: Feminist Ethnographies of South Asian Women* (Walnut Creek, CA: AltaMira Press, 2004), 2.

13. These essays were the first versions of what later became the authors' dissertations and ultimately groundbreaking books in the field—Studlar's *In the Realm of Pleasure: Von Sternberg, Dietrich, and the Masochistic Aesthetic* (New York: Columbia University Press, 1993) and Lawrence's *Echo and Narcissus: Women's Voices in Classical Hollywood Cinema* (Berkeley: University of California Press, 1991). According to Kinder, who directed both dissertations, the success of these initial essays encouraged subsequent graduate students to submit their work to *Spectator* and develop dissertations and books along similar paths.

14. Susan Sontag, "Notes on 'Camp,'" *Partisan Review* (Fall 1964): 515–530.

15. Alexander Doty, *Making Things Perfectly Queer: Interpreting Mass Culture* (Minneapolis: University of Minnesota Press, 1993), 16.

16. Henry Jenkins, *Textual Poachers: Television Fans and Participatory Culture* (New York: Routledge, 1992); Constance Penley, "Feminism, Psychoanalysis, and the Study of Popular Culture," in *Cultural Studies*, edited by Lawrence Grossberg, Cary Nelson, and Paula A. Treichler (New York: Routledge, 1992), 479–494; and Camille Bacon-Smith, *Enterprising Women: Television Fandom and the Creation of Popular Myth* (Philadelphia: University of Pennsylvania Press, 1992).

17. Natalie Fisher, "Is *Star Wars* Setting Up Poe Dameron as Its First Queer Protagonist?," Hypable, December 24, 2015, http://www.hypable.com/star-wars-poe-dameron-queer-protagonist/.

18. Transmedia storytelling has special resonance at USC, since the concept was first introduced by Marsha Kinder in 1991 in her book *Playing with Power in Cinema, Television, and Video Games* (Berkeley: University of California Press, 1993), greatly expanded by Henry Jenkins in his work on convergence, and strongly encouraged by USC's new graduate program in media arts and practice.

19. For an early iteration of an ongoing series of feminist critiques of Hollywood, see Anita Sarkeesian's vlog about the Bechdel Test's validity in the twenty-first century: Anita Sarkeesian, "The Bechdel Test for Women in Movies," Feminist Frequency, December 7, 2009, http://feministfrequency.com/2009/12/07/the-bechdel-test-for-women-in-movies/.

PART I Revisiting Film Subjects and the Pleasures of Cinema

ONE

Feminine Discourse in *Blackmail*

AMY LAWRENCE

This article proposes to analyze Alfred Hitchcock's 1929 sound film *Blackmail* according to the presence and power allotted to feminine discourse in the film. By the term "feminine discourse," I mean narrative techniques used in a particular film that confer some degree of control over the narrative to a female character.[1] Through an examination of all the scenes involving the main character Alice, we will be able to consider: (1) the narrative logic of the film (which is built around Alice); (2) the device of suspense, which is primarily focused on Alice's words; and (3) the continuing comparison between silent film and sound film as it is projected onto the characters. These issues place Alice within a male-dominated system and make the subject of speech (particularly female control of speech and environment) central to the film.

In the classic film noir, the detective, representative of the Law, searches for the Truth through snares and obstacles set up by duplicitous women. In *Blackmail*, however, it is the woman (and the audience) who knows the Truth, while the detective's job (the purpose of the Law) is to prevent the revealing of the Truth, i.e., to keep the blackmailer and the woman silent. In this way, *Blackmail* illustrates how the Law and the patriarchy are founded on the suppression of the Truth, and shows the degree of hypocrisy needed to maintain Victorian patriarchy in the twentieth century—especially in suppressing women's sexuality as a means of preserving the status quo of male control. *Blackmail* does this through both

Figure 1.1. *Blackmail* (1929)

form and content, most suggestively through the relation between sound and image.

As the first sound film made in England, *Blackmail* presents a rare opportunity to begin at the beginning. The year 1929 was rather late to be a "first" sound film, but Hitchcock was able to turn out an advanced meditation on the possible uses of sound while demonstrating the pros and cons of the argument of the day—sound versus silence/silent. The conceit of this sound film is an attempt to keep a man silent (paying a blackmailer). The heroine spends over a third of the film virtually speechless. The dialogue is laughably banal, yet the right word can cut like a knife. The silent opening—a chase—is immediately contrasted with an interminable, static dialogue scene. But before we glibly assume silent were "better movies," sound becomes a powerful emotional tool and a moral force while silence is linked with corruption and moral lassitude.

Hitchcock's Heroine: The Problem of Choice

Our feelings on "sound plus image" versus "image alone" are carefully paralleled with our feelings for Alice White. She is introduced as a chatterbox. After a violent assault, she becomes almost catatonic. Finally, she accepts speech as a moral imperative, achieves maturity and the audience's respect before slipping back under patriarchal control. Alice is the personification of the course the sound film must take.

Visually, Alice is first defined by her clothes. In her initial appearance, she is wearing a black and white dress in the fashion of a flapper. The flapper stood outside class distinctions; she could be a debutante or a shopgirl. Beyond this, she represented the unharnessing of women's sexuality. The flapper did not submit to Victorian morés governing male/female sexuality. While young men drank bootleg all night, it was the female jazz baby who caught the attention of society. Alice's new freedom is why Hitchcock has us identify with her—because she has a choice. She can choose the stolid conservative policeman Frank, or the bohemian artist, or a whole new set of rules. But Alice is more modern still. Her image (like the film stock itself) now reaches beyond black and white; it speaks. Alice's character and the major points of the film are thus communicated through (1) how we see her (dress), and (2) how we hear her.

Frank, the detective, is totally caught up in his male world of work, the function of which is to maintain law and order—the status quo. Frank, half an hour late, greets Alice by telling her the great (male) machinery of Scotland Yard cannot be rushed for a woman. Frank's idea of a good time is seeing a movie called *Fingerprints*—about Scotland Yard. (Fingerprints, incidentally, are visually perceived physical imprints—like the silent film image—that allegedly tell who is guilty or innocent. In the case *we* are about to see, fingerprints would be totally inadequate in determining guilt.)

As they walk outside the Yard, Alice pouts, then begins to giggle. Frank asks her what she's thinking, but she keeps it to herself. The sound suggests there is something beneath the surface. At dinner, Alice is again dissatisfied with Frank. The Artist, on the other hand, has sent her a note saying how *he* will wait to *see her*. While Frank is clearly and consistently the force of order (safe, secure, predictable), the Artist attracts Alice with a bohemian quality that suggests he is free of Victorian expectations and constraints. Yet Alice has trouble deciding. Should she stay safely subordinate or step out? Verbally, all she does is equivocate. An exasperated Frank walks out (making her choice for her), and she leaves with the Artist.

Going to a man's apartment is a further step out of the prescribed morality, but, after minutes of indecision and evasiveness, she accedes. She says, "I think a woman knows instinctively when she can trust a man."

Here, a Victorian audience raised on "good girls don't" would moan with foresight, "She's going to get what's coming to her." Culturally, all lone males were love wolves, "artists" especially. The camera's following Alice and the Artist up a tortuous staircase suggests she is in over her head. Watching the film without this Victorian bias, a contemporary audience must agree with Alice. The Artist so far is unhurried, kind, and enjoys her company. The series of uninterrupted, static long takes in the scene gives their exchanges a sense of naturalness noticeably absent from the stilted restaurant scene with Frank. The scene's limited camera movement, in contrast to the audible "opening up" (the use of music, verbal wit), allows the characters to constantly experiment with their positions (where they are and what they say), thus also increasing the sense of freedom.

However, this scene is gradually revealed as a subtly graded series of attempts by the male character to control both the female's image and her discourse. Alice draws a face that could be either male or female. The Artist, controlling her hand, adds a sexy female body. Alice toys with the idea of putting on a fancy dress and asks if it will fit. She may sound a little silly, but she clearly feels free to try new things. He urges her to try on the dress and Hitchcock indulges/accuses his/our voyeurism as she undresses behind a black screen but is visible to the camera. This creates a split-screen effect. Alice looks like an idea in the Artist's mind, a projection of white on black, a silent image in his "all-singing, all-talking" one. He sings a song about the twenties' "wild youth" ("There's no harm in you, Miss of Today"), and when Alice steps out, he informs her, "That's you," defining her in the lyrics of the song. While Alice takes dressing up as part of her adventure, one of the possibilities opening up to her, the Artist uses it as an excuse to kiss her, implying that her willingness to experiment with her own image shows she has, in fact, agreed to accept the image *he* has given her. The kiss upsets Alice and she wants to leave, but the Artist dominates her further. He prevents her from leaving by her dress. Finally, he totally dominates her discourse; dragging her out of the frame, despite her physical reluctance and objections. He terms her words "silly."

Up to this point, Alice's words have had little individual impact. They have been a series of clichés, slang phrases, and expressions of indecisiveness indicating she doesn't know her own mind. The irony is that when she definitely says "no" it is discounted. The futility of her discourse, her attempt to establish an independent identity in the face of male domination, is now introduced forcefully. By cutting to a static medium long shot of a draped bed, Hitchcock reduces the image's power, eliminating its ability to tell us simple facts of plot or action. The only moving image is Alice's hand, fingers flexing against air, literally unable to come to grips with the assault taking place. The emotional force is thus displaced from image to sound. Alice screams, "No. Let me go!" over and over. Her attacker doesn't listen; the policeman outside is oblivious; Hitchcock doesn't spare her. If words, vocal expression, and physical resistance are ignored, Alice can only decide: (1) to allow herself to be victimized, or (2) to resort to violence. Music at full volume, Hitchcock returns power to the image with a close-up of Alice's hand finding the knife that will free her.

In image and discourse, the betrayal of the female by the artist is linked with the exploitation of women by male directors like Hitchcock. This aspect of the film is not avoided by Hitchcock. After the attack, he recalls our salacious interest in the "unveiling" scene when Alice removed her dress and rebukes us for it. Alice emerges from the hidden attack in the same short, white slip, so sexy earlier, but now reminding us of a frightened baby—all innocence. Here, the significance of the "innocence" (whiteness) of her slip is more important as a symbol than for its "authenticity" within the context of the assault. In spite of the violent attack culminating in the stabbing, Alice's clothes are neither torn nor bloody. (This also implies her sexual innocence.)

"When Will She Speak?": Asserting the Feminine Discourse

Alice's reaction to both the attack and to her violent response is presented in both sound and image. Visually, she reverts to childhood, hiding in the clothes and actions of a little girl safely back in the confines of her home. She hides in bed until Mother comes to wake her. Throughout the scene, the amplified chirping of a caged bird mocks her. Rising, Alice breaks her powder case, subconsciously rejecting her flapper makeup, and dresses in the unappealing and frumpish dress of a hausfrau or shopgirl—the obedient daughter. Her dress also reasserts her place in a specific social class as well.

Verbally, Alice is reduced to near-catatonia. She can barely speak. Her one moment of verbal catharsis, when she expresses her full horror immediately after the attack, is taken from her by a cut. Wandering the streets until dawn, Alice comes upon a man's body in a doorway. She screams. Hitchcock cuts to the Artist's landlady finding his body. The effect is that another person (the landlady) takes over Alice's screams. By robbing Alice of this moment of full vocal expression, Hitchcock makes her (and the audience) wait for a later time when she can express what has happened from a base of knowledge rather than emotion.

The power of words—proved so impotent when used by Alice in the rape scene—is imposed on her at breakfast when she is, presumably, in "the bosom of her family." As Alice sits down, a local gossip relates in gory detail the heinousness of the "murder." The words fade to a murmur while the word "knife" is amplified, sharpened. The blurring/accenting technique shows how most words are unnecessary, but the *right* one can figuratively cut like a knife. The breadknife (highlighted visually) also functions as an extension of Alice's effort at control. She used the first knife to regain control of her environment, to stop the attack; here, she unconsciously tries to deny she ever had control of the original knife by suddenly flinging the breadknife to the floor.

At this point in a classical Hollywood film the hero would enter and take over—speaking for the heroine, protecting her, explaining situations, devising scenarios, and verbally controlling the world for both of them. However, Hitchcock insists on Alice's discourse. Although she is often speechless, instead of turning to the detective to relate the "Truth" and take charge, Hitchcock makes us wait for Alice. As Frank waits, Alice (center of the frame) plays with her sweater, looks away, and shakes her head. No music fills the space.

Thus, the dramatic structure of the film has been transformed. The suspense now rests entirely on Alice's asserting her version of events, her discourse—the truth. This is the need established in the audience which must now be satisfied. Not "who done it?" but "when will she speak?"

But Alice finds it extremely difficult to speak except in the near-nonsensical utterances of a young lady at tea. At one point, the blackmailer, pressuring Alice and Frank and raising the suspicions of Alice's parents, brazenly invites himself to breakfast. With all eyes on her, the only thing Alice can finally say is, "Would you stay for breakfast?"—clearly inadequate to the tense situation, but for the moment all she can handle.[2]

Patriarchal Suppression of the Truth

Frank finally decides to take charge and starts by blackmailing the blackmailer. Alice rejects his attempt but is unable to make him listen. She is trapped between them, motionless, or shoved against the left side of the frame where she attracts our attention by pathetically pulling Frank's sleeve or making small sounds with short disconnected words, "But . . .

oh. . . ." Far from helping Alice overcome her fear of speech, when Alice succeeds in getting out a word, Frank snaps, "Don't interfere." It's her life, but it's his *job*, which from the beginning has taken precedence over Alice. Just as the Artist would not concede Alice the control of her image or validity of her speech, Frank also tries to suppress her. Visually, he and the blackmailer work together, surrounding Alice or forcing her to the edges of the frame. Dramatically, the blackmailer and Frank are both engaged in an effort to keep Alice's actions secret. After all, Frank protects Alice (and society) from the public admission that she chose her own male companion and assumed the authority to say whether or not she would have sex.

Where the goal of the standard film noir detective is to find (and thus establish for us) the Truth, here Frank knows the Truth. His job—to suppress the Truth—defers to an even greater goal—the Victorian patriarchal control of women's sexuality. In this case, preserving the illusion of control is what counts the most. Alice must be ushered back into the fold.

While it may seem that Frank (earlier so dedicated to the Yard and police technique) would have scruples against hiding evidence, Hitchcock (never a fan of cops) reveals that it is surprisingly easy. To keep things quiet, Frank will consider paying blackmail. Instead of seeking justice, he finds it more appealing to frame an innocent man. This underscores the fact that his job never was to find the truly guilty party but to maintain law and order, the status quo—appearances. Caught in his failure to control Alice, Frank simplifies the situation, saying in effect, "Shoot now, ask questions later" (when words can say anything we want them to). The police will believe one of their own rather than an ex-convict blackmailer; forced to run, he dies in the chase.

This example of police procedure refers us back to the opening scene. Now we see the lack of moral commitment, moral thoroughness, that results when action (visual only) proceeds without verbal (moral) qualifiers; the power of force is celebrated over the power of reflection. In the opening scene, the police push their way into the room of a man who looks typically "criminal" (unshaven, surly). However, the man's neighbors object to his being taken and crowd around the police. Who is this man? What is the charge? Why do the people defend him? What do we know about him except the stereotype of the silent film "thug"? Silence shows us the surface, but we never do find out what was at the bottom of the arrest. This foretells the end of the film's second chase. The wrong man dies in a mindless, impurely motivated chase, persecuted *by* the police because it is convenient *for* the police. They pursue the matter no further.

Once the action has been carried out, they wash up and head home (as in the first scene).

Discourse as Moral Imperative

Formally, the respective moral sensitivities of Frank and Alice are thus linked to cinema. The framing of the blackmailer is the dilemma that forces Alice to speak. The chase is intercut with Alice. Given a moment to reflect alone, she decides. By writing a morally courageous note, she refuses to participate in what amounts to a lynching. She says she must "speak up" to save "this poor man."

Alice arrives at the police station again dressed fashionably and attractively. She is wearing white, in effect asserting herself (Alice White) and the basic goodness of her image (Alice is white). Rejecting Frank's simplification of dilemmas through dependence on visuals alone, Alice is here to synchronize her image with a moral voice. She makes full use of the moral choice offered to her by the sound film's techniques and conventions.

The station is a male cloister where a woman must apply to the doorman in writing (!) for admittance. The sergeant (who knows her as Frank's girl) laughs at the thought of a young lady knowing anything about a "murder." Alice is led to the Chief Inspector's office, where Frank interrupts her to tell his superior that what she says can't be important. The Chief interrupts her by taking a phone call in the middle of her statement and delegates Frank to decide whether what she has to say is worthwhile. Alice breaks down outside and tells Frank her action was in self-defense, but what she says clearly does not matter. Out of convenience, the forces of law and order have blamed a dead man. Frank has returned Alice to her constrained place within the patriarchy. She has been forced to submit herself to the judgment of the police, to "confess" her "crime," and her confession has been totally contained by the system. As Mildred Pierce's story is dismissed by the police, who reveal they knew the *real* truth all along and send Mildred back to her husband's control, Alice's story is dismissed (the *real* truth) and she is turned over, in effect, to Frank's custody.

Surrendering to the Status Quo

As a last comment on male/female relations in such a social structure, the ending resoundingly denies any romantic resolution. The sergeant jokes with Frank, "Did she tell you who did the murder?" Frank thinks, and gives a very considered "yes." By their thoughtfulness, both he and Alice emphasize the difficulty of speaking in a world filled with loaded questions, dominated by a male order that predetermines what the answers can be. (For one thing, it wasn't murder at all, but self-defense.)

The sergeant's last joke is, "Next they'll be having lady inspectors." Standing between Frank and the sergeant (literally surrounded by the police), Alice joins in the laughter. She is back in line and won't step out again. Another policeman takes the Artist's portrait of a clown to be filed away. The pointing clown reminds Alice of her newfound knowledge: Alice stops laughing.

Why does Alice accept her position under male control so quietly at the end? The flapper's revolt against society's standards was a personal one. Alice has no friends, no women confidants, no one to support her emotionally. As a flapper, she demands her moment of freedom, but when the party's over she meekly settles back into the status quo—the trap. Alice's surrender is an act that will become all too familiar in the conclusions of numerous films of the forties and fifties.

The final edge that encourages us to disregard Alice's discourse is the fact that "Alice" cannot speak. The actress who played Alice (Anny Ondra) had a heavy Czech accent and, consequently, a British actress was hired to re-dub all of Alice's dialogue. A "Woman" was constructed according to the male production team's idea of what a woman should be—half-agreeable appearance, half-acceptable accent. Consequently, the desire to dub Anny Ondra was created by a cultural/realist demand ("local English girls don't talk like that") and the subsequent economic demand (the public won't "buy" a Czech "posing" as a Chelsea shopgirl).[3] Nevertheless, we still like, sympathize with, and eventually respect Alice. But the final institutionalized irrelevance of Alice's discourse—with this commercial twist—comes through loud and clear.

Notes

1. E. Ann Kaplan, ed., *Women in Film Noir* (London: BFI, 1980); I am indebted to this source for the authors' exegesis of how these techniques are wedded to the dramatic form of the detective story, which then serves as a vehicle for reestablishing both male control over women's discourse and the patriarchal control of any ultimate "Truth."

2. As E. Ann Kaplan points out in her article, "The Place of Women in Fritz Lang's *The Blue Gardenia*" (in Kaplan, *Women in Film Noir*, 85): "Women in patriarchy do not

function competently at the level of external public articulation and thus may appear 'stupid' and 'uncertain.'" This encapsulates Alice's position, and underlines what she is up against.

3. Charles Barr, "*Blackmail*: Silent and Sound," *Sight and Sound* (Winter 1982–1983). A reproduction of the film's British poster states, "See and Hear Our Mother Tongue as it *should* be spoken!" (italics mine).

TWO

Venus in Furs

Masoch, Deleuze, and the Films of von Sternberg

GAYLYN STUDLAR

IN A WORLD OF ILLUSIONS, HIS CAMERA SUGGESTS EVERYTHING IS POSSIBLE AND NOTHING NECESSARY. POETRY TRANSCENDS PLAUSIBILITY.[1]

ANDREW SARRIS

HUMAN BEINGS CANNOT SUBSIST ON THE SCANTY SATISFACTION WHICH THEY CAN EXTORT FROM REALITY.[2]

SIGMUND FREUD

The film world of Josef von Sternberg is a creation of sublime visual beauty, mystery, and sensuality. Dreamlike chiaroscuro and stifling decorative excess form the backdrop for melodrama in which nothing dominates more securely than a diffuse sexuality. This world blatantly defies our expectations of the "real," so much so that it has been compared to surrealist art.[3] Von Sternberg himself once iconoclastically declared, "Verisimilitude, whatever its virtue, is in opposition to every approach to art."[4] This is a very different philosophy from that which motivates surrealism, and von Sternberg's films emerge as being neither realistic nor surrealistic, but as film fantasies that embrace the paradoxical. As many critics have observed, his films are poetic but not symbolic; melodramatic and even tragic, but characterized by a detached, ironic humor. In these narratives dominated by passion, even passion takes on a curiously distancing coldness. In the films with Marlene Dietrich, von Sternberg adds the paradox of the dazzling, if sometimes strangely androgynous, female who is both moral and amoral, eminently proper and irredeemably decadent. As a result of these layers of paradox, the fascinating ambiguity of emotion, and the almost transcendental visual beauty of these films, von Sternberg's work has become the center of ever-increasing critical interest.

For years, many critics regarded von Sternberg's films as gorgeous but meaningless melodramas, or, as Richard Schickel once scathingly called them, "trash dressed up as art."[5] That view has radically changed; von Sternberg's place in the "Pantheon" has been assured, but the controversy surrounding his work has not lessened. His films have been described as everything from "emotional autobiography . . . in which exoticism is . . . a pretext for objectifying personal fantasies,"[6] to *Cahiers'* declaration that von Sternberg's *Morocco* is the exemplification of "erotic fiction itself entirely determined by the ideology."[7] While Laura Mulvey uses von Sternberg's *Blonde Venus* as an example of the kind of film representation of the female that oppresses women for the sake of the patriarchy's fetishistic aims,[8] Robin Wood argues that the very same film offers a subversively anti-patriarchal and daringly radical feminist stance in which, "Every myth of Woman is *exposed* not celebrated."[9]

In spite of such controversy, von Sternberg's films have not been the subject of a systematic approach that would illuminate the films without forfeiting a sense of the richness and complexity of the work. What is needed is an examination of the specific aesthetic framework that serves as the underpinning of these films, so that von Sternberg's work may be understood as more than just the expression of a "baroque" sensibility or the product of the overwrought aestheticism of a director whose tendency towards self-indulgence pulled him across the forbidden threshold into the no-man's-land of trivialized "camp."

The purpose of this study is to offer a new way of approaching the complex, ambiguous work of Josef von Sternberg. This approach is derived from Gilles Deleuze's *Masochism: An Interpretation of Coldness and Cruelty*. Deleuze proceeds from what he calls "an almost deductive psychoanalysis," which attends "first of all to the formal patterns underlying the processes, viewed as formal elements of fictional art."[10] Deleuze's study focuses on the literature of Leopold von Sacher-Masoch, for whom the pervasive masochism was named. Deleuze identifies his "masochistic aesthetic" operating in Masoch's novels and presents a revised concept of masochism as a clinical, theoretical, and aesthetic entity.

With their emphasis on fantasy, disavowal, fetishism, and suspension, and in their stylistic traits, narrative pattern, and emotional dynamics, von Sternberg's films are the cinematic equivalent to the masochistic aesthetic as represented in literature by Masoch. Not only do von Sternberg's films bear uncanny formal resemblance to Deleuze's description of the masochistic aesthetic in literature, but von Sternberg's work also partakes of the same heritage of German Romanticism as Masoch. Like Masoch's novels, von Sternberg's films can be described as a "mystical play of flesh, fur, and mirror."[11] Other interpretations of von Sternberg's films have acknowledged the role of fantasy, fetishism, and the erotic, and have discussed the relationship between their style and content; yet the appreciation of Deleuze's masochistic aesthetic in von Sternberg's work provides a comprehensive understanding of the dynamics of visual pleasure created by the films, their style, and the psychoanalytic substructure that affects their narrative and visual strategies.

The sexual dynamics in von Sternberg's films have often been labeled "sado-masochistic," and the emphasis on psycho-sexual concerns within the films is obvious, yet the psychological and emotional dynamics of the films have not been explored in depth. Additionally, the characteristics of fantasy, fetishism, and disavowal, all recognized by several critics as present in von Sternberg's films, have not been related to a total aesthetic that simultaneously accounts for the psychic and formal structures of his work.

In order to determine the form and function of the masochistic aesthetic and its relationship to von Sternberg's films, it is necessary to carefully delineate the exact meaning of the term "masochism." Sadism and masochism were linked by several of Freud's predecessors in psychosexual inquiry, including [Richard von] Krafft-Ebing, who gave Leopold von Sacher-Masoch's name to the perversion in his landmark study on aberrant sexuality, *Psychopathia Sexualis*. Krafft-Ebing defined masochism as "the opposite of sadism . . . the wish to suffer pain and be subjected to force," and declared the parallelism between masochism and sadism to be "perfect."[12]

Freud discussed masochism, which he called "the lust of pain," in several essays. After several major shifts of opinion, Freud finally concluded that despite its confusing clinical and theoretical complexities, masochism consisted of the turning around of the superego upon the ego as a result of guilt. The masochist's submission to pain served to punish the unresolved infantile conflict that held sway over the person's psyche.

The child's incestuous desire, first for the mother and then transferred to the father, results in the desire to be punished. The ego allows itself to be subjected to the "heightened sadism of the superego."[13] Consequently, Freud continued to pair sadism and masochism, even though he considered it possible for a primary masochism to arise directly out of the death instinct.[14]

As with other adult perversions, masochism reflects the failure of the individual's defensive mechanisms and so is the opposite of a neurosis. Unlike the neurotic, the masochist tolerates an open fantasy which he acts upon. This fantasy, rooted in the demands of infantile sexuality, merely evidences the individual's failure to outgrow the normally perverse inclinations of childhood sexuality.[15]

To identify a perversion such as masochism as an aesthetic is to suggest a discourse in which form and content are affected by a specific infantile family structure. Just as fantasy forms the basis for dreams, it also becomes the basis for symptoms,[16] and, as Freud noted in his essay "Creative Writers and Daydreaming," for art as well. The work of art represents "a yield of pleasures which he (the artist) offers in the presentation of his fantasies."[17] The acting out of fantasy in a perversion is not far removed from integrating conscious experience with unconscious fantasy in the creation of art.

The complexity of issues involved in the question of masochism, including the reversal of instinct (passive-active), the role of the Oedipus complex in the fantasy, the link between pain and pleasure, and the role of the death instinct and guilt, has provided the impetus for numerous reconsiderations of the perversion. Deleuze's study is unique because his goal is to reintegrate the clinical/psychoanalytic concept known as masochism with its literary context and to correct the misconception of a sado-masochistic entity. To Deleuze, Freud's and subsequent theorists' tendency to consider masochism and sadism as complementary, as mere reversals of each other, has obscured the definition of masochism. Deleuze regards the commonality of the pleasure-pain complex in them as a highly questionable justification for linking the two. Deleuze believes masochism should primarily be considered as a formal entity rather than a material or moral one, and, consequently, he condemns any approach that abstracts either masochism or sadism from its specific self-created universe.[18] Deleuze regards masochism as a particular form of desire, a particular means of reaching pleasure that creates a very specific pattern of fantasy and a unique combination of formal characteristics to express that pattern.

Through his comparative literary analysis of the novels of Masoch and Sade, Deleuze determines that masochism is distinctly separate from sadism, both as a psycho-pathology and as a foundation for a specific aesthetic form.

Deleuze's analysis of Sade's work is startlingly similar to Roland Barthes's description in *Sade/Fourier/Loyola*. Barthes regards Sade's work, in spite of its pornographic nature, as totally lacking in eroticism. This is the result of Sade's scrupulous avoidance of "the striptease . . . that apologue essential to modern eroticism."[19] Barthes and Deleuze both conclude that the Sadian world is dominated by order, apathy, and institutionalized vice. Detailed, often ironic, and invariably obscene descriptions of sexual violence predominate. To Barthes, Sade's denotative language is an unconventional one that serves to "thwart" interpretation and symbolism.[20] Deleuze notes that Sade's narrative structure, dependent as it is on repetition and acceleration of cruel and obscene acts, defies the limits of human physicality and human evil. Sade's world could have no referent in the real world. Barthes and Deleuze agree that Sadian master and victim are rigidly locked into their appointed status. Deleuze emphasizes that contrary to the popularly held notion that there is a sado-masochistic bond, the libertines in Sade's texts do not want a masochistic victim, for as the character Justine declares, "They wish to be certain their crimes cost tears; they would send away any girl who was to come here voluntarily."[21] Sade creates a fantastic world of mechanistic negation of Nature based on the rule of reason. The psychoanalytic foundation of this world, according to Deleuze, is the negation of the mother and the exaltation of the father to a place above the law. In an Oedipal construct, it is the father and child who bring about the destruction of the mother.[22]

In contrast to the Sadian world, masochism creates a distinctive vision based on fantasy, disavowal, suspension, and fetishism. Its language, rather than being imperative and descriptive like Sade's, is mythical, persuasive, and dialectical. Masoch's world is centered around the idealizing, mystical exaltation of love for the woman who punishes. In the masochistic aesthetic, imagination, not reason, reigns supreme. Its beauty and "super sensuality" of description replace the ironic humor of Sade's shocking homage to Negation through reason. Sade exalts evil; the masochistic aesthetic exalts beauty. Unlike the Sadian world of accelerated repetition of tortures and obscene acts in ever-changing patterns, the masochistic text freezes desire into vignettes of veiled sexuality and masquerades of misunderstanding. In *Ideology and the Image*, Bill Nichols remarks on the evocation of the erotic in von Sternberg's *Blonde Venus* through "the flash of skin between two folds of clothing."[23] Such an eroticism has no place in Sade's world of institutionalized fornication, but is very relevant to the masochistic aesthetic which needs no censor because the control of desire is the essence of masochism's need to suspend pleasure. Suspension of gratification is the temporal fundamental of masochism's narrative scheme. The rigidity of order and identity of the Sadian world is in complete contrast to the masochistic text's transformations of identity through role-playing and masquerade.

In the masochistic aesthetic, the female is not the object of torture, but the object of almost mystic contemplation that disavows female castration and fetishizes her. Danger and reassurance are mixed in the fetishized female who is intelligent, brave, and capable of great love, but who is also quite capable of driving men to heartbreak, insanity, and death with her coldness and infidelity. Sade's destruction of the female is replaced by the positive disavowal of woman. Dramatic suspense replaces Sadian repetition and acceleration; intimacy between mutually consenting partners replaces the impersonal, institutionalized orgy, just as eroticism replaces obscenity.

At the psychoanalytic core of the masochistic aesthetic is the Oedipal triangle in which mother and child are united in alliance to expel the father's genital likeness in the son. Deleuze, in a major revision of Freudian theory, believes that it is this infantile fantasy that produces masochism. At the center of this fantasy is the masochistic ideal of the cold oral mother who inflicts pain, but who can also become the recipient of pain in the easy transference typical of masochism. The female is the ambivalent maternal figure who punishes the dependent infant but also provides love and sustenance. The father is perceived as a threat and must be expiated. As Deleuze remarks, "The father is nothing, in other words, he is deprived of all symbolic function."[24] The mother superficially assumes the father's superego function. In her ideal form in the masochistic aesthetic, the female is not sadistic, but inflicts cruelty in love only because she must fulfill her role as the necessary element of pain. Just as the sadist does not want a masochistic partner who would not enjoy pain, the masochist could not tolerate a sadistic partner who would undermine the masochistic scheme of mutual contracted agreement. Deleuze concludes that it is the superego, represented by the father, that is destroyed and the ego that finally triumphs. The masochist, in controlling his orgasmic pleasure by suspending it, accomplishes ego's narcissistic triumph over the demands of the superego that would prevent or punish pleasure.[25]

In *Shanghai Express*, Magdalene/Shanghai Lily represents all the virtues of the masochistic ideal female type, but she has "wrecked a dozen men up and down the Chinese coast." Her past relationship with Doc Harvey is largely left a blank (thus increasing her alluring enigma). Doc admits to suffering loneliness in various exotic locales after their smashup. Lily's only spoken regret after five years as a prostitute is that she has bobbed her hair. Initially, she appears to represent Masoch's Grecian woman who is pagan, sensual, and independent. Lily is both "imperious and coquettish," just as Masoch described a character in his novel *The Siren*.[26] Although aloof and cynical, Lily eventually proves her love for Doc, who must accept her back on her terms as Lily raises her function as a prostitute to a level of sacrifice. This paradoxical idealization of women through degradation is characteristic of von Sternberg's films and Masoch's novels. The good oral mother assumes and transforms the functions of the bad mother (punishment, prostitution, etc.). To save Doc from the threat of blinding, Lily offers herself to the villain, Chang. Doc sees her stay with Chang and assumes that Lily has her "professional" reasons for doing so. He must accept her back without proof of her motives. Knowledge through visual proof must defer to disavowal's "I know but nevertheless" structure of acceptance. The film ultimately is a paean to faith, which could be considered just another form of disavowal.

Much has been made of the "sadism" of the central female in the von Sternberg/Dietrich films. Raymond Durgnat identifies the sadism of Concha in *The Devil Is a Woman* as being the result of "class vindictiveness" and asks of Catherine's actions at the end of *The Scarlet Empress*: "Isn't she now a female Sade?"[27] Deleuze explains that in the masochistic aesthetic, the female's actions may appear to be "sadistic," but they are only the pseudo-sadism of the female's necessary assumption of superego function. True sadism could not exist within the masochistic world. At the end of *The Scarlet Empress*, Catherine becomes a woman of stone; she achieves the masochistic ideal of coldness, buried sentimentality, and death.[28] In Masoch's novels, the masochistic male signs a contract with a woman and persuades her to assume the role of torturess. In the world of von Sternberg's films, either the individual male or the patriarchal society can make the woman assume the same role. In the transformation of the German princess Sophia into the "Messalina of the North," the female is manipulated by the system's political structure until she is the icy mother, the terrible Tsarina who replaces Peter and, ironically, becomes the relative good in a corrupt system. In one of Masoch's novels, a girl dreams of being an executioner, yet she is still described as "reasonable and kind."[29] In *The Scarlet Empress*, Sophia begins life as an innocent who wants to be a "hangman" like the kind of executioner who tends her. Renamed Catherine, she becomes a female "brood mare" in the Russian court. Finally, Catherine leads Cossacks as she takes the throne and replaces male rule. Her attainment of power results from her manipulation by and then of the system, just as the female in Masoch's novels is also manipulated into playing the role of torturess.

In keeping with the masochistic aesthetic, the women in many of von Sternberg's films embody the malleability of the female in contrast to the fixation and stasis of the male. The ambivalent female's capacity for role-playing finds its source in the fantasy figure of the seducing-rejecting mother who is created by the dependent, controlled child. The child projects his hostility onto the mother figure. In masochism, the fetishization of the female (the oral mother figure) disavows the female castration that would mark her sexual difference and rob her of the symbolic power of the phallus. It freezes the moment in which belief in the mother's phallus was still possible for the child and denies knowledge of sexual difference by the substitution of the fetish.

Women's protean nature is foregrounded in von Sternberg's films through several means—the masquerades of revelry or spying in *Dishonored* and *The Devil Is a Woman*, the "performance" of prostitution in *Blonde Venus* and *Shanghai Express*, and the stage performance sequences in virtually all of the von Sternberg/Dietrich films. Role-playing becomes a matter of survival, as it does for Catherine in *The Scarlet Empress* and Helen Faraday in *Blonde Venus*. Catherine survives the intrigues of the Russian court because she accepts the necessary roles. At one point she tells Alexei, her frustrated lover, that she likes Russia now that she has "learned how Mother Russia expects me to behave." With the end of *The Scarlet Empress*, Catherine assumes male attire and male power. She is the phallic female whose presence disavows female castration, yet, paradoxically, Catherine's "castration" as a female has permitted her to attain a dominant position. She has seduced the Russian army. Through her possession of, as Freud called it, the "inferior organ" of woman which her officer's uni-

Figure 2.1. *Blonde Venus* (1932)

form would seem to disavow, she has assured her survival and subjugated the male to her icy rule.

In *Blonde Venus*, Helen Faraday, like Catherine, assumes male attire at the pinnacle of her "success" in the male world. A client at the Parisian nightclub where she performs tells Nick Townsend, her former lover, that Helen's rise to fame has been secured by her exploitation of men. "She's as cold as the proverbial icicle," he adds. At her lowest, in a miserable flophouse, Helen swore that she would "find a better bed." We are led to believe that she has found several. She has left behind her role of good mother who prostituted herself for the welfare of both husband and child. Now she is like Masoch's Grecian woman, a hermaphroditic figure who denounces the permanence of love and lives only for pleasure. In a poster that advertises her appearance at the club, she is depicted as an abstracted deco nude, as female object for the male gaze. On stage, however, she is more than discreetly covered in a gentleman's white tuxedo. Her costuming renounces her audience's expectation that her body is of chief interest in her performance. With her costume, Helen, like Catherine in *The Scarlet Empress*, denies the sexual difference that has ensured her success in a male world. She has become a mirror reflection of man's manipulative power. Helen tells Nick that she has no more feelings, but what would appear to be a sadistic negation of feeling is only a disavowal. The chains of emotion are unbroken; with the end of the film, Helen is restored to her maternal function as the ideal oral mother. She is reunited with her husband, but, more importantly, with her real primary love object, her son, whose sexualized relationship with his mother is in keeping with the masochistic fantasy core of the alliance between the desiring infant and the oral mother.

The model offered by Deleuze seems a promising one. Too often Freudianism or Freudian based psychoanalytic approaches have been employed in film criticism to the apparent exclusion of other models. Deleuze's approach opens avenues for close textual analysis of von Sternberg's films that can include consideration of narrative structure, mise-en-scène, specific motifs, as well as the dynamics of pleasure created by the films.

To study the relationship between a perversion and its expression as an aesthetic and psychologically governing principle in films is not only to examine the expression of a certain type of power/pleasure relationship portrayed through narrative events and character types, but to open up the possibility of examining the complex phenomenon of spectator/film text relationship and the generation of cinematic pleasure in general. The masochistic aesthetic suggests, not only the creation of a unique type of film discourse based on a certain way of structuring infantile sexual conflict (unconscious) and conscious adult conflicts (cultural and sociological concerns) into art, but also the creation of a specific mode of perception and form of visual pleasure in the spectator. The masochistic aesthetic depends upon fantasy, disavowal, suspension, and fetishism in the formation of its formal structure—the very same factors that enable the classic narrative cinema to produce visual pleasure in its audience. This study's approach holds fascinating possibilities for dealing with films that centralize the place of violence or sexuality and therefore have an obvious link to a masochistic or "sadistic aesthetic"; it also has important ramifications for the exploration of visual pleasure and film.

Notes

1. Andrew Sarris, *The Films of Josef von Sternberg* (New York: Museum of Modern Art, 1966), 29.

2. Sigmund Freud, "Introductory Lecture on Psycho-analysis," in *The Complete*

Psychological Works of Sigmund Freud (Standard Edition), edited and translated by James Strachey (London: Hogarth Press, 1953–1966), 16:372.

3. Ado Kyrou, *Le Surréalisme au cinéma* (Paris: Éditions Arcanes, 1953), 123–127.

4. Josef von Sternberg quoted in Peter Wollen, *Signs and Meaning in the Cinema* (Bloomington: Indiana University Press, 1969), 137.

5. Richard Schickel quoted in Josef von Sternberg, *Fun in a Chinese Laundry: An Autobiography* (New York: Macmillan, 1965), 262.

6. Andrew Sarris, *The American Cinema: Directors and Directions 1929–1968* (New York: E. P. Dutton, 1968), 77.

7. "Morocco," *Cahiers du Cinéma* 225 (November–December 1970), in Peter Baxter, *Sternberg* (London: BFI, 1980), 91.

8. Laura Mulvey, "Visual Pleasure and Narrative Cinema," *Screen* 16, no. 3 (Autumn 1975): 14.

9. Robin Wood, "Venus de Marlene," *Film Comment* 14, no. 2 (March-April 1978): 63.

10. Gilles Deleuze, *Masochism: An Interpretation of Coldness and Cruelty*, translated by Jean McNeil (New York: George Brazilier, 1971), 63.

11. Ibid., 61.

12. Richard von Krafft-Ebing, *Psychopathia Sexualis*, translated by F. J. Ribman (reprint, New York: Special Books, Inc., 1965), 131, 217.

13. Sigmund Freud, "The Economic Problem in Masochism," in *General Psychological Theory: Papers on Metapsychology*, edited by Philip Rieff (New York: Collier Books, 1963), 191.

14. Ibid., 190–192.

15. Deleuze, *Masochism*, 39.

16. Sigmund Freud, "The Unconscious," in Rieff, *General Psychological Theory*, 138.

17. Sigmund Freud, "Creative Writers and Daydreaming," in Strachey, *Standard Edition*, 9:144.

18. Deleuze, *Masochism*, 39.

19. Roland Barthes, *Sade/Fourier/Loyola*, translated by Richard Miller (New York: Hill & Wang, 1975), 26.

20. Ibid., 134.

21. Marquis de Sade, *Justine*, quoted in Deleuze, *Masochism*, 36.

22. Deleuze, *Masochism*, 115.

23. Bill Nichols, *Ideology and the Image* (Bloomington: Indiana University Press, 1981), 123.

24. Deleuze, *Masochism*, 83.

25. Ibid., 42–54.

26. Masoch, *The Siren*, quoted in Deleuze, *Masochism*, 42.

27. Raymond Durgnat, "Six Films of Josef von Sternberg," in *Movies and Methods*, edited by Bill Nichols (Berkeley: University of California Press, 1970), 268–271.

28. Deleuze, *Masochism*, 49.

29. Masoch, *The Aesthetic of Ugliness*, quoted in Deleuze, *Masochism*, 45.

THREE

"You Don't Know What It Is to Look White and Be Black"

The Black Press Mediates Race in the Classic Hollywood Studio System, 1930–1940

ANNA EVERETT

UNCLE TOM HAS DROPPED HIS HAT; AUNT JEMIMA HAS REMOVED HER BANDANA; PICKANINNIES ARE WEARING SHOES AND SLOWLY BUT SURELY, HOLLYWOOD FILMS ARE GROWING UP.

FAY M. JACKSON (1934)[1]

IN ALL CLASS SOCIETIES, THE DOMINATING CLASS RULES BY CONTROLLING THE INSTRUMENTS OF CULTURE, ALONG WITH ECONOMIC AND POLITICAL POWER. TO TALK OF PURE AND UNBIASED ART UNDER SUCH CIRCUMSTANCES IS SHEER ROT AND NONSENSE. ART IS A WEAPON IN THE HANDS OF THE WHITE RULING CLASS.

CYRIL BRIGGS (1933)[2]

Since most writing on blacks in Hollywood during the classical studio era centers on the representation of African-Americans in mainstream films, the focus has been on image criticism and negative racial stereotypes as considered retrospectively by such important writers on the topic as Donald Bogle, Thomas Cripps, Henry Sampson, Mark Reid, bell hooks, Ed Guerrero, among others. As important as the literature and criticism produced by these scholars and writers is to the study of American film history, it represents the proverbial tip of the historical iceberg where writing on black participation in Hollywood during the studio era is concerned.

For example, one area of exploration into this period that has suffered chronic inattention is the enormous amount of writing on the cinema produced contemporaneously by black writers who lived through and wrote about the black experience in Hollywood during the thirties and forties. Much of their film criticism and commentary, due to the segregated nature of publishing at that time, was restricted to the newspapers and journals comprising the national black press network.

Although many of the epoch's black writers producing film criticism were journalists with local prestige, a significant number enjoyed national and international reputations, and some were well-renowned and well-respected members of that elite literary circle dubbed the "black literati" of Harlem Renaissance fame—writers such as James Weldon Johnson, Melvin B. Tolson, and Alain Locke. Other important writers from the period who contributed to the literature were poets Sterling Brown and Langston Hughes, and cultural anthropologist Zora Neale Hurston. Even independent filmmakers Oscar Micheaux and Juli Jones wrote film criticism for the black press. While some of the contemporary writers have consulted the historical literature produced by black critics of the thirties and forties, often the focus has not been on the literature itself but rather on the factual or evidentiary information the writing provides. What is still needed is an analysis of the black press writers' engagement with the technical, social, and artistic controversies of the period.

The black film criticism produced during the ascendancy of Hollywood's classic studio system is prolific, complex, and deeply imbricated in the political, social, and economic upheavals of the Great Depression era. Significantly, this literature bifurcates along familiar lines in African-American political thought: that duality of accommodation and radicalism. Along the accommodationist axis is criticism and commentary concerned with effecting a progressive reform of Hollywood attitudes on the race question; along the radical line are those critiques defined by a politics of opposition to dominant filmmaking practices and their attendant bourgeois and Eurocentric ideologies. Whereas the former is marked by an integrationist tendency designed to increase black participation in the Hollywood mainstream, the latter often mobilizes radical political ideologies, such as Marxism, socialism, and alternative proletarian art aesthetics,[3] to redirect the black political consciousness away from the lure of "false consciousness" offered by Hollywood's escapist and often racist cinematic productions.

Sound and Censorship

The innovation of sound technology in 1927 played an important role in shaping the film literature of the thirties, for Hollywood developed a new interest in black talent. The successful wave of black-cast stage productions in Northern theaters, such as *The Emperor Jones*, *The Green Pastures*, and *Porgy*, influenced this interest. A number of black performers, including Bill "Bojangles" Robinson, Duke Ellington, and Ethel Waters, were pressed into service in mainstream Hollywood fare during the first few years of the sound revolution. Thus Hollywood's cooptation of black musical idioms for its sound films led white and black critics to the presumption that a new era in black cinematic representations had finally arrived.[4] Furthermore, African-American performers, critics, and activists anticipated the opening of greater opportunities for blacks in Hollywood.[5]

A telling comment by African-American performer Geraldyn Dismond provides the best indication of black critics' attitudes regarding the potentially revolutionary impact of sound technology. In the August 1929 issue of the British journal *Close Up* (a special edition devoted to blacks and the cinema), Dismond discussed the limitations of and possibilities for new cinematic articulations of race and representations of blackness. "The talkie, which is being despised in certain artistic circles, is giving [the African-American] the great opportunity to prove his right to a place on the screen."[6] Dismond's and other writers' criticisms appearing in the special *Close Up* edition were occasioned by Hollywood's 1929 releases of not one but two all-black-cast films, MGM's *Hallelujah* and Fox's *Hearts in Dixie*. Dismond states: "It is significant that with the coming of talkies, the first all-Negro feature pictures were attempted by the big companies. . . . The movie of yesterday, to be sure, let him dance, but his greatest charm was lost by silence. With the talkie, the Negro is at his best. Now he can be heard in song and speech."[7] In the main, the critics expressed a guarded optimism that despite these films' perpetuation of "the way down South in the land of cotton idea,"[8] "the present vogue for negro films was inevitable."[9] As for some critics in the black press who sought to capitalize on the big studios' "inevitable" demand for novel approaches to the special requirements of sound technology, the moment had indeed arrived to press for a wider integration of African-Americans in Hollywood and, by extension, in the mainstream of American civil society.

While the sound revolution gave particular impetus to the dominance of what can be described as the integrationist logic in the black press's literature, a number of black writers who focused on Will Hays and the film industry's Production Code Administration (PCA) were not as accommodating. Giving voice to concerns about the hegemonic function of Hollywood's self-policing agency were the film critics who wrote for Cyril Briggs's left-wing newspaper the *Harlem Liberator*, later rechristened the *Negro Liberator*. The *Liberator*'s two film columns routinely presented scenarios confirming suspicions that, even after the institution of the PCA's Seal of Approval in 1934, exceptions to the rule of the PCA were not uncommon, especially if box-office receipts indicated public demand for anti-code material, particularly anti-code material that did not undermine or disparage capitalism or the nation's racial attitudes. The *Liberator* writer, pseudonymously called "Camera-Eye," presents one clear example of the code's double standard where nudity and sexuality are at issue. Writing in the column "Screenings," Camera-Eye demonstrates the hypocrisy of the Hays Office in its approach to censorship on the grounds of nudity. Supposedly, "nudity of all sorts" was absolutely prohibited.[10] Camera-Eye illustrates in the January 27, 1934, column that this decency taboo was elastic when race entered into the equation. How else to account for the nonapplicability of the nudity taboo to cinematic representations of the black female body? "Will Hays's boys are on the rampage again with blasts against too-naked women. But it's Okay when African women appear with the proverbial G-string. Morals are funny things."[11] The point Camera-Eye makes is well taken, though understated. Presumably, American spectators understood that nudity was disallowed by "the code" in films at all times. Yet, with the exception to the rule being the *de facto* acceptability of black nudity, it is apparent that the Hays Office and the studios found yet another way to construct racial binary oppositions in representations that privileged whiteness. On the one hand, the code's morality clause shielded nude white bodies from the prurient gaze, while on the other, the fetishized "primitive" black body, positioned outside the code of human morality and decency, was at once made an acceptable site for sexual titillation and sanctioned racial degradation.

Whereas Camera-Eye takes aim at the diegetic manifestations of the code's duplicitous uses, the *Liberator*'s other columnist, Dave Platt, takes on Will Hays directly in a parodic utterance designed to reveal Hays's actual function as the studios' rubber stamp instead of as a guardian of the public morals. In his column published on March 24, 1934, Platt considers Will Hays and his official duties:

> Will Hays once again says the movie companies must keep the moral code or suffer severe penalties. . . . Hays has been saying this for many years now and the movie companies have been paying him handsomely for it . . . but still we get the same old pictures day after day. . . . It's just a game of tag with them. . . . Hays knows too well that if he steps out of bounds just once, he's through. . . . That is [why] this "moral code" business is such a big joke.[12]

Platt is intent on revealing the chief "moral code" enforcer's own lack of morality. By reminding readers that Hays is not an independent agency, but one wholly beholden to powerful film moguls, Platt, like Camera-Eye, bares the economic and ideological motives behind the Hays Office's highly selective use of its immense powers of censorship. This is an important emphasis that takes on added significance when viewed in the context of both columns' critiques of specific instances where films were censored for political reasons. For example, on December 23, 1933, Platt criticizes the Hays Office for banning a film exposing the conditions of a squatters' camp known as "Hooverville." Officially the film was banned for a violation of the morals code because it depicted a common-law relationship between an unmarried couple. But Platt contends that this was a mere pretext used to foreclose the circulation of cinematic references to the crisis of unemployment.[13] To illustrate the hypocrisy of this instance of censorship, Platt states that "Mae West and her whole tribe are permitted all kinds of salacious liberties in their films without encountering any trouble whatsoever from Mr. Will Hays." Platt observes a similar tendency on the part of the censors when the subject of lynchings appears in the films.

In his March 31, 1934, "Drama—Movie: Movie Snapshots" column, Platt opens with a reference to the recent release of a Universal Studios horror film, expected to be a major hit because it features Hollywood's most famous monster icons, Bela Lugosi's "Dracula," Boris Karloff's "Frankenstein," and Lionel Atwill's "Doctor X," together in one film, *The Suicide Club*. After framing his main discussion in terms of the upcoming cinematic monster fest, Platt shifts his focus to a consideration of what he terms the nation's true monstrosity. Platt writes:

> But the biggest monstrosity of them all is not manufactured by make-up men in Hollywood, but is right here in our midst doing some real blood sucking and bone breaking. I mean that gigantic monstrosity called Capitalism. Will Hays believes that Walt Disney's "Three Little Pigs" put an end to the Big Bad Wolf of the Depression. Hays sees signs of prosperity all around his palatial

residence in Beverly Hills. According to Mr. Hays the Depression which put fifteen million honest workers out of work was started by Miss Betty Boop singing "The Sun Is Going Down." That's upper class ideology for you.[14]

Platt's wicked humor is extremely effective here because it successfully recodes Hollywood's fictitious monster discourse to make it symbolize the economic bloodletting visited upon real victims of economic depression. In this way Platt forces readers and spectators to refocus their attention onto their own actual pain and suffering caused by the specialist capitalist interest that men like Hays represent. His aim is to make film audiences understand the different lenses through which the unemployed, presumably themselves, and the over-employed, individuals such as Hays, see the realities of the Depression. Of course, Platt insists, Hays and his class cannot see accurately the depths of the Depression from their "palatial" residences in Beverly Hills, and he, Platt, is just as insistent in his interpellation of the suffering masses so that they can see how ridiculously inadequate Hollywood's escapist film fare is for a nation caught up in this crisis of capitalism.

While blacks writing from an accommodationist viewpoint saw the progressive potential of talking pictures, the advent of sound on the eve of the Great Depression brought untold catastrophe for the black independent filmmakers. The prohibitive costs associated with the conversion to sound in the wake of the stock-market crash of 1929 proved insurmountable indeed for the fledging independent black film companies. Many historians have considered the crisis wrought by the technology on both the white independents and the major and minor Hollywood film studios.[15] Yet, even in the wake of revisionist historiographies of the period, no adequate accounting of sound's near-total decimation of the black independents has been forthcoming.

We can deduce the deleterious and the far-reaching consequences of sound technology on the black independents by their coterminous disappearance. Some telling comments appear in a 1931 *New York Age* article. "Sidelights on New Picture, 'The Exile,'" is a brief discussion of Oscar Micheaux's first sound film, *The Exile*, which was produced in that same year. Micheaux's particular case becomes synecdochial for the entire independent black film industry: "The difficulties of creating talking pictures were so great, however, that he [Micheaux] was hardly able to get started."[16] As the article progresses, it goes on to stress some of the costly sound production elements that increased the financial expenditures associated with the pursuit of harnessing the technology for the "race-films" market. Micheaux's "lack of funds" resulted in a partnership arrangement with white theatrical manager Frank Schiffman. Unfortunately, most black independents, such as the Lincoln Motion Picture Company, were not as resilient as Micheaux. Consequently, they failed to make the expensive transition to sound. However, Micheaux's interracial alliance with Schiffman was double-edged in that it saved the mercurial company from bankruptcy, but that salvation had a Faustian dimension. As Mark Reid describes it in *Redefining Black Film*, "even though Micheaux retained his name in the Micheaux Film Corporation, the corporation was financed and controlled by two whites."[17] This transfer of power in the Micheaux case was symbolic of an even greater transformation impelled by the advent of sound. The "Schiffman-Brecher-Micheaux union," with its successes, "presaged later interracial [filmmaking] collaborations,"[18] but most importantly, the flood of white-controlled film companies into the lucrative "race-films" market, conjoined with the sound revolution and the economics of the Depression, engulfed and ultimately supplanted the last vestiges of the black-owned and -operated independent film companies.

Imitation of Life and the Black Press

When Universal Pictures released its cinematic adaptation of Fannie Hurst's best-selling novel *Imitation of Life*, at the end of 1934, the general consensus in the black press mainstream was that the film portended "A New Departure in Movies." At least this is the sentiment as expressed in a *Pittsburgh Courier* editorial of December 22, 1934. As a film that centered on the lifelong friendship and professional partnership between two widowed, single mothers, one black (Louise Beavers) and one white (Claudette Colbert), this highly successful social problem film did represent a departure from the usual Hollywood films featuring black characters. In terms of casting alone, this film broke new ground, and on several fronts. First of all, it is the first interracial buddy film featuring a black actor in an important role. Second, it is the first to feature a representation of "the modern black woman." And though she was "still a servant," Donald Bogle reminds us that this particular celluloid servant was figured as a modern black woman "imbued with dignity and a character that were an integral part of the American way of life."[19] Third, in casting Fredi Washington and giving her narrative range and agency as Louise Beaver's mulatta daugh-

Figure 3.1. *Imitation of Life* (1934)

ter, Peola, the film is the first to treat sympathetically the psychosocial dynamics of the tragic mulatto issue from the perspective of the mulatto character.[20] Lastly, on this subject, this is one of the first interracial Hollywood films to permit the white and black characters to occupy positions of relative parity insofar as the narrative emplotment was concerned. In terms of locale and setting, this is the first mainstream film with a central black story line that is not confined spatially to a Southern plantation, although it is important not to overlook the Southern antebellum ethos that drives this melodramatic plot of race, lies, and pancake fortune.

The film's transcendent value for black audiences of the thirties, however, is best summed up by this editorial commentary published in the *Courier*:

> When before has any screen or stage drama for general attraction pondered the pertinent question of the "colored" girl who can pass for white? . . . When also has the question of the proper relations between a white and colored person in a business partnership been propounded? . . . When before have colored people appeared as dignified, intelligent, well-dressed human beings and not as jovial cretins on the silver screen? Here are Negroes who go to college, have beautiful churches and dignified religious services quite contrary to the libelous nonsense of "The Green Pastures." . . . Imagine! A moving picture with Negro actors, and yet no hoofing, no blues singing, no vociferous horselaughs, no razor wielding, no barnyard amours! There is much in "Imitation of Life" which is dreadfully superficial and needlessly sentimental and far-fetched, but it will really set America to thinking furiously. It is dynamite.[21]

The *Courier* reports that the black response to the film in Chicago was so overwhelming that it was "held over for a second week at the Metropolitan Theatre." The manager of the theater is reported as saying, "We have done more business with the motion picture 'Imitation of Life' and Fredi Washington, one of the stars making a personal appearance with the film, than any other week in the history of Warner Brothers Metropolitan Theatre. So eager were the people to see the picture with their own stars that hundreds paid for standing room." This situation was duplicated in New York, according to entertainment critic Chappy Gardner.

To account for the immense popularity of this film among African-Americans, it is useful to examine some of the specific issues that bear on the film's allure for 1930s black spectators. The fact that the film is among the first to set its tale of interracial cooperation against the backdrop of the Great Depression must have resonated forcefully with this financially weary audience. But that surely was not enough to motivate them to part with their meager resources for the privilege of paying for standing room only to see this film. However, we get an indication of just what Depression-era black audiences found so compelling in *Imitation of Life* from *Courier* critic Fay M. Jackson.

Writing on December 15, 1934, shortly after the release of the film, Jackson uncovers the one element in the film that triggers the black audiences' affective response: in two words, Fredi Washington. Washington's powerful performance in the film made her "the great black hope."[22] Far beyond the limits of the tragic mulatta icon, Washington's Peola generates a signifying chain of highly complex social, historical, economic, racial, and psychical meanings for black spectators. In her review, "Fredi Washington Strikes New Note in Hollywood Film," Jackson describes many of these coordinates as they converge to produce the Peola discourse:

> In "Imitation of Life," Fredi Washington . . . utters a cry. "I want the same things other people enjoy." . . . That found an echo in the hearts of 12 million smoldering Negroes throughout the United States and probably has been since their so-called emancipation from chattel slavery. Actress though she be, Fredi Washington expresses the desire for freedom and equal justice in this picture that is more convincing than any mere performer could have voiced. True to her own life, the injustices of color and race prejudice have retarded and prohibited a fuller life and freedom of expression. . . . You feel some of the weight of the bars of race prejudice in this country when you see, probably for the first time, the true symbol of the American Negro struggling

against these bars as Fredi Washington portrays the role of "Peola" in "Imitation of Life."[23]

As Jackson patently illustrates, black audiences responded so favorably to the fair-skinned Washington because the actress's own racial identity imbued the character with an authenticating aura unavailable to a Caucasian actress attempting to pass for black attempting to pass for white. It was precisely Washington's degree zero of representational whiteness[24] that made Peola's cry, as Jackson writes it, "I want the same things other people enjoy," so forceful and shrill. Surely, black audiences understood the subtext at the bottom of such a yearning. My own screening of the film at this writing did not confirm the above statement that Jackson attributes to Washington's Peola character. What I can confirm is that Peola says, "You don't know what it is to look white and be black," an equally powerful statement that appears in the film when Delilah and Peola have their final gut-wrenching encounter. Ultimately, for black audiences of that era, the point is that if an African-American could possess all that America holds dear, education, good lucks, youth, vitality, and above all, luminous white skin, and still be denied the "same things other people enjoy," then what chance has the darker African-American? Peola's simple utterance interjected in the mass consciousness of a racist nation was tantamount to an act of sedition. The subversiveness of the quote, in either case (what Jackson heard, or what I heard), is somewhat confined within the tragic mulatta problematic. Still, it functions as a potent demand for the nation to acknowledge the fact of black humanity. Jackson and Bogle concur on the point that Washington's "Peola absolutely symbolized the 'New Negro' demanding a New Deal."[25] In 1934, at the height of the Depression, one can imagine that this utterance alone was worth the price of standing room only. When we consider the implications of one particular test of the film's allure in the black community, one episode is especially revealing: "'Imitation' faced strong [competition] from Duke Ellington at the Regal Theater, half a block away, when it opened [in Chicago], but toward the end of the week 'Imitation' was still jamming them in with plenty of vacant seats at the Regal."[26] This cultural contest for the leisure time and money of Chicago's "Black Belt" gives us an index of the power of the Peola discourse.

Of course, while Jackson's review provides evidence of black spectators' transgressive readings of the film's racist ideologies, contrasted particularly by the Peola character, it is doubtful that Hurst, Universal, or director

John Stahl imagined Peola as a subversive element, a "rebel against the system."[27] Donald Bogle points out the fundamental differences between the black and white interpretations of the Peola discourse. "The explanation for Peola's rebellion," in the white imaginary "is that she wants to be white," whereas the black interpretative community understand "that she wants white opportunities."[28] It matters little whether or not either interpretation accords with the narrative intent of the character's construction as a literary or cinematic object. What is certain about such interpretive contests regarding the social meaning of texts is that "one cannot appeal to the text, because the text has become an extension of the interpretive disagreement that divides them [*sic*] and, in fact, the text as it is variously characterized is a consequence of the interpretation for which it is supposedly evidence."[29] Put more plainly, we cannot arbitrate successfully between these two perspectives on the grounds of textual "fact" because, ultimately, black and white audiences saw in the film's mulatta character "facts" or evidence that corresponded to the dictates of their racially and socially constructed outlooks. We can, however, credit the production of the film and its sympathetic portrayals of Beavers's and Washington's characters to the nation's new spirit of liberalism, impelled in large part by the realities of the Depression economy, the Great Migration, and the "New Negro."

While Beavers's breakout performance in the film must have warmed the hearts of black audiences as well, it is doubtful that this audience found Beavers's modern "mammy" compelling in its own right. Whereas the *Courier* found the mere suggestion of a black and white business partnership in this film as propounding a step forward for race relations, its failure to see the Delilah character's rejection of her fair claim to financial compensation in the business venture as the equivalent of two steps backward and as an insidious narrative redeployment of the antebellum master-slave relationship is curious. Perhaps this is one of the "far-fetched" elements to which Jackson's review alluded. If *Imitation of Life* was teaching blacks and whites a vulgarized class solidarity in the "fight for better living conditions,"[30] in the words of Arthur Draper, it likewise was undermining the cause of racial equality by reconstructing white supremacist ideology in the black and white characters' domestic relations.

Apparently *Courier* critic Bernice Patton recognized that this flawed logic constituted a bitter pill for black audiences. But Patton, as representative of the accommodationist press, opted for the most conciliatory gloss in her film review entitled "Critics Weep at the Preview of 'Imitation of Life.'" Even though she concedes that "naturally there are sequences in the film that will grieve my people,"[31] Patton goes on to articulate a position of acquiescence that one would expect from *Imitation of Life*'s modern mammy, Delilah. Eschewing the more critical stance, Patton continues:

> But I beg of them to be tolerant. . . . Don't spoil your economic advantages and possibilities in the movies by intolerant criticism. You must remember that this film gave you your first real star, Louise Beavers, fabulous financial gains to the race and opens the way for other Negro artists in the films. I think the epic really serves its purpose, inasmuch as it proves to white people that they have been unkind and unjust to their American brother of African descent. The picture gives them a more human understanding and love for the Negro.[32]

It is interesting that after admonishing black critics and spectators against expressing their just dissatisfactions, Patton would hold up Beavers—the new and improved modern mammy—as evidence of good faith from "the industry that aims to erase the color-line." In attempting to justify her untenable position, Patton advances this questionable appeasement: "The making of the picture has been a delicate task, because the plot involves the social and economic problem of the Negro. The kind, sympathetic Stahl was a mighty brave man to produce the stirring, daring drama. He took every precaution not to offend either race. . . . Throughout the screen version, he struck out the word 'nigger.'"[33] Patton either conveniently neglects to mention or is unaware that the excision of the epithet was the result of pressure from the NAACP that was brought about at the behest of Louise Beavers.[34]

Interestingly, Patton's and Jackson's differing perspectives on the film's meaning as conveyed through the two black performers almost reenact the philosophical split that exists between the film's characters Delilah and Peola. Whereas Jackson's review foregrounds the subversive potential of Washington's portrayal of a would-be modern black woman, one impatient with the slow pace of racial justice, Patton's review preaches patience and acquiescence to the status quo in terms resonant with Delilah's acceptance of "her place." Although Jackson and Patton assess the film's merits differently, they both endorse the film. Still, the recognition that each woman approaches the film from opposing critical positions leads us to a more nuanced appreciation of the often unruly and multifarious nature of the accommodationist literary mode.

The *Crisis* magazine's criticism of *Imitation of Life* is also instructive on this point. In the June 1935 edition, Howard University professor Mercer Cook wrote a review of the film from Paris, France. Cook's critique is fascinating because his own reception of the film is conditioned by the zeitgeist, if you will, of a foreign national culture. More importantly, Cook's exposition is not confined to issues of the pro-filmic or the narrative diegesis. His review is enlarged by its anthropological function. In addition to communicating his own feelings about the film, Cook relays and interprets the French audience's response to the film for his American readers back home.[35] To this end, Cook opens the discussion with this observation, "The reaction of the spectators at last night's performance was one of perplexity rather than of enthusiasm. Nevertheless, from the Negro's point of view, the showing of the film in France is significant and deserving of passing comment."[36] Having said that, Cook then explains the perplexing cultural and linguistic factors that in all probability would prevent the film from enjoying "great popularity in Europe." For one thing, "the subject is too foreign," Cook says. "The action drags at times," and "the French subtitles are in several instances extremely unsatisfactory," he adds.

The cultural barriers Cook finds most significant have to do with "the difference between American and French conceptions of race relations."[37] This explains much in the way of accounting for the insufficiencies in the French subtitles. For as Cook points out: "There is, for example, no French equivalent for the word *Mammy*." The translator, therefore, was "unable to render the idea intelligible for the French audiences." As confounding as that example is, Cook goes on to relate an even more glaring cultural dissonance revealed by the French subtitles concerning the peculiarly American racial problematic known as "passing":

> Less excusable, perhaps, is the error in the scene in which Delilah visits Peola's school. The latter, ashamed to let her comrades know she is colored, hides her face so that her mother will not recognize her. Delilah, seeing her, asks the teacher: "Has she been passing?" The translator, confused at this point, misconstrues this meaning of the verb *to pass*, with that which indicates success in one's studies. . . . In like manner, when Delilah explains, on reaching home: "Peola was passing, and I spoiled everything," here again the subtitle reads: "She was studying well, and I spoiled everything."[38]

Cook finds similar hermeneutic difficulties with "the rendition of Delilah's dialect."

Despite these "exceptions," Cook is relieved that "the version is reasonably exact, and the French spectator is able to follow the story." It could have been much worse, he assures us. The film could have been dubbed with French voices. The only time French was audible at the screening was during the film's introduction in which a benshi-like discussant "states in a few words the situation of the Negro in the United States, explaining how discrimination, segregation and prejudice often made his life unbearable." Cook found this innovation, and the fact that it was deemed necessary, proof of the French people's more enlightened attitudes on matters of race and difference. Cook reports that the French journal reviews were, for the most part, positive. But he was not willing to assume that these "flattering" assessments represented the attitudes of the general French audience. After sampling a few glowing reviews of the performers, Cook found the French reviewer's renunciations of "American race prejudice" to have even "greater significance." He gives these examples: "One deplores the 'redoubtable and cruel problems created in the United States by the tragic condition of Negroes.' Another remarks: 'Yes, Peola, who finally understands, has been criminal, but how much more criminal yet are those atrocious prejudices!'" He goes on to make these comments relative to his own spectatorship:

> I do not know how the Negro press reacted to this film when it was shown in the United States; there were in all probability, objections concerning the segregation of the daughter at her mother's funeral. Nevertheless, as propaganda favoring the American Negro in his struggle for recognition as a human being, no picture has been as effective.[39]

This quote's abbreviated judgment suggests that his main focus was a cross-cultural reception study of the film and its implications for evaluating African-Americans as global cinematic subjects.

It is unclear if Cook knew that his colleague and fellow Howard University professor, Sterling Brown, led the charge in denouncing the film in America. Brown's critique of *Imitation of Life* ran two months earlier in the National Urban League's *Opportunity* magazine in March of 1935:

> It takes no searching analysis to see in *Imitation of Life* the old stereotype of the contented Mammy, and the tragic mulatto; the ancient ideas about the mixture of the races. Delilah is straight out of Southern fiction . . . the director would not even let Delilah die in peace. She must speak. . . . I have heard dialect all my life, but I have yet to hear such a line as "She am an angel." . . . The music of the quartet is stirring, although it is unfortunately synchronized

> with Delilah's dying, and is another instance of Hollywood's poor imitation of life. . . . It hardly seems anything to cheer about.[40]

Brown's review, "Imitation of Life: Once a Pancake," appears in the *Opportunity*'s book review section, "The Literary Scene: Chronicle and Comment." Brown was a frequent contributor to this department of the journal. His analysis stands apart because unlike the others he compares Hurst's literary text and Hollywood's cinematic adaptation and points the way to one of the most important features of the radical discourse—a disruption and rejection of the accommodationist compromise. Brown was incredulous at the promotional hype touting the film's "novelty": "Remembering the book, I was unprepared to believe the theatregoers and critics who urged the novelty, the breaking away from old patterns of the picture. Of course they had reasons." In fact, the only recuperative impulse that tethers Brown to the discourse of accommodationism is his assessment of the performances of Beavers and Washington. Beavers's cinematic portrayal of Delilah is less objectionable for Brown than is Hurst's literary characterization (perhaps the "intrinsic dignity of Louise Beavers kept down the clowning"). Further, Brown surmises that if given the opportunity to speak dialogue consistent with the character, "Miss Washington could have risen to heights in its delivery."[41] Even with such guarded praise, he disrupts the accommodationist discourse by refusing to recommend the film: "It hardly seems anything to cheer about."

Regarding the most significant distinction between film and book, Brown apprises us that in the literary universe Peola is successful in her "passing" quest, which is not true in the film. After giving us the necessary background story contained in the novel but absent in the film, Brown states that "the characterization and ideas, however, are little changed."[42] He then proceeds to discredit the film on its own "realist" terms, and here Brown's interrogation is trenchant. For example, in disclosing the glaring inconsistencies in Delilah's character and speech that undergird what Mikhail Bakhtin might describe as an "ideologically freighted discourse" that exists to espouse "a particular way of viewing the world,"[43] Brown demonstrates the racial economy that this character's speech and actions serve, namely the reification and naturalization of black inferiority:

> Delilah . . . [while] less abject than in the novel, . . . is still more concerned with the white Jessie [the white child in her charge] than with Peola [her own daughter]. She has little faith in Peola's capacities: "We all starts out smart; we don't get dumb till later on." Resignation to injustice is her creed. . . .

> When she refuses her twenty percent (not because it was too little) she is the old slave refusing freedom: "My own house? You gonna send me away? Don't do that to me[!] . . . I's yo'cook. You kin have it; I make you a present of it." . . . She is canny about the ways of men and women where Miss Bea is concerned; but when her daughter is yearning for music and parties, she says, "Come on, honey, I'll dance with you."

Brown is on to something here. What he captures in this analysis is the black character's necessary internal panopticism. In other words, Delilah and Peola are constructed in such a way that the white masters do not have to exert their racial privilege and power because the black characters police their own racial boundaries and act accordingly.

Brown does not stop at pointing out the logical fallacies governing the construction of the black characters; he also presents an astute semiotic analysis of the film's spatial dimensions. Brown has noticed the racialized nature of the characters' spatial environments and how they convey the nation's race and class hierarchies:

> There is one scene where Miss Bea [the white heroine] goes upstairs while Delilah goes down. It is symbolic of many things. One is that in *Imitation of Life* where Claudette Colbert has a role to bring out all that there is in her, both Miss Beavers and Miss Washington have, so to speak, to go downstairs; Miss Beavers to a much greater childishness, and Miss Washington a much greater bewilderment.[44]

Upstairs, for Brown, symbolizes an upward social and economic mobility that is unavailable to the black characters, whereas the downstairs domain signifies black social and economic stasis, which is not attributed to racism but to the black characters' personal limitations, hence Delilah's infantilization and Peola's delusions. Brown's analyses are incisive because they clearly engage with the text's manifest and latent meanings, meanings always heavily sedimented with racial mythemes (see figure 3.2).

Brown observes that even though the manifest content of the film's racial discourse purports to evacuate "ancient ideas about the mixture of the races," they are smuggled back in through the film's latent significations of racial difference and separation. As Brown observes: "The bandana has been exchanged for a white chef's cap," and "cabins and cottonfields are a long way from the suite (downstairs) of Delilah. Both Delilah and Peola can dress up, after a fashion." While "all of these things are undoubtedly gladdening to our bourgeois hearts," Brown reminds us

Figure 3.2. *Imitation of Life* (1934)

that "that doesn't make them new."[45] For all the film's pretense to racial equality, Brown aptly demonstrates how it still preserves the primacy of racial separation, especially through the latent economy of space; upstairs and downstairs suites, the races do "not ride side by side in the same automobile"; and in the psycho-dynamics of the characters, especially Delilah's self-sacrificing, volunteer servitude signified by her refusal to accept even a paltry twenty percent of the business built entirely on her own "recipe and skill." According to Brown, these deep-structural elements provide unintentional truths about "the ways of America."[46]

Conclusion

In juxtaposing Cook's and Brown's opposing views on the same film, we can see the range of opinions held by these black intellectuals, and by extension, the larger black community, regarding cinematic depictions of blackness during the interwar and Depression years. Brown's review is more structural in its concern with various levels of signification, script, music, performance, and dialogue. Cook's project, in comparison, is more journalistic and sociological. When conjoined with the literature produced by female journalist critics Jackson and Patton (and the more radical critique of the American cinema in general represented by writers such as Dave Platt and "Camera Eye"), Cook's and Brown's responses to the film render glimpses of historical black spectatorial engagement that clearly dispel the notion of an essential black viewing subject, at least as one might be theorized in 1934. Moreover, these writers problematize any conception of black spectatorship that does not theorize effectively what I term "the recalcitrant gaze," rendered unruly by a historically radicalized subjectivity always impossibly multiple, always shape shifting, and always in constant self-redefinition that *is* the negotiation of what W. E. B. Du Bois calls "double consciousness."

By the 1940s the mainstream black press, including the *Crisis*, had become markedly less strident in its opposition to Hollywood, and in subsequent decades the political critiques of film among black writers would resume with little historical context. Still, the black press's dialectical engagement with the Hollywood cinema during the classical studio era becomes the discursive precondition out of which subsequent oppositional black film literary formations emerge.

Notes

1. Faye Jackson, "Fredi Washington Strikes New Note in Hollywood Film," *Pittsburgh Courier*, December 15, 1934, 8.

2. Cyrill Briggs, "Art Is a Weapon," *Harlem Liberator*, September 9, 1933, 2.

3. In his essay "Art Is a Weapon," Cyril Briggs, the editor of the *Harlem Liberator*, is insistent that African-American "artists and intellectuals have a significant contribution to make in the liberation struggles of the oppressed black masses" (2). In an adjacent column of that September 9, 1933, edition, J.C.L. advocates the necessity for African-Americans to produce "their own films," as well as write protest letters to studios condemning stereotypes and sponsor "well-organized boycotts" (2).

4. This was particularly true of white leftist film critics in Britain. Kenneth McPherson, the editor of the film journal *Close Up*, devoted an entire issue (August 1929) to cinema and Africa and African diasporic representation. This journal edition is notable for its inclusion of criticism written by African-Americans in addition to its own critical discussions on the issue. See also the British Film Institute's journal *Sight and Sound*, which included "articles on the negro and the cinema by Georg Noble and William Harrison" (14–17) in its Spring 1939 edition; and in 1935 the left-oriented journal of theater *The New Theater* included an interview with Duke Ellington, the important African-American jazz musician. Here, Ellington discusses his critical opinion on the play *Porgy*, which was adapted to film in 1959 by Samuel Goldwyn and the Universal Studios as *Porgy and Bess*.

5. "A New Departure in Movies," *Pittsburgh Courier*, December 27, 1934, 12.

6. Geraldyn Dismond, "The Negro Actor and the American Movies," *Close Up* (August 1929): 97.

7. Ibid., 119.

8. Robert Herring, "Black Shadows," *Close Up* (August 1929): 101.

9. Harry A. Potamkin, "The Aframerican Cinema," *Close Up* (August 1929): 108.

10. David A. Cook, *A History of Narrative Film* (New York: W. W. Norton, 1990), 299.

11. Camera Eye, "Screenings," *Harlem Liberator*, January 27, 1934, 6.

12. Dave Platt, "Drama—Movie: Movie Snapshots," *Harlem Liberator*, March 24, 1934, 6.

13. Dave Platt, "Drama—Movie: Movie Snapshots," *Harlem Liberator*, December 23, 1933, 6.

14. Dave Platt, "Drama—Movie: Movie Snapshots," *Harlem Liberator*, March 31, 1934, 6.

15. See, for example, Pam Cook, ed., *The Cinema Book* (New York: Pantheon Press, 1985), 6–7, 26–27; "The Coming of Sound, 1926–32" and "The Sound Film and the American Studio System," both in David Cook, *A History of Narrative Film* (New York: W. W. Norton, 1996), 253–354; and Robert Sklar, *Movie-Made America* (New York: Vintage Books, 1994), 152–154.

16. "Sidelights on New Picture, 'The Exile,'" *New York Age*, March 7, 1931, 6.

17. Mark Reid, *Redefining Black Film* (Berkeley: University of California Press, 1993), 18.

18. Ibid., 18.

19. Donald Bogle, *Toms, Coons, Mulattoes, Mammies, and Bucks* (New York: Continuum, 1973, 1989), 57.

20. The image of the mulatto does appear in Griffith's *Birth of a Nation*. I see these characterizations separate and apart from those proffered by *Imitation of Life*. In the first place, Griffith's mulattoes are portrayed by whites in brown-face, and they are not sympathetic characters.

21. "A New Departure in Movies," *Pittsburgh Courier*, December 27, 1934.

22. Bogle, *Toms, Coons, Mulattoes*, 60.

23. Jackson, "Fredi Washington Strikes New Note," 8.

24. In fact, Washington looked white. "Press releases described her as looking French or Italian." Bogle, *Toms, Coons, Mulattoes*, 60.

25. Ibid., 60.

26. "Imitation Sets New Record at Chicago's Metropolitan," *Pittsburgh Courier*, 23 February 1935, 8.

27. Bogle, *Toms, Coons, Mulattoes*, 60.

28. Ibid.

29. Stanley Fish, "What Makes an Interpretation Acceptable?" in *Contexts for Criticism*, edited by Donald Keesey (Palo Alto, CA: Mayfield Publishing Co.), 348.

30. Arthur Draper's essay "Uncle Tom Will Never Die" considers the adverse effects of plantation drama films on the attitudes of white workers who were beginning to join together with black workers in forming sharecroppers', mineworkers', and steelworkers' unions.

31. Bernice Patton, "Critics Weep at the Preview of 'Imitation of Life,'" *Pittsburgh Courier*, December 8, 1934, 8.

32. Ibid.

33. Ibid.

34. Bogle, *Toms, Coons, Mulattoes*, 64.

35. I am borrowing Bill Nichols's conception of the function of the documentary film that "attempts to explain or describe some aspect of another culture to members of the [explicator's] own culture" to discuss Cook's interaction with the reception issue as it pertains to the French audiences; see Nichols, *Ideology and the Image: Social Representation in the Cinema and Other Media* (Bloomington: Indiana University Press, 1981), 238.

36. Mercer Cook, "'Imitation of Life' in Paris," *Crisis* (June 1935): 182.

37. Ibid.

38. Ibid.

39. Ibid.

40. Sterling Brown, "Imitation of Life: Once a Pancake," *Opportunity* (March 1935): 88.

41. Ibid.

42. Ibid., 87.

43. Mikhail M. Bakhtin, *The Dialogic Imagination*, edited by Michael Holquist (Austin: University of Texas Press, 1981), 333.

44. Brown, "Imitation of Life: Once a Pancake," 88.

45. Ibid., 87–88.

46. Ibid., 87.

FOUR

Joe Dallesandro—A "Him" to the Gaze

Flesh, *Heat*, and *Trash*

STEPHEN TROPIANO

AND [NOAH] DRANK OF THE WINE, AND WAS DRUNKEN; AND HE WAS UNCOVERED WITHIN HIS TENT. AND HAM, THE FATHER OF CANAAN, SAW THE NAKEDNESS OF HIS FATHER, AND TOLD HIS BRETHREN WITHOUT. AND SHEM AND JAPHETH TOOK A GARMENT, AND LAID IT UPON BOTH THEIR SHOULDERS, AND WENT BACKWARD, AND COVERED THE NAKEDNESS OF THEIR FATHER; AND THEIR FACES WERE BACKWARD, AND THEY SAW NOT THEIR FATHER'S NAKEDNESS. AND NOAH AWOKE FROM HIS WINE, AND KNEW WHAT HIS YOUNGER SON HAD DONE UNTO HIM. AND HE SAID, CURSED BY CANAAN; A SERVANT OF SERVANTS SHALL HE BE UNTO HIS BRETHREN.

GENESIS 9:21–25

Over the past fifteen years, gay film studies has been limited to a small body of writing, devoted primarily to issues of representation and pornography. While feminist film criticism continues its theoretical inquiry into issues surrounding spectatorship, pleasure, desire, and the position of the female in the Oedipal narrative, gay film studies has ground to a halt, preoccupied with separating the "positive" gay images from the "negative," without addressing or questioning for ourselves not only our positioning within the filmic text, but the positions we occupy outside as well as spectators. In challenging Laura Mulvey's initial assertion that "active/passive division of labor has similarly controlled narrative structure," Teresa de Lauretis questions whether the pleasure of the text is simply Oedipal: "How or with which positions do readers, viewers, or listeners identify, given that they are socially constructed as women or men"?[1] De Lauretis's line of questioning can be extended further to examine what constitutes the gay male spectator in relation to the gaze and desire. Does the male homosexual receive pleasure from the text in the same manner as the heterosexual male? Can the male image be positioned as the erotic object of the gaze of not only gay but also bisexual and heterosexual male spectators as well?

Three films produced by Andy Warhol and directed by Paul Morrissey—*Flesh* (1968), *Trash* (1970), and *Heat* (1972)—appropriate the cinematic codes of gay pornography to challenge the dominant cinema's restrictions on the display of male nudity and the expression of male sexuality, which has been traditionally linked to neurosis, violence, and death. More than any other filmmaker, Warhol was a groundbreaker in his frank and liberating representations of the male body and male sexuality, blazing the trail for John Waters, Rainer Fassbinder, and Pedro Almodovar. The fixation of voyeur extraordinaire Warhol on the male body was central to the artist's early filmmaking ventures. Warhol's *Sleep* (1963) featured John Giorno's nude body resting comfortably for six hours, while later efforts, notably *Blow-Job* (1963), *Couch* (1964), *The Thirteen Most Beautiful Boys* (1965), *Fifty Fantastics and Fifty Personalities* (1965–1966), and *My Hustler* (1965), featured the erotic antics of the Factory's male superstars. As the artists loved porno ("the real dirty, exciting stuff"), and took Polaroids of the male Factory visitors ("no matter how straight looking"), and moved towards commercial feature-length filmmaking with Morrissey as director, the camera's erotic attention remained fixated on the body of superstar Joe Dallesandro up through *Frankenstein* (1974) and *Dracula* (1974).[2]

The three Morrissey films featuring Dallesandro are part of a subgenre of erotic cinema which puts male sexuality on display. As Stephen Koch observes, Joe and "his naked body, curving buttocks, gangling genitalia, classic torso and good-boy face are the center of the camera's erotic attention."[3] The sexuality of Dallesandro is on the brink of what Ihab Hassan identifies as the shift from genital-centered, phallocentric modernist representations of sexuality to the more polymorphous and androgynous sexuality characteristic of postmodernism.[4] Joe is an anti-hero, an isolated creature who hustles women and men in *Flesh*, can't perform sexually in

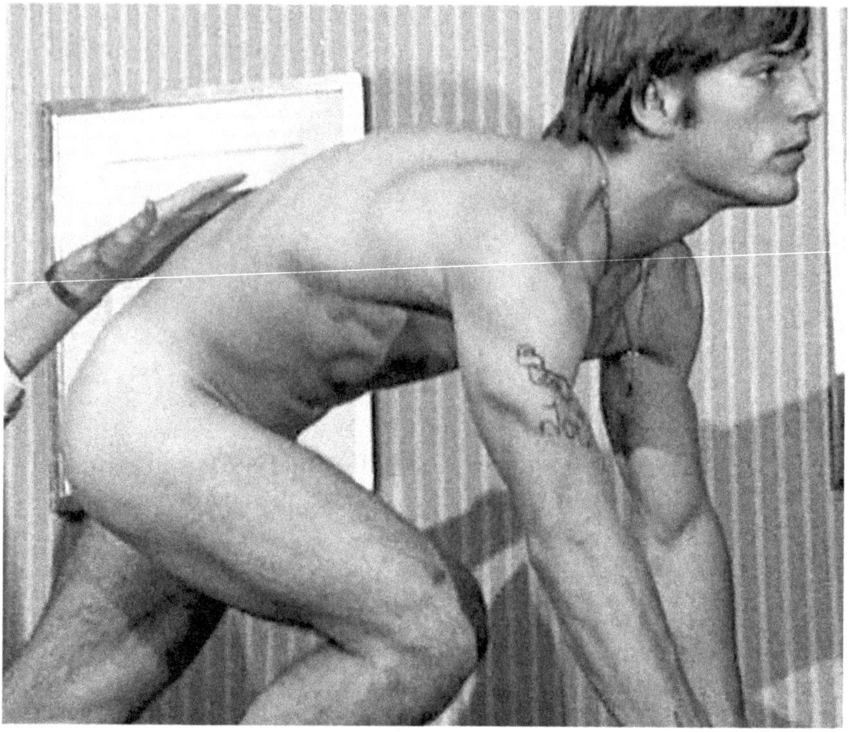

Figure 4.1. *Flesh* (1968)

Trash, and uses his body to further his acting career in *Heat*. By employing these stylistics of gay pornography and the narrative codes designed specifically to put the male body on display, Morrissey positions Dallesandro's body as the object of the camera's gaze. The films never reach, however, the level of hard-core pornography in the depiction of sexual activity. Strictly speaking, this refers to images of erection of male genitals and the actual act of intromission. Morrissey titillates the spectator with the possibility and threat of explicit homoerotic activity but maintains the position of merely teasing the viewer without any real fulfillment of those expectations.

The Male as Erotic Object

As feminist film critics challenged Mulvey's omission of the female spectator in "Visual Pleasure and Narrative Cinema," several film critics focused their attention in the early 1980s to Mulvey's denial of the male image as the erotic object of the gaze. In his essay "Difficulty of Difference," D. N.

Rodowick accuses Mulvey of "falling back on biological essentialism" in reducing the male to the active-voyeur and the female to passive object choice. Mulvey's denial of the legitimacy of the male as the object of the erotic gaze is highly problematic for Rodowick because she makes no differentiation between the male as identity figure and object choice, "nor does she consider the significance of authority in the male figure from the point of view of an economy of masochism."[5]

In "Masculinity as Spectacle: Reflections on Men and Mainstream Cinema," Steve Neale supports Rodowick's assertion that there is an oscillation on the part of the spectator between the male image as identity figure and erotic object. Neale doesn't find it surprising that male-oriented genres (the western, gangster, and war films) "involve sado-masochistic themes, scenes, and phantasies that male heroes can at times be marked as the object of the erotic gaze."[6] Using Paul Willemen's analysis of the films of Anthony Mann, Neale argues that the cinematic spectator experiences visual pleasure when the male image is positioned as the object of another male's gaze, which stems, as Willemen asserts, from a repressed homosexual voyeurism derived from seeing the male in activity (riding, fighting, etc.) and later mutilated.[7] Neale argues that Willemen's conclusion is based on an "unstated thesis" that "in a heterosexual and patriarchal society the male body cannot be marked explicitly as the erotic object of another male: the look must be motivated in some way, its erotic component repressed."[8] As Neale points out, in a Sergio Leone western, male bodies are marked in a shoot-out sequence as spectacle, stylized and fragmented by close-ups, but cinematically unmarked as erotic objects and mediated by the fearful, hateful aggressive looks of the other characters, thus disavowing the eroticism of the look.[9]

Neale's model runs into trouble when he discusses the male body in nonmale genres, specifically Rock Hudson in Douglas Sirk melodramas and John Travolta in *Saturday Night Fever* (1977). Neale classifies these two male protagonists as "feminized" male bodies, with the look of the camera usually marked by a female character. Although Neale doesn't define "feminization" in any specific terms, he implies that the illness of Rock Hudson in *All That Heaven Allows* (1955) and John Travolta's solo dance numbers in *Fever*, which, in Neale's words, put his body "unashamedly" on display, function in the same manner as the violence and sadism in male-oriented genres in terms of disavowing the erotic gaze towards the male.[10] Neale concludes that when the body is displayed as spectacle the body is "feminized." What Neale fails to acknowledge is that it is not the display of the body but the cinematic code of the gaze itself which operates to feminize the male body. Neale asserts that the "feminization" of the male is an "indication of the strength of those conventions which dictate that only women can function as the objects of an explicitly erotic gaze." The real strength of the gaze, however, lies in its complexity. The same conventions of the code of the look are utilized to eroticize the male body. This is accomplished, however, through the eyes of the female voyeur in the circuit of the fetish. When the male spectator looks at the male body through the gaze of the female protagonist, the female character stands in as the sadistic voyeur for the male spectator, who traditionally casts the sadistic look upon the female body. The screen males who are repeatedly being looked at by female protagonists, James Dean, Marlon Brando, and Montgomery Clift, are masochistic—psychotic, injured, castrated, or neurotic. Thus, these stars are eroticized by Hollywood, which integrates these characteristics into their on-screen sexuality.[11]

The male movie stars of the 1950s (Marlon Brando, James Dean, Burt Lancaster, William Holden), are examples of what Joan Mellen describes as screen males "crackling with undirected energy, sexually alive precisely to the degree that they do not conform," are frustrated, confused, and, above all, vulnerable, which on the screen was "not merely acceptable, but desirable, and an indispensable aspect of male sexuality."[12] According to Mulvey's model, the male unconscious can escape the threat of castration by turning the female star into a fetish so that she becomes reassuring rather than dangerous. Masochistic male characters, however, do not pose a threat to the male spectator as identification figures because these characters descend from a long line of masochistic/castrated males in Western culture, including Jesus Christ, Oedipus, and Prometheus. The sexuality of Dean, Clift, and Brando is channeled by Hollywood through their masochism without disavowing their objectification as erotic objects.

When and how a male can look at another male in the cinema is socially and culturally coded. Even in television, as Margaret Morse concludes in her analysis of sports programming, men can look at men playing football because of the balance between "play and display . . . every look of the man . . . is transformed into scientific inquiry into the limits of human performance."[13] The emphasis on statistics and the justification of sport as a hermeneutic process ("Who will win?") makes it possible for men to look at other men and "render it harmless."[14] While the disavowing of the erotic gaze on the male body in both television sports and the cinema is socially and culturally endorsed, both representations are constructed entities, mediated by the absent one—the director. Instead of concentrating on strategies of disavowal, our attention should turn to the very fact that the cinema is a mediated process, opening up the possibilities for a homosexual look to be constructed through the cinematic codes of the dominant Hollywood cinema or through the construction of a "radical" look.

The former can be exemplified in a scene from Ken Russell's *The Music Lovers* (1970), in which the homosexual composer Tchaikovsky (Richard Chamberlain) refuses to consummate his marriage to his nymphomaniac wife (Glenda Jackson). On their wedding night, the gaze he casts upon her is not motivated by sexual desire, but characterized by repulsion and nausea. What Russell constructs is clearly a "homosexual" gaze because it is through the very pre-coded look by which women have been eroticized, that he reinforces Tchaikovsky's sexual preference for men. An even more radical look is constructed in Paul Morrissey's mediation of the camera as it concentrates on the body of Joe Dallesandro.

Andy Warhol Presents . . . Joe Dallesandro

The opening shot of *Flesh* is exemplary of Joe Dallesandro's positioning as the erotic object of the camera's gaze. The song "Making Wiki Waki Down in Wakiki" chimes over the soundtrack during a two-minute-and-thirty-second close-up of Joe's face, which cuts to a medium shot of Joe's nude body sprawled over the bed. As Stephen Koch observes, "The camera's task is simply to pay attention to that body and the relation between subject and object couldn't be simpler. Visually, the camera wants. Visually, Dallesandro delivers."[15]

According to Warhol, Dallesandro made his first film appearance by accident when he wandered into the Greenwich Village apartment where Warhol was shooting *The Loves of Ondine* (1967). When Morrissey later saw Joe's face on the screen, he became convinced, in Warhol's words, that Joe was "another Brando or James Dean—a person with the same kind of screen magic that'd appeal to both men and women."[16] Dallesandro soon joined the ranks of other Warhol pretty boys, who appeared together in Warhol's campy western *Lonesome Cowboys* (1967), and then became the leading player in Morrissey's subsequent works. Warhol ended his filmmaking career and became satisfied with being the name above the title (Andy Warhol presents . . .) with the hope of being the new Walt Disney, whose name, Warhol believed, transformed everything into gold. During this transitional period, the Factory was relocated and transformed into an office. The Superstars and hangers-on defected or were eliminated by Morrissey, who ran the new Factory and restricted its cinematic output to commercial filmmaking.[17]

Consequently, Morrissey moved towards more narrative works, with Joe's body at the center of each story. In *Flesh*, Joe (Dallesandro always played himself) is a street hustler who is told by his wife to go out and make $200 to pay for her girlfriend's abortion. After sexual encounters with both men and women, he returns home to find his wife in bed with her girlfriend, who doesn't really need the money after all. In *Trash*, Joe is an impotent heroin addict in search of his next fix who lives with his girlfriend in an apartment furnished with street trash. Joe is former child star Joey Davis in *Heat*, who returns to Hollywood to resume his career and meets "an aging, minor, practically unknown star" à la *Sunset Boulevard*'s (1950) Norma Desmond played by Sylvia Miles. She seduces Joe in exchange for helping him with his career, but when she learns of his affair with her lesbian daughter, she goes after him with a gun.

Although the protagonist of each story, Joe is a passive figure—the object of the other characters' desires, both male and female. They look at him, talk about his body, offer to pay for him, providing Joe with ample opportunity to undress for the camera, whether it be for money, drugs, or employment. Joe is a commodity for the other characters as well as for the erotic gaze of the camera, a gaze which is marked, through Morrissey's utilization of the codes of gay pornography, as a "homosexual" look being cast upon Joe's naked body.

The Codes of Gay Pornography

The structures and cinematic codes of two distinct types of gay erotic cinema—the posing film and the narrative film—are employed by Morrissey to position Joe's body as the object of the camera's gaze. In "Hard to Imagine: Gay Erotic Cinema of the Postwar Era," Thomas Waugh analyzes the tradition of gay erotic cinema which was distributed in the 1950s and 1960s through magazines and mail-order houses. Waugh describes the posing film as "the most naked, frontal enactment of the sexual pleasure of looking at the male body," consisting of models, completely naked or wearing a posing strap, standing in front of the camera in various poses:

> The presentational, frontal quality of the poses constantly accentuates the spectatorial status of the consumer. The posing film, refusing the spectator

all entry into the frame through fantasy or identification, at the same time relegates the model's proud exhibition of his strength to be a commodified sexual display.[18]

There are instances in which the subject acknowledges the camera's gaze. In *Spike Adams at Home* (from the Athletic Model Guild, circa late '50s), Spike wakes up in the morning and smiles at the camera, inviting the spectator to watch him brush his teeth and eat his breakfast. Most films, however, as Waugh describes, involve an awkward look by the subject into the camera at an invisible director (and the subject). In *Gable Bordeux Poses* (Athletic Model Guild circa late '50s), Gable stands on a diving board and wavers between smiling into the camera and looking away from it. While Morrissey never directs his actors to look into the camera or acknowledge its presence, he does position Joe in various poses distinctly for the camera's gaze. Before going out to work in *Flesh*, Joe sits in the nude on the floor and plays with his baby son. The camera captures Joe in several poses—sitting, squatting, lying on the floor—linked together by the strobe cut (editing in the camera at the time of shooting). His body is fragmented by a series of close-ups of his tattooed bicep, his smile, his chest, etc. The shots last only a few seconds, thus framing the various parts of his body as still images.

In a later sequence, Joe literally poses for a middle-aged artist (Maurice Bradell), who picks Joe up off the street and pays him $100 to stand in classic positions (the sprinter's starting position, the discus thrower), while he sketches and takes pictures of him and lectures about the importance of body worship. In a seemingly endless diatribe, Bradell explains that body worship is behind "all art, all music, all sex, all love—if you cut it for any reason, you deprive yourself of one great chunk of life." "No sooner is Body Worship launched," Greg Ford observes, "than its practice seems annulled in *Flesh*, if only because such a high percentage of what is preached by the funny fossilized old windbag is unmistakable gibberish."[19] Rather than annulling the practice, as Ford suggests, I would argue that the artist's speech not only enhances the self-reflexivity of the sequence by commenting on the very practice the spectator is engaging in, but directs the spectator's focus on Joe by diverting attention away from the soundtrack.

The artist/subject setup is exemplary of early gay narrative films, which Waugh describes as "thin contrivances for getting the models to disrobe, pose and fight" which include "innumerable bathing scenes, waking and sleeping scenes," and "'artist' plots in which the problems of sculptors, photographers and painters with their nude models invariably provided the hinge of the plot."[20] In *Trash*, Joe breaks into an apartment to steal money, but finds a delighted Jane Forth instead. Joe undresses and takes a bath while Jane looks on and comments on his body ("Oh, my, you have such strong arms! . . . Oh, you're rather large!"). The camera pans back and forth between Joe and Jane as she describes how she was nearly raped by an artist she and her husband picked up. When Joe stands up in the bathtub and begins to wash his hair in the shower, Jane's eyes remain fixed on Joe, while the camera moves in for close-ups of his chest, biceps, and face.

In a later sequence, Joe shoots up for the camera, while Jane and her husband begin to quarrel over whether she was a virgin when they were married. The strung-out Joe collapses on the floor, but the camera remains on his naked body, only to open up the space by cutting to an overhead shot. As Greg Ford observes, "The transfer from eye-level to overhead viewpoints is hardly discernible since Morrissey never ceases to use Joe's nude physique as the median vertical guidelines for his compositions."[21] In *Heat*, Joe's body is again eroticized as the camera remains relatively fixed on his muscular form. A conversation between motel manager Pat Ast and a tenant is visually interrupted by Joe's appearance at the top of the stairs. The camera follows Joe while the conversation continues and is eventually sidetracked to a discussion of Joe's looks. ("Isn't he pretty?" the tenant remarks to Ast, who reduces Joe's rent in exchange for sexual favors.)

In terms of aesthetics, Morrissey employs cinematic techniques characteristic of pornography. The flat lighting, long takes, and minimal editing work in conjunction with one another to create a less idealized image. As David E. James observes, the lack of sound continuity and classical cutting prevents the spectator from being sutured into the diegetic time and space: "The spectator is stranded upon his or her self-consciousness."[22] The fragmentation of Joe's body by the constant zooming and panning to his body is not being constructed in the way the classical Hollywood cinema has depicted women's bodies in fragmented pieces. The voyeuristic camera of male patriarchy has been disavowed by the blatant exhibitionism of Joe's body. James asserts that Joe is like a Hollywood heroine because he "can never look, only be looked at," which reduces him to "an object of visual consumption . . . in the film and for the film, producing moments of metaphoric reflexivity when his relation to the viewer is figured intradiegetically."[23] I would argue that it is the use of the narrative and cinematic codes of pornography, this "metaphoric reflexivity" within the text in conjunction with the blatant exhibitionism of Joe's body, that is actually what distinguishes Morrissey's display of Dallesandro from Hollywood's classical construction of the female body.

The Body as Signifier

In his essay "Signification of the Phallus," Jacques Lacan positions the phallus as being an intrinsically neutral signifier. "The phallus in Freudian doctrine is not phantasy . . . nor is it such an object," Lacan writes. "It is even less the organ, penis or clitoris, which it symbolizes."[24] When Lacan speaks of the "phallus," he is referring to a power, which, Kaja Silverman asserts, is a "signifier for the cultural privileges and positive values which define male subjectivity within patriarchal society, but from which the female is isolated."[25] Consequently, male homosexuality is theorized as double on the side of desire. This is extremely paradoxical in relation to Joe and the erotic gaze of the camera, a homosexually constructed gaze which positions Joe's body as the object of desire, because he is void throughout the three films as having any sexual desires towards anyone. Sex is a commodity in *Flesh*; it pays the rent and can potentially advance his career in *Heat*. Joe is impotent in *Trash* and displays little interest in sex at all. ("Don't you miss it?" someone asks. "I haven't really thought about it," he replies.)

The result is a desirable figure for the homosexual and bisexual spectator and a potentially less threatening one for the male heterosexual because while desire is being projected onto Joe, he does not reciprocate, in addition to avoiding the depiction of male-to-male contact. While the Oedipal myth has been the framework for Western culture, the homosexual abduction myth and initiation ritual of Oedipus's father Laius and King Pelop's son Chrysippus, which occurs prior to Oedipus's birth, is continually suppressed by the dominant Hollywood cinema.[26] Morrissey is constantly setting up homosexual and other culturally taboo images, only to diffuse them, thereby subverting the spectator's expectations. The stage is set for an older man/younger boy scenario when Joe visits Louis Waldron in *Flesh*. Instead of erupting into a highly charged sexual encounter, the two look at male physique magazines as Waldron tries to convince Joe to move in with him.

As in Warhol's *Blow-Job*, in which the fellated penis is the focus of attention while the camera remains on the recipient's face, Morrissey offers the thrill without the danger, the excitation without the release.[27] Joe is the recipient of oral sex in the three films, but the action itself, as in *Blow-Job*, is never shown. *Trash* opens with a close-up of Joe's backside while a young woman kneels in front of him. During the blow-job sequences, the camera remains on Joe's upper body or on a close-up of his face, which reveals what the dominant Hollywood cinema refuses to show—the expression of the male face in a state of pleasure or ecstasy. In addition, *Flesh*, *Heat*, and *Trash* expose the signifier of desire to the viewer in full view of the camera. In the opening of *Flesh*, Joe's wife tries to convince him to get out of bed and go to work. The couple begins to make love and at one point his wife playfully wraps his penis up with a scarf and tries to convince him to leave it on when he goes to work. The veiling of the penis (the covering of what has already been revealed) emphasizes not only its importance as the object of desire, but the threat of its potential power. "The phallus is the signifier of this *Aufhebung* [that which is sculpted, erased] itself," Lacan writes, "which it inaugurates (initiates) by its disappearance. This is why the demon of Shame arises at the very moment when, in the ancient mysteries, the phallus is unveiled."[28] Hollywood has, thus, performed a duty similar to Shame (and Shem in the covering of Noah's nakedness).

Conclusively, issues surrounding gay spectatorship need to be examined further so we may better understand not only how we are being represented, but also our positioning as spectators. By limiting our analysis of the objectification of the male image to systems of disavowal, we are theoretically shortchanging ourselves. As an analysis of the Morrissey films demonstrate, we must turn our attention to individual texts, explore their codes and conventions, and, consequently, begin to formulate for ourselves how the male body can be objectified and eroticized and how we derive pleasure from the filmic text.

Notes

1. Laura Mulvey, "Visual Pleasure and Narrative Cinema," *Screen* 16 (Autumn 1975): 6; Teresa de Lauretis, *Alice Doesn't: Feminism, Semiotics, Cinema* (Bloomington: Indiana University Press, 1984), 121.

2. Andy Warhol and Pat Hackett, *Popism: The Warhol Sixties* (New York: Harper & Row, 1980), 294.

3. Stephen Koch, *Stargazer* (London: Calder and Boyars, 1973), 49–50.

4. Ihab Hassan, *The Postmodern Turn* (Columbus: Ohio University Press, 1987), 91.

5. D. N. Rodowick, "The Difficulty of Difference," *Wide Angle* 5, no. 1 (1982): 8.

6. Steve Neale, "Masculinity as Spectacle," *Screen* 24 (November–December 1983): 8.

7. Paul Willemen, "Anthony Mann: Looking at the Male," *Framework* nos. 15–17 (Summer 1981): 16.

8. Neale, "Masculinity as Spectacle," 8.

9. Ibid., 14.

10. Ibid., 15.

11. Ibid., 14.

12. Joan Mellen, *Big Bad Wolves* (New York: Pantheon, 1977), 191.

13. Margaret Morse, "Sports on Television: Replay and Display," in *Regarding Television*, edited by E. Ann Kaplan (Los Angeles: American Film Institute, 1983), 45.

14. Ibid.

15. Koch, *Stargazer*, 50.

16. Warhol and Hackett, *Popism*, 239.

17. Koch, *Stargazer*, 50.

18. Thomas Waugh, "Hard to Imagine: Gay Erotic Cinema in the Postwar Era," *Cine-Action!* (Fall 1987): 67.

19. Greg Ford, "'You Name It, I'll Eat It': A Monologue Discussion of Morrissey's *Flesh*, *Trash*, and *Heat*," *Cinema* 1 (1973): 29–37.

20. Waugh, "Hard to Imagine," 70.

21. Ford, "'You Name It, I'll Eat It,'" 21.

22. David E. James, *Allegories of Cinema* (Princeton, NJ: Princeton University Press, 1989), 79.

23. Ibid.

24. Jacques Lacan, "The Signifier of the Phallus," in *Écrits* (New York: Oxford University Press, 1982), 285.

25. Kaja Silverman, *The Subject of Semiotics* (New York: Oxford University Press, 1982), 183.

26. Bernard Sargent, *Homosexuality and Greek Myth* (Boston: Beacon Press, 1984), 67–68.

27. Koch, *Stargazer*, 50.

28. Lacan, "The Signifier of the Phallus," 288.

PART II Speaking Up and Sounding Out

FIVE Unheard Sexualities?

Queer Theory and the Soundtrack

SCOTT D. PAULIN

It is by now a commonplace of film music criticism to bemoan film theory's privileging of the visual and relative inattention to matters of sound. While this imbalance is gradually being redressed through the efforts of film scholars and musicologists alike, it has largely been reproduced in the field of gay and lesbian film theory. Queer film theorists display as little concern with sound and music as scholars of the audiovisual do with queers. Both tend to be preoccupied with their particular absences: the "invisibility" of gay men and lesbians in cinematic representation, or the "unheard melodies" of film music.[1] Traditionally conceptualized as the most nonrepresentational and abstract of the arts, music may seem to have little relevance to queer film theory, which has generally investigated questions of representation, epistemology, and authorship, and has been dedicated to locating homosexuality in or behind the diegesis, whether in the concrete form of queer characterizations or in the more nebulous realms of ideology and psychology. However, a conversation is indeed possible between queer theory and film sound criticism, for music often participates directly in constructing on-screen representations of desire and sexuality, usually encouraging the audience to identify with a (hetero)sexual relationship and to desire its consummation.[2]

A rereading of Alfred Hitchcock's *Rope* (1948) alongside D. A. Miller's gay theorization of the film, "Anal *Rope*," will suggest ways in which the consideration of film music through queer theory can be fruitful.[3] Miller's formulations—and by extension, those of any queer film theorist—are both enriched and challenged by attention to the soundtrack as an essential component of film. To address the three-way intersection of film theory, musicology, and gay and lesbian theory more extensively, an investigation follows of the use of music in films—*Rebel Without a Cause* (1956) and *Sunday Bloody Sunday* (1971)—that either implicitly or explicitly represent a bisexual love triangle, a narrative in which a character is emotionally drawn toward or erotically attached to both a man and a woman.[4] This structure allows the comparison within individual films of the relative imbrication of music with both heterosexual and homosexual desire, ultimately demonstrating that music is instrumental in suppressing the homoerotic in film, as well as in potentially allowing it to emerge.

Aural *Rope*

While he gives fair weight to the script of *Rope*, D. A. Miller is fairly emphatic on the primacy of the visual image in locating homosexuality in the film: "Of course the most sustained evocation of the possibility of such explication [of gay material] occurs at the level of the image. . . . Not just more constant, the visual teasing is also more charged than the verbal kind."[5] Miller thus posits a strict binary relationship between the visual and the verbal, as if together they constituted the entirety of a film. Another binary opposition, the principal one in Miller's argument, is that of denotation and connotation. In representations of homosexuality, Miller implies, both verbal and visual signifiers operate either in the register of literal denotation (hypothetically, the statement, "I am gay"; or the depiction of a sex act), or in the murkier realm of connotation, allusion, and implication (in *Rope*, the statement that the telephone is "in the bedroom," implying that there is only one such room in the apartment shared by two men; or the depiction of two male bodies in strangely close proximity).[6] Miller is correct to argue that visual representation can be a powerful signifier in a way that sound cannot, that relations between male bodies on-screen can function as an "index" of gay sex: "A-man-standing-too-close-to-another signifies homosexual behavior by being an instance of it."[7] However, Miller's binaries of visual/verbal and denotative/connotative are deceptively tidy and all-inconclusive. Privileging the former team in each dyad for political reasons—denotation is "out" while connotation remains closeted[8]—Miller avoids acknowledging a more ambiguous and floating term that belongs on neither side of either binary, and thus has the power to rupture both of them: music, along with other nonverbal sound. Limited neither to connotation nor denotation, music is unable to signify the homoerotic as the image or the word can. Rather, music's power and potential meaning occupies a different register altogether, one grounded in the bodies and fantasies of its auditors both on-screen and in the theater, complicating Miller's and other theorists' strategies to locate queer content in film. Music constructs desire and opens up a space in which fantasies can be projected; the absence of music can be as telling in this respect as its presence, and may explain why many film representations identified by theorists as gay or lesbian often go unnoticed as such by spectators who have internalized the overdetermining conventions of film music.

Rope features two significant musical elements: first, the *Mouvement perpetuel* No. 1 (1918) by Francis Poulenc, performed diegetically by the pianist Philip (Farley Granger) and appearing nondiegetically in an orchestral version over the opening and closing credits; and second, a medley of popular songs performed by The Three Suns in a diegetic radio program, which provides background music for a portion of the evening's party. Aside from the credit sequences there is no "unrealistic" nondiegetic music, and most of the film is devoid of music completely. As if he realized that even mentioning music in his analysis would rupture his formulae, Miller overlooks ways in which it operates in part on a simple connotative level in *Rope*. By making Philip a musician (which he is not in the original play on which the film is based), Hitchcock and screenwriter Arthur Laurents tap into the metonymic linkage of musicality—through sensitivity, emotional expression, solipsism, and effeminacy—to the connotation of homosexuality. As Philip Brett writes, "Music has often been considered a dangerous substance, an agent of moral ambiguity always in danger of bestowing deviant status upon its practitioners."[9] Further, Brandon's libidinal investment in Philip is mediated through Philip's music: Brandon (John Dahl) will see that his roommate is "locked up to make sure he practices six hours a day," and has "finally wrangled a debut for him" at Town Hall.

But the music Philip obsessively plays takes us beyond connotation. Whether or not Hitchcock was aware of composer Francis Poulenc's homosexuality,[10] the choice of Poulenc's *Mouvement perpetuel* No. 1 is remarkable for its opposition to the norms of classical tonal music—in short, for its deviance.[11] Over a moderately paced *ostinato* bass (the "perpetual motion" of the title) Poulenc writes a series of brief, unrelated melodies, some of which are highly chromatic and clash rather dissonantly with the unchanging bass. After a return "home" to the opening theme (Poulenc's one nod to classical form: a recapitulation) the music ebbs away, finally rising to close on a quiet but dissonant tone-cluster. The ending is tentative and inconclusive, and the pleasures of the work are those of momentary harmonic colors and shifts—not of a steadily building tension which is finally and cathartically resolved, as in classical tonal procedures. (Philip, however, never plays the piece through to its conclusion.) Not connoting homosexuality in any simple or precise way, Poulenc's composition in its original form provides a space where non-goal-oriented, non-teleological, non-(re)productive fantasies (all implying a distance from rigid heterosexual norms) can be projected and pleasures can be found.[12] In the film, Philip's investment in such fantasies is displayed in his second on-screen performance of the work. Conversing with his former teacher Rupert (James Stewart) at the same time, Philip deconstructs the Poulenc work into small fragments, lingering on certain moments, oscillating between notes, repeatedly returning to the beginning. Rupert recognizes Philip's special relation to this composition, saying at one point, "You're very fond of that little tune, aren't you?" Rupert then switches on a metronome at high speed as he begins to antagonize Philip with loaded questions, hoping to disorient him, but Philip persists in his slower pace, introducing *rubatos* rather than struggling to keep up with the metronome.[13] Eventually he gives up, irritated by the metronome and by Rupert, but he does not cede his own interpretation, his private pleasure, or the secret of his guilt to Rupert's superegoic demands.

The unacceptability of this refusal is registered in the nondiegetic orchestration of Poulenc's piano piece. Over both the opening and closing credits, much of Poulenc's pungent harmony is rewritten in a more tonal framework, and is further diffused through a broader instrumental palette which romanticizes and softens melodies which seem altogether more acerbic and brittle when played on the piano. Most striking of all, the film ends with the defeated Philip slowly picking out Poulenc's melodic line with one finger, as if to attempt to relocate his pleasure, his joy in music, but the theme is taken up by brass and strings and given an emphatic and triumphant tonal cadence in a major key over the words "The End." Such a cadence is impossible within the harmonic language of Poulenc's work—just as such an "end," a productive goal, is often considered to be absent from gay sexuality[14]—and this cadence or goal is quite literally imposed from outside here, with Poulenc's harmonic freedom reinterpreted as sterility. This nondiegetic closure "corrects" Poulenc's deviation from the prescribed norms, but it also assimilates the music to the dominant paradigm, as if to deny that such deviance had ever existed. By enunciating the norm in this way, *Rope* negates the oppositional force of fantasy which the music had offered—in other words, the (musical or sexual) other was never really there; and if it was, it is easily corrected or erased.

The presentation and final undercutting of the Poulenc composition is evidence of *Rope*'s extremely self-conscious use of music, and the employment of other musical elements in the film similarly reveals an awareness of music's potential to act as an affective background, promoting specific emotional responses in the characters and the audience. This is explicitly foregrounded in the film's script, which twice alludes to music's power to bring about a desired condition in the listener. Near the end, when Brandon hypothetically asks Rupert how he would go about killing David (which, of course, Brandon already has done), Rupert responds, "I'd try to make him at ease. Philip would play the piano or something." Philip's musicality would thus be the key to seducing David into complacency and danger. Earlier, just before Hitchcock isolates Kenneth and Janet (formerly a couple, now the late David's best friend and girlfriend) for an extended dialogue, Brandon turns on the radio and says to them, "A little atmospheric music goes a long way," his voice dripping with insinuation. The romantic tunes by The Three Suns do indeed provide a background for Kenneth's and Janet's partial reconciliation, renewing their mutual desire, and allowing them to communicate once again. Despite their suspicion of Brandon's motives (Kenneth: "Brandon and his atmospheric music"; Janet: "Bringing us back together again with sweet music"), progress is made in the resurrection of their romance, and they do finally leave the party together.

What is particularly important here is that music is used (by Brandon and by Hitchcock) to endorse and promote the flowering of heterosexual passion. In other words, The Three Suns not only put Kenneth and Janet "in the mood," but also arouse the audience's desire for their coupling. The love song signals the audience that this is "more" than just an ordinary conversation. But by calling attention to Kenneth and Janet's relationship in this way, the film also generates a parallel absence by not marking the possibly homosexual relationship between Brandon and Philip through music. It is almost too obvious to state that a visual image of two men or two women will seldom be accompanied in mainstream cinema by a ballad or theme that can be interpreted as generating a romantic affect. To do so would be to violate the ideological tenet that romance is impossible between a same-sex couple, while film music's exploitation of the convention of the "love theme" is otherwise so thorough as to suggest that romance between a man and a woman is all but inevitable. Through this structural imbalance, film music is complicit with censorship and the representational strategy of connotation, Miller's focus in his analysis of *Rope*, in suppressing homoeroticism in film. Going beyond connotation's ability to relegate homosexuality to the level of half-articulated allusion, however, film music has the power to direct our attention, our emotions, our fantasies, and our desire toward one thing, while articulating through its very absence that another thing is precisely nothing.

But as implied above, music always has the power to act as a gateway to intense emotional experience, and thus to imply or promote deviance, to corrupt. As Royal S. Brown notes, "The erotic instinct is not focused just on the look alone: it is also focused on the act of hearing, and hearing music in particular."[15] In a sense, it would be overkill to accompany an image of two men—which has, as Miller suggests, an *a priori* erotic connotation as an index of gay sex—with romantic music. In the same sense, romantic music is *always* overkill, providing supplementary evidence that an inherently erotic visual image is, indeed, to be interpreted as erotic, and attempting to control the type of fantasy the audience will project.[16] It is this explosive potential at the point of intersection between visual and musical erotics that dictates the need, as per the ideology of compulsory heterosexuality,[17] to clearly mark heterosexual romance through the presence of music and, by contrast, to disavow the possibility of homosexual romance through music's absence. And it is also the intersection between visual and musical erotics that prevents the complete success of this ideological operation, as will be seen/heard in *Rebel Without a Cause*, for music is not always easily contained by the director's or composer's intentions, and can cause the emergence of the homoerotic spectacle it seeks to suppress.

The Bisexual Love Triangle

The relationship of homoeroticism to film music could surely be investigated in many genres of film—the western, the combat drama, the buddy picture, the gangster film, and the road movie all come to mind. But the divergence between film music's construction of heterosexuality and its more reluctant interaction with homosexuality can be seen and heard with greatest clarity in films—regardless of genre—with narratives hinging on a bisexual love triangle, juxtaposing a heterosexual with a same-sex relationship. In Nicholas Ray's *Rebel Without a Cause*, Jim Stark (James Dean) is at the center of a triangle, linked to both Judy (Natalie Wood) and Plato (Sal Mineo).[18] Within the narrative, Jim's relationship to Judy is clearly defined as romantic, while his bond to Plato is only homoerotic in the realm of connotation, in the looks they direct at each other, the tenderness of their interactions, the sexual charge of two male bodies framed by the camera.[19] Plato is coded as gay, a "mama's boy" with a picture of Alan Ladd in his locker whose desire is directed at other men. Jim may pursue Judy, but Plato pursues him with equal vigor, while Jim seems to return Plato's feelings without perhaps being fully aware of the implications thereof. Yet the gay implications of Plato's role can be easily ignored, and probably often are, in favor of a textually denoted reading that stresses his desire for a father figure, not for romance, and that sees a nuclear family structure reproduced among the three teenagers instead of a love triangle. Any threat of homosexuality is removed by Plato's convenient death, however, after which Jim and Judy are firmly united as the only acceptable couple. The triangle is thus never more than implicit, any greater degree of denotation being prohibited by Hays Production Code–era censorship.

Leonard Rosenman's musical score attempts complicity in the erasure of homoeroticism from *Rebel* and is very successful. The film's main theme is introduced in a dramatic form at the opening of the credits, played by unison brass and punctuated by crash cymbals. After a jazzy interlude featuring saxophone and trumpets, during which we see a drunken Jim Stark stumbling down a deserted street, the opening theme returns in a very different form. Now it is soft and gentle yet warm, performed on violins with a lushly arranged and harmonized accompaniment—in other words, it returns in the form of the classic romantic "love theme." It rises with ardor (hinting at both the Lydian mode and the pentatonic scale, a standard signifier of the "exotic" in music) and falls with resignation—with a lingering *rubato* stretching out almost every bar.[20] This pattern is repeated and then transposed to a lower pitch level before the entire eight-bar phrase is repeated an octave higher, after which a contented cadence is reached.[21] The other principal recurring musical motif that emerges from the often athematic matrix of Rosenman's score is first hinted at in the bluesy swing trumpet melody of the middle section of the overture, and emerges in full in the opening scene in the police station. This motif does not have the striking melodic profile of the "love theme"; rather, it obsessively focuses on a single note, decorated by neighboring tones that oscillate around it but are always drawn back to it as if by a gravitational force. The motif is tense and anxious, appears in a variety of orchestrations, occasionally with altered rhythms, and serves various narrative functions; thus, I shall refer to it as the "narration motif."[22] It is used as a musical bridge between scenes; often accompanies travel via automobile; serves as a background signifier of tension within scenes, with or without dialogue; and seems to reflect both the confusion in Jim's mind and his problems with other people. While the love theme is tied exclusively to Judy, the narration motif is not bound to a single character. It appears in relation to Jim's parents, to his enemies at school, in some cases to Judy, and to Plato.

Following the overture, the love theme is almost inevitably present in scenes featuring Jim and Judy together. In the opening police station scene, the first time Judy is seen, a note is sustained in a dissonant suspension on the soundtrack, as if the love theme is about to begin; shortly thereafter, the theme appears in a rather anxious form. The next day, as they speak for the first time, the theme is reintroduced when Jim recalls having seen her at the station the previous night. Later, at the observatory, Jim is confronted by the gang of quasi-delinquent youth of which Judy is a member; the otherwise tense music is briefly interrupted here by a fragment of the love theme as he directs a question at her. In the ensuing sequences depicting Jim's conflicts with the gang, the love theme often appears when Judy enters the frame (for example, when Jim calls her to his car and asks her for dirt to rub on his hands). After Buzz's death, the two reach out to each other and finally clasp hands (framing Plato, who stands alone in the background); the theme is first hinted at, then stated as they walk away together. Later that night, the theme occurs when Jim attempts to telephone Judy, and Jim and Judy's subsequent meeting is accompanied by a complete statement of the theme, leading to a full cadence—this scene breaks down the physical barriers between them as well, as they sit close together, and he kisses her forehead. The theme is also prominent in their subsequent romantic rendezvous in the abandoned house. The spectator/auditor is thus directed to link this lovely, languorous melody with the equally lovely spectacle of Natalie Wood. The viewing perspectives of the audience and the protagonist are aligned with that of the camera—all are directed at Judy—and the love theme (which could almost better be thought of as an "objectification theme") encourages us both to share Jim's desire for her and to anticipate the consummation of their relationship. While the linkage of the theme to the presence of Judy's body may lead us to misapprehend it as a melody that issues directly and intrinsically from her, its connection to her is not so natural. The theme is, of course, applied to her from the outside, generated by Jim's (and the camera's) desiring look at her and further suturing the audience's identification with Jim and his desire. It would be incorrect to describe the theme as Judy's *leitmotif*, for it is more properly linked to the presence of Judy within Jim's thoughts and his (and our) field of vision. The music tells us both that Judy is the object of Jim's conscious desire (the only individual marked in this way) and that, well before their relationship begins, she has already been incorporated in this way into his symbolic network.

If the love theme coincides with moments of contemplation when Judy appears to Jim as an object of spectacle who is in a sense already "possessed," the narration motif underlies more ambiguous situations where some form of conflict is played out. For example, it appears in Jim's interaction with authority figures such as his parents and the police, figures against whom he rebels. More curious, then, is the use of this motif in conjunction with Jim's friend Plato—who is thereby linked to other forces of conflict and confusion in Jim's life. The narration motif's first post-overture appearance occurs at the police station, as Jim offers his jacket to the shivering Plato, and it is introduced again when Jim passes Plato at his locker, and Plato, seeing Jim in mirror reflection, looks back with fascination. It recurs in too many and various situations through the remainder of the film to list here, and returns for the last time, on the oboe in fragmented form, near the end as Jim laments Plato's death. Several things are noteworthy about the linkage of this theme to Plato. First, Plato does not receive his own theme as Judy does; even though he is tied to this motif, it is not uniquely bound to him. The specificity of his relationship to Jim is denied, along with the implicit erotics of that relationship—he is subsumed into the narrative flow, and his own desire is not articulated with the affective power of music. As suggested above with regard to *Rope*, the absence of a certain type of romantically coded music effects the partial erasure of homoeroticism. Second, by giving Plato the generic narration music which is also applied to Jim's parents and other figures of antagonism, the score positions Plato as another problem to be resolved. The narrative reinforces this by placing a gun in his hands and ultimately organizing a manhunt to capture the increasingly deranged boy, solving the "problem" of Plato by finally killing him. Not coincidentally, his death also resolves the problem of his desire, ensuring that homoeroticism will no longer threaten to emerge. The tense narration motif expresses Jim's uneasy relationship with authority and his frustration with his marginal position, and in its linkage to Plato it implies Jim's uneasiness with Plato, with Plato's manifest desire for him, or perhaps even with his own unnamable feelings for Plato. Like the authority figures in Jim's life, Plato demands something of him—namely the reciprocation of his desire. Plato's demand places Jim in an untenable position, passive and powerless; only in relation to Judy can Jim be "on top," the active subject of desire. If the love theme places Judy as a clearly defined and already attained goal, the narration motif weaves Plato into a network of discomfiting and antagonistic forces impinging on Jim's life.

The most interesting appearance of the narration music, however, and the one in which it most calls attention to itself, occurs in a rather different context. Jim and Judy have left the sleeping Plato in order to "explore" the abandoned house. Alone in another room, their romantic relationship reaches its diegetic climax through a combination of their physical entwinement in a tightly framed shot, their discussion of love, and the affective background of romantic music. Not surprisingly, the love theme is present in this scene, supporting Judy's declaration, "I love somebody." Following this admission, the musical score crescendos with a prominent upward harp *glissando* as it becomes obvious (visually, narratively, and musically) that a passionate kiss is about to take place. Indeed it does, but while one might expect the film's love theme to accompany this image, it is in fact the narration motif which appears on the soundtrack as the endpoint of the dramatic anticipatory *crescendo*. (This motif has on occasion accompanied previous conversations between Jim and Judy, but has almost always led into the love theme, not served as a climax itself.) It is important to note at this point that the two main themes of the score are audibly constructed from related musical elements. The three-note upbeat, repeated several times in the love theme, is a transposed inversion of the three notes that lead back to the central pitch of the narration motif, and both figures resolve up a major second to their goal pitches. Frequently, the narration motif is fragmented such that these three notes and the goal they lead to are removed from the larger context of the motif. Also, since each theme has long, sustained pitches at the beginning of many measures, juxtaposed with shorter notes moving to another held pitch, there are several occasions in the film where it is momentarily unclear which of the two themes will be generated from a sustained pitch.

It is in the love scene, however, that this inherent ambiguity is foregrounded, with the active expectation for one theme frustrated by the appearance of the other. This surprising development has several possible implications which interpenetrate each other: Jim's relationship to Judy is "problematic" for him in some way, just as his interactions with other people are; when Jim kisses Judy, his mind is elsewhere, focusing on his other troubles, one of which may be Plato; when Jim has finally kissed Judy, his desire is satiated and is ready to move on to another *objet petit a*, in the Lacanian sense of shifting and receding objects of desire. Jim's world is structured by his anxieties, including his sexual anxieties—just as the film is advanced and structured by the narration motif—and these anxieties naggingly emerge in the form of this motif at the moment which should be the realization of Jim's greatest pleasure. Rather than affording him an intense enjoyment—as if to imply that such perfect enjoyment, the satisfaction of desire, is impossible—his encounter with Judy is coterminous with the realization of his lack and his unresolved anxieties.

It would be too facile to claim that it is simply Jim's latent homosexuality or desire for Plato that emerges when the narration motif, so often linked to Plato in the film, is juxtaposed to Jim and Judy's intimate moment. The music cannot signify so specifically. But the music does indicate Jim's confusion and ambiguity, which are linked through the film's narrative to his sexuality. This ambiguity is even expressed musically by the narration theme that "moves on" perversely and refuses to be fixed teleologically or productively. Contrary to the likely intentions behind it, *Rebel*'s score (and in particular, the narration motif) suggests a dissatisfaction with rigid heterosexuality—and thus allows the possibility of homosexuality to emerge—by implying, using the same musical tools that have inflected Jim and Plato's homosocial friendship, that there is something missing from Jim's experience of heterosexuality. If the love theme represents his fantasy, the theme's absence at this moment reflects the fantasy's failure to be commensurate with reality. And in the love theme's final occurrence, as Jim introduces Judy to his parents at the film's end, it is played simultaneously in counterpoint with the narration motif, bringing the fantasy down to earth, integrating it within Jim's conflicted experience of reality. The soundtrack's final utterance, a dissonant and noisy pile-up of notes that has previously appeared in the film's scenes of violence, goes even further to suggest that Jim's trials are not yet over.

In contrast to *Rebel Without a Cause*, John Schlesinger's *Sunday Bloody Sunday* depicts a fully realized bisexual love triangle. Young artist Bob Elkin (Murray Head) is somewhat grudgingly shared by middle-aged gay doctor Daniel Hirsh (Peter Finch) and a divorced woman, Alex Greville (Glenda Jackson), but ultimately leaves them both behind when he jets off to America. Bob's sexual relations with both partners are clearly denoted visually, so music is not used here simply to call attention to an eroticism which cannot be explicitly depicted—nor could music's absence at various significant (romantic, erotic) points disguise the homosexual desire that is unmistakable in this film. Of the many musical elements in *Sunday Bloody Sunday*—Ron Geesin's pop guitar score and synthesizer cues, alongside diegetic music including a church organ, a Jewish cantor, and Alex's singing pianist neighbor, among many others—the most prominent is the trio "Soave sia il vento" ("May breezes blow lightly") from Mozart's opera *Così fan tutte*, appearing no less than seven times in a variety of diegetic and nondiegetic, fragmented and nearly complete forms, culminating in a full performance over the closing credits.

Even though the Mozart trio is scored for two soprano voices and a bass (in contrast to the film's trio of two men and a woman), one of its effects is to offer an aural counterpart to the narrative situation. Over gently rocking strings the three voices join in different combinations, connected to each other in shifting harmonic and contrapuntal relationships. A familiarity with the Mozart work may cause one to link its appearance here with the trio's text (sung in Italian), which is a farewell and an expression of sadness at loss—clearly relevant to Daniel's and Alex's impending loss of Bob, and to the terms of their triangular relationship by which each of them is constantly losing Bob to the other. Even in the more likely event that the trio and its text are not familiar to the audience, the music's slowly unfolding, mostly descending melodic lines provide much the same affect, of beauty tinged with sorrow and imminent loss. Despite its major key, the music sounds like a lament, bittersweet at best. "Soave sia il vento" becomes the closest approximation of a "love theme" in this film, but instead of arousing desire and leading to a climax, it reflects a desire which already contains its own disappointment. Significantly, the same music, and thus the same affect, is applied both to heterosexual and homosexual relations in *Sunday Bloody Sunday*, but linked only to these three characters—Alex's encounter with another man is backed instead by a lightly rippling piano piece.

One oddity in the text-setting of the Mozart trio, surely not accidental, is that it places particular stress on the final word, *desir*, holding it out twice as a dissonant suspension, and ending with four repetitions of the text's last line. This preoccupation with desire, problematized by dissonance, is preserved in the passages from the trio which have been selected for use in the film. In all but one instance, each appearance of the music leads up to and is cut off after one of the invocations of *desir*. Mozart's setting does more than emphasize this word, however; it also creates a double entendre. Taking the text at face value, the desire is strictly meteorological, a call for favorable winds at sea: "Let the elements respond benignly to our wish [*desir*]." Mozart's setting, in the context of the opera's narrative of faithlessness and romantic betrayal, excavates the subconscious significance of the situation by shifting the meaning of *desir* from "wish" to "desire" and evoking the sexual connotations thereof. Thus Mozart's musical strategy here is not that different from the frequent use of music in film to betray the undercurrents of a situation (in particular, a sexual one) which is only implicit in the script or in visual representation.

It is under Daniel's control that the Mozart trio is first introduced in *Sunday Bloody Sunday*. Alone in his apartment, he puts on the record. The camera lingers on the rotating turntable and dropping needle, and the surface noise of the vinyl is clearly audible before the music begins. This prolonged setup focuses our attention intensely upon the music, which is heard nearly complete in its first appearance (bars 1–29 out of Mozart's 41). From its concrete origin as source music in time and place, however, it continues nondiegetically as Daniel—who first contemplates the sculpture Bob has built in his backyard, presumably also contemplating Bob's absence—proceeds to take out the garbage and the music carries over to accompany the next scene, in Alex and Bob's bed. In appearances of the Mozart intervening between the first statement and the final credits, all nondiegetic:

1) Daniel and Bob look through a book of photographs and discuss religion; Bob removes his shirt and gets into bed with Daniel; Daniel's hands are shown clasping Bob's back; they are interrupted by the telephone (one of many always-too-loud telephone rings in the film) (Mozart bars 6–25);
2) Alex watches through the curtain as Bob showers, and they subsequently embrace as Alex apologizes for her jealousy; Bob jokingly (?) calls Alex a "silly tart"; this time Alex's hands are shown clasping Bob's back (Mozart bars 2–18);

3) Bob massages Alex's forehead as she falls asleep, after which he draws and makes a phone call (Mozart bars 2–23);
4) Daniel ascends the stairs, finds Bob asleep in his bed; has a brief, hallucinatory vision of a feverish Bob, ill in bed; undresses and joins him; Bob wakes and they speak briefly; Daniel: "I wonder if you'll miss either of us"; Bob: "I'll be back . . . sometime"; they look into each other's eyes and Daniel cradles Bob's face in his hands (Mozart bars 1–36); and
5) Alex arrives at a mutual friend's house and finds Daniel's car outside; the music is obscured in this final case, as if in an echo chamber (Mozart bars 35–38).

The appearances of the trio chart a series of failed encounters. Despite the presence of desire and intimacy, and regardless of the sexes of the parties involved, these encounters are unsatisfactory for a variety of reasons—interruption, distrust, exhaustion, the knowledge that a lover is about to or has already abandoned them, or the presence of the romantic rival. Never accompanying a successful sexual encounter, it may seem curious to designate the Mozart trio as a sort of love theme. True, it does not function as a typical romantic melody might, for rather than romanticizing sexuality, "Soave sia il vento" locates a sadness and lack at the root of desire, echoing the film's depiction of the inadequate relationships people—gay, straight, or bisexual—are always forced to settle for and to find some meaning in. For once, the tendency of filmmakers to chop pieces of preexisting music into tiny fragments has a concrete effect—until the final credits, the Mozart trio is always interrupted, often fading out on a dissonance, never allowed to run its course to its sublime conclusion. Beyond the affect of the music, the form in which it is presented, with closure disallowed, also reinforces the film's depiction of what Lacan would call the "impossibility" of the sexual relation.

Equally interesting is the film's occasional refusal to introduce music of any kind in certain situations where we might expect, in a more conventionally encoded film, a surging romantic theme. In Alex and Bob's sexual encounter, early in the film, and shortly afterwards when Daniel and Bob kiss passionately, there is no background music to contribute affect or emotion to the images. Like the use of Mozart's trio, the absence of music here represents a refusal to romanticize. In both cases, but especially in the lengthy, tightly framed kiss, we are forced to confront a raw spectacle of sexual desire without the comfortable distance from the image that music often affords such scenes. Without the power of music to direct our emotions, there is no fantasy screen erected; we are forced to surrender to the much more discomfiting "realness" of the visual image. A potential audience reaction to Bob and Daniel's kiss encompasses an aversion to homosexuality and intergenerational relationships (Daniel is nearly old enough to be Bob's father), and Schlesinger's frank depiction is doubly uncompromising by virtue of his refusal to offer the audience an escape from the spectacle of homosexuality through the romantic affect of music.[23] And Schlesinger's sense of equity in this matter is manifest in his earlier comparable treatment of the heterosexual love scene, just as the equivalence of Daniel's and Alex's relationships to Bob is later implied musically: when each of them drives past Bob's apartment, the same waltz is emitted from both of their car radios, the triple meter of the music once again calling up the image of the love triangle. What *Sunday Bloody Sunday* ultimately suggests, in its narrative and its soundtrack, is that while these relationships are based in equivalent and equally valid desires, it is impossible for any of the individuals to come together in any mutually satisfactory combination. This intrinsic truth of relationships is visible only when conventionally overpowering musical fantasies are silenced.

Conclusion: Queering the Soundtrack

For much of the history of film and film theory, both homosexuality and music have occupied marginal positions, structurally inherent in and necessary to film in a variety of ways, but very little discussed, always secondary to what film is "really" about: heterosexuality (man's objectification of woman, as well as the obvious narrative privileging of the heterosexual couple), and the visual image and narrative. Both music and homosexuality are dangerous enough on their own—music for its effect on the emotions and the body, homosexuality for its potential to upset hegemonic notions of patriarchy and masculinity—but together they are practically explosive. Music has the capacity not simply to connote or denote homosexuality in the cinema, but more powerfully, to invoke it, to call it into existence, to endorse it, to construct an audience's desire for it. It is small wonder then that this capacity has seldom been explored (even in *Sunday Bloody Sunday*, there is not so much an affirmation of homosexuality as an equalization between similarly bleak forms of sexuality), and that music's powers have instead been directed to maintain the illusions of ideology, to actively construct socially acceptable forms of sexuality and to passively obscure their unacceptable counterparts. For example, even in a more recent bisexual love triangle film, *Three of Hearts* (1992), the female couple rarely even shares the screen, their sexual relationship relegated to a prediegetic past, but the male-female couple copulate at length to the strains of a romantic ballad, "Shape of My Heart," sung by Sting.

But even in the decidedly nonradical cinema of Hollywood, these ideological illusions are not impeccably maintained. Much effort needs to go into the work of constructing heterosexuality. Even when attention is not explicitly called to music's role in this process (as in *Rope*: "A little atmospheric music goes a long way"), the work can become audible—the love theme and the dramatic background for the kiss may suture us into position, but it takes only a moment of detachment to recognize the transparency of these clichés, to see the lengths to which filmmakers go in order to ensure audience identification with and desire for the inevitable heterosexuality of the figures on-screen.

Leaving the intentions (conscious or otherwise) of filmmakers and composers aside, it is essential to note that music only exists insofar as there is a listener to apprehend it, and that the ultimate meaning of any music is ultimately made in the body, mind, and fantasies of the listener. Music is inherently perverse, promiscuously penetrating the bodies of its auditors and offering a strictly goal-less pleasure in and for itself. An attempt to embody a particular meaning—or to construct a single, universal fantasy—through music in a film is doomed to partial failure. Music inhabits a space of semiotic excess, "representing" that which is strictly unrepresentable or at least unspeakable. Sexuality as a whole falls into this latter rubric, of course—and film music thus becomes yet another Foucauldian discursive instrument consigned to eternally articulating sexuality—but homosexuality occupies a limited position within this discourse by virtue of being the most perennially unspeakable and undenotable object of all. Merely by allowing music into a film, no matter how strictly it is controlled, a window has been opened for a multiplicity of interpretations and fantasies, emanating from or projected (by the audience) upon nonnormative subjects such as Philip and Brandon in *Rope*, Jim and Plato in *Rebel Without a Cause*, and Daniel and Bob in *Sunday Bloody Sunday*. If music does not endorse these fantasies, neither can it foreclose them, for it is responsible in part for their arousal.

Thanks to Michelle Lekas, Carolyn Abbate, and Mary Kearney for their guidance and suggestions in the writing and revision of this essay.

Notes

1. The latter terminology is Claudia Gorbman's in her *Unheard Melodies: Narrative Film Music* (Bloomington: Indiana University Press, 1987). For representative work in gay film theory, see, for example, the essays collected in *Out in Culture: Gay, Lesbian, and Queer Essays on Popular Culture*, edited by Corey K. Creekmur and Alexander Doty (Durham, NC: Duke University Press, 1995).

2. See, for example, Royal S. Brown, *Overtones and Undertones: Reading Film Music* (Berkeley: University of California Press, 1994), 85–91, on the fetishization of the female in the film score. On film music's construction of the feminine, see Caryl Flinn, *Strains of Utopia: Gender, Nostalgia, and Hollywood Film Music* (Princeton, NJ: Princeton University Press, 1992), especially 51–69. On the relation between desire for musical closure and sexual consummation, see Susan McClary, "Sexual Politics in Classical Music," *Feminine Endings: Music, Gender, and Sexuality* (Minneapolis: University of Minnesota Press, 1991), especially 61–62.

3. D. A. Miller, "Anal *Rope*," in *Inside/Out: Lesbian Theories, Gay Theories*, edited by Diana Fuss (New York: Routledge, 1991), 119–141.

4. The films I have chosen to deal with in depth all concern male homoeroticism, and my conclusions may not be generalizable to films with lesbian plots or connotations. Further investigation would be necessary to characterize the use of music in such films, which are probably quantitatively rarer. In mainstream film, the greater emotional freedom accorded to representations of women may encourage a use of music as affective backing for scenes between women which is more likely to eroticize those relationships than in similar scenes between men; but by the same token, the tendency in films with explicitly erotic scenes between women is to use an operatic duet for two female voices on the soundtrack; in particular, such a duet from Léo Delibes's opera *Lakmé* has been used in Tony Scott's *The Hunger* (1983), among other films. I have yet to see a film which draws on the erotics of male vocalization to parallel on-screen physical coupling in such a way.

5. Miller, "Anal *Rope*," 130.

6. Ibid., 124, 130.

7. Ibid., 131.

8. The value Miller implicitly ascribes to being "out" is mapped literally onto semiotic terms in a rather problematic way. The latter is not an intrinsically repressive means of representation, though it becomes one under conditions where it is enforced as *the* means of representation.

9. Philip Brett, "Musicality, Essentialism, and the Closet," *Queering the Pitch: The New Gay and Lesbian Musicology*, edited by Philip Brett, Elizabeth Wood, and Gary C. Thomas (New York: Routledge, 1994), 11.

10. Which is by now so generally accepted a fact as to pop up casually in CD liner notes. For example, with regard to delays in Poulenc's completion of an opera, "letters recently published show that a deeper cause was the homosexual Poulenc's troubled relationship with a young man, Lucien Robert." Roger Nicholas, liner notes, *Dialogues des Carmélites* by Francis Poulenc, Orchestre de l'Opéra de Lyon, conductor, Kent Nagano (Virgin Classics, 1992), 29.

11. The style of Poulenc's piece may not have been unusual in the context of modernist composition of the time, especially in Paris, and this work in particular is indebted to Erik Satie. Nevertheless, for most audiences at the time of its composition, at the time of the making of *Rope*, and probably today as well, the *Mouvement perpetuel* would be likely to seem strange to listeners accustomed to the still prevalent norms of tonality.

12. In addition to its difference from goal-oriented, "productive" musical narrative, it should be noted that this type of musical stasis has often been used by European composers without an Orientalist discourse. The East has long been construed by Europeans as eternally static, as Edward Said has written: Orientalism has proceeded "without ever changing its mind about the Orient as being always the same, unchanging, uniform, and radically peculiar object." Said, *Orientalism* (New York: Vintage Books, 1978), 98. In music, especially in opera, representations of Asia and the Near East have relied on harmonic methods marked by their difference from traditional total harmony. Said writes elsewhere of "the airlessness and immobility" of Giuseppe Verdi's opera *Aida* (set in Egypt), its emphasis on ritualized spectacle rather than dramatic impetus. Said, "The Empire at Work: Verdi's *Aida*," in *Culture and Imperialism* (New York: Alfred A. Knopf, 1994), 124. An analysis along these lines with more specific musical examples is Ralph P. Locke, "Constructing the Oriental 'Other': Saint-Saëns's *Samson et Dalila*," *Cambridge Opera Journal* 3 (1991). Locke notes, for example, the French opera's "hypnotic rhythms" (266), the "looping arpeggios" and "obstinate (40-bar long) pedal" of the music associated with the Philistines (277), and "an over-simple cantus firmus in exact canon suggesting archaic rigidity" (286). The connection I would like to make here (suggested in conversation with Carolyn Abbate) is that music of this type can be coded in terms of various types of "otherness," whether this means "not Western," "not male" (given the frequent feminization of the East), or "not heterosexual." A similar mapping onto each other of sexual and racial "otherness" is explored with regard to the operas of gay composer Benjamin Britten in Philip Brett, "Eros and Orientalism in Britten's Operas" (in Brett et al., *Queering the Pitch*, 245): "Orientalism is one of the means by which desire unacceptable to or feared by the (Western) Subject can be projected on to the Other." The use of Poulenc's music, which asserts its own difference in relation to the largely Germanic canon of tonal art music, taps into this multivalent nexus of "othernesses" when it is introduced on the soundtrack to *Rope*, where its correlation with gay connotations in the film supports an interpretation of the music in this light.

13. *Rubato* is the musical term for a flexibility of tempo, an expressive speeding or slowing of speed at the performer's (or orchestral conductor's) discretion. Royal S. Brown seems to misapprehend the action in this scene as he writes that "the young men's symbolic undoing comes when Philip loses control of the music's 'perpetual motion' as . . . Rupert . . . sets a metronome at an ever increasing pace, ultimately making it impossible for Philip to continue playing." Brown, *Overtones and Undertones*, 75. Rupert does not continually increase the rate of the metronome, and Philip makes no attempt to keep up with it. The metronome is an irritant, but Philip retreats into the world of his music and holds his own against Rupert's oppressive tempo for quite some time.

14. A definition of "perversion" dating at least back to Freud. On the link to homosexuality, see Jonathan Dollimore, *Sexual Dissidence: Augustine to Wilde, Freud to Foucault* (Oxford: Clarendon Press, 1991), especially 174–182.

15. Brown, *Overtones and Undertones*, 85.

16. The warning against a relationship of mere "redundancy" between the sound and image tracks has been a frequently recurring topic in film music criticism nearly since the birth of sound cinema. In 1939, Rudolf Arnheim wrote that a "'double track' will make sense only if the components do not simply convey the same thing." Arnheim, "A New Laocoön: Artistic Composites and the Talking Film," in *Film as Art* (Berkeley: University of California Press, 1957), 215. Theodor Adorno and Hanns Eisler similarly find the musically illustrative supplement extraneous: "Why should one and the same thing be reproduced by two media? The effect achieved by such repetition would be weaker and not stronger." Adorno and Eisler, *Composing for the Films* (London: Athlone Press, 1994), 66. Largely heedless to such advice, mainstream cinema has tended to practice a modified level of "parallelism" between sound and image, of which the convention of the "love theme" accompanying the romantic couple is but one example.

17. See Adrienne Rich, "Compulsive Heterosexuality and Lesbian Experience," in *The Lesbian and Gay Studies Reader*, edited by Henry Abelove, Michele Aina Barale, and David M. Halperin (New York: Routledge, 1993), 227–254.

18. For a conventional gay reading of *Rebel Without a Cause*, see Vito Russo, *The Celluloid Closet: Homosexuality in the Movies* (New York: Harper & Row, 1987), 109–110.

19. And potentially at a point of cinematic "excess" where the "real-life" Dean and Mineo, both rumored to have been gay or bisexual, intersect with their screen roles.

20. The Lydian mode is an alternate scale with roots in the system of medieval church modes—a major scale with the fourth degree raised a half-step—and the pentatonic scale is an imitation of Asian scales using the five black keys on a keyboard. See note 13 for *rubato*.

21. Here as elsewhere, Rosenman's score bears clear indebtedness to Leonard Bernstein's score to *On the Waterfront* (1950). The opening of *Rebel*'s love theme is almost identical to a phrase from *Waterfront*'s.

22. I give it this name in part for its musical and functional resemblance to what Brown identifies as a "narration theme" in *Double Indemnity* (1944), though *Rebel*'s "narration motif" does not act so rigidly as a marker of narrative construction through voice-over and transition between sequences. See Brown, *Overtones and Undertones*, 125–126.

23. On music's power to mitigate the force of images, Brown writes, for example, that the disturbing scene of Marion Crane's murder in Hitchcock's *Psycho* (1960) is made bearable only by interaction with Bernard Hermann's music. "By forming an interactive whole in which the spectator can become totally immersed, the separate components become more palatable." Brown, *Overtones and Undertones*, 25.

SIX

The Articulation of Body and Space in *Speak Body*

CHRISTIE MILLIKEN

Introduction: Film, Abortion, and Representation

If superstitions and taboos are motivated by a reaction to events which elude human control/mastery, and which are ultimately mysterious and frightening, it comes as no surprise that abortion would be steeped in taboo. Not that the "fact" of abortion in itself is beyond control strictly speaking. But its practice engages in a direct confrontation with the "uncontrollable" semiosis of the body. Oscillating within a dialectic which simultaneously involves the process of sign production (pregnancy and the prospect of birth) and the end of all representation (the termination of potential life), abortion as an "event" points to and interrogates the very limits of representation. Small wonder it has been given so little attention in a medium which deals heavily (though not exclusively) with the visual.

And yet how odd that the issue has been so infrequently addressed by recent feminist filmmaking practice, being, as it is, so central to the movement. This reluctance may be linked not only with the problem of visual presentability, but with the frustration of finding any decisive settlement (by philosophical, religious, or scientific means) to the issue itself. Daniel Callahan summarizes the problem succinctly:

> The mixture of facts and values, the "is" and the "ought" is as thoroughgoing here as in any other moral issue that can be imagined. Many competing interests, perspectives of the self and the world, biological and psycho-

> logical data, notions of gender and moral theories and traditions interact at the abortion debate.[1]

Speak Body (1979, directed by Kay Armatage) is important not only because it deals with this issue, but because it does so in a manner that is conscious and critical of the language and controversy around which abortion is framed. Rather than submit to a heated battle over the rights of women vis-à-vis those of their unborn children, Armatage structures the film as an exploration of the experience of pregnancy and abortion as it is discussed by several women (voices) who are never visually present in the diegesis of the film. This is not to say that the filmmaker avoids the ethical issue of abortion, as I will show. She instead demonstrates how the material conditions of women in society are inextricably bound to the specificity of their experience. Issues of reproduction and family are not avoided within the context of abortion, but, in fact, are made central to the problems positioning women on either side (and within the debate).

Feminism and Form in *Speak Body*

If the absence/repression of women in discourse has been one of the ways in which male dominance/suppression has perpetuated itself, *Speak Body* addresses this issue by giving space and dialogue to women. In this way, it falls into the category of feminist documentary outlined by Julia Lesage:

> Consisting almost entirely of self-conscious, heightened, intellectual discussions of role and sexual politics [*Speak Body*] gives voice to that which has been spoken for women by patriarchy.[2]

Yet *Speak Body* is not exactly a documentary. While it is true that as spectators we consider this dilemma to be a very "real" one, the form of the film avoids the problematic positioning of a "talking heads" interview style, and makes us fully aware of its construction.

As a result of this, the realist-formalist debate is superseded. In Eileen McGarry's words:

> Reality is coded long before the filmmaker arrives. But the filmmaker is not dealing with reality, but with that which has become the pro-filmic event: that which exists in front of the camera.[3]

The pro-filmic event, though most obviously controlled in the fiction film, is an unavoidable component of the nonfiction film as well, where the technology of filmmaking (no matter how "unobtrusive" a role it plays) and the ideology of the filmmakers (choice of subject matter, decisions about representation, choice of location, angle, etc.) are the key ingredients. It is because of the problem posed by preexistent codes of reality, developed out of capitalist notions of representation, that Claire Johnston claims that cinema of nonintervention or vérité filmmaking is actually dangerous for feminists. To her peril:

> . . . is that it promotes a passive subjectivity at the expense of analysis. Any revolutionary strategy must challenge the depiction of reality, it is not enough to discuss the depiction of women within the text of the film; the language of the cinema/the depiction of reality must also be interrogated.[4]

In other words, because realism as a style incorporates the old, dominant, status quo consciousness, it cannot challenge consciousness. It is only by confronting the depiction of reality within their films that feminist filmmakers can show how "real" representations are manufactured.

In *Speak Body*, Kay Armatage creatively blends audio and visual techniques (formalism) with an experiential approach to abortion. The film begins in blackness; the camera is tilted downward into what looks like a thin cloud of smoke. The mysterious tone of this image is amplified by an eerie chorus of voices which loom over the visual space of the film in the soundtrack. The camera tilts down further—the smoke is hair—continuing over a solemn woman's face (with eyes cast downward) across her heavily shadowed neck, onto the chest, to her brightly lit breast which is protected from complete exposure by her hand.

While remaining physically passive, the body in this shot is semiotically active. The movement of the camera seems to establish this image as an assertive "probing" of the nude body, but "shielding" the breast is a counterpoint to this voyeuristic positioning. It is as though this gesture acknowledges the presence of the camera (and the spectator) even though the woman's gaze does not. This confounds the objectification of the body that seems, at first, to be established.

On another level, the visual brightness of the breast (a traditional symbol not only of sexuality but of life and nourishment), contrasted by its shadowy protection, may be seen to imply a certain self-determination in the woman (object into subject) at whom we are gazing. Could this deliberate covering/control signify her desire for procreative autonomy?

One other point regarding this shot deserves mention as an argument in favor of formalism's explanatory power and as a counter to Bazin's ontological theory of the long take as faithful rendering of the event in its own time and space. Brian Henderson puts it concisely: "Bazin did not consider nor admit that long take styles, short of pure sequence shot, also break down or analyze the event, and that they necessarily do this."[5] This extended shot from darkness over the woman's body becomes, as it were, a montage sequence of images from blackness, to smoke, to hair, to a "portrait" of the face and the framing of a breast. It "breaks down" and "analyzes" this body into a montage of bodily parts emphasizing how the long take is as much a deliberate construct as a fragmented sequence of individual shot pieces.

This shot is quickly juxtaposed with black leader which flashes the words "Speak Body" in bright white. There is an urgency to this image, an aggressiveness in contrast to the motionless (almost) passive positioning of the body in the previous shot. These two images are followed by the visual narrative of the film. The woman's face is never in the frame again until the second-to-last image of the film. Instead, we see fragments of a body, a hand leafing through a journal (a missed period, the question of pregnancy), a hand fidgeting with a pen (the wait), a hand reaching for the telephone (establishment of communication/action), and so on.

Voice-Over/Voice-Off: The Sound of *Speak Body*

Although we never actually see the physical bodies (or at least their reflected images) who discuss abortion in this film, they may be said to act as voice-off (or space-off) characters in contrast to the voice-over narrator. Taking Mary Ann Doane's definition, voice-off "refers to instances in which we hear the voice of a character who is not visible within the frame."[6] Yet we don't question their existence; we have the impression that they are "just over there," "just beyond the frameline," in a space which the camera does not choose to show. If techniques of sound tend to confirm the cinema's function as a mise-en-scène of bodies, sound in *Speak Body* emphasizes a "mise-en-espace" of voices.

Not only is it disengaged from its traditional space in the visual image, but so is the space of the voice disrupted through the effect of sound looping. The crosscutting of voices as they detail the events surrounding discovery of pregnancy and the experience of abortion has the effect of exposing how voice-off is edited to correspond with the visual narrative in the film. One example is the sequence representing a medical examination. Here the camera is positioned from the perspective of a woman flat on her back with her feet in gynecological stir-ups.

Visually, the shot contains only a bright flood of light in high angle to the camera. A voice says: "In the glare of the examination room my emotions took precedence." A crying voice permeates the soundtrack. Another voice says: "It was like a B movie," a comment which resonates rhetorically for the spectators, reminding us of our relation to this film artifact. The next voice quotes her physician, who warns: "If you don't have this child, you might never have another child again." During this comment, the examination light takes on the personality of the presumed doctor, looming unsteadily back and forth in the frame, probing forward to an extreme, invading position and then retreating back to a distance. Interestingly, the camera becomes a transparent body in this sequence without having recourse to physical representations.

This shot, with its subjective intervention of the doctor, posits a significant point regarding women as passive recipients (objects) of the medical gaze. To begin with, a woman's right to choose abortion (self) seems always to be circumscribed by a doctor's willingness to perform it (other). Moreover, one may ask whether it is ethically appropriate for obstetricians and gynecologists (who deal in a life-giving specialization) to be holding the monopoly on abortion services.

Notwithstanding the supposed liberation of contemporary society, public attitudes remain fixed. It is extremely difficult for women to express their negative attitudes and feelings toward a pregnancy that is actually in progress (since this implies a refusal to identify with motherhood and the maternal, an essentialist fate to which femininity has all too often been reduced). Armatage deals with this by means of a voice-over narrator. The voice-over in *Speak Body* functions in a similar relation to its text as the voice-over relation described by Bill Nichols in his analysis of *Roses in December*. The narrator:

> . . . offers a supplemental moral response that fuses fact and value, body and meaning, that heals the breach between self and other opened by clinical professionalism or voyeurism.[7]

In *Speak Body*, the voice-over narration brings order to the conflicting voices within the text, merging the issues of private self (here selves) within woman's total situation (public self).

For example, during the shot in which a hand fidgets with a pen, a datebook and an unidentifiable book (all symbols of communication) are placed within the frame, and the narrator's voice becomes part of the discourse of voices as she says: "Every night for the next three weeks I sat at the kitchen table feeling my body changing." During the image which follows, a close-up of a telephone (communication), the narrator's voice moves out of the diegetic space and becomes voice-over commentary, presenting facts about inadequate day care facilities, single-parent families, and the widening pay scale differential between men and women. This oscillation between voice-off (personal experience) and voice-over (socioeconomic experience) reflects a moral, nonhierarchical positioning which strives toward collectivity. By placing the voice-over commentary in a mutual position to the other voices in the film, *Speak Body* mediates a strategy of containment, a politicization of the personal.

Negative Space and Absent Bodies

The visual reconstruction of abortion is probably the most critical aspect of *Speak Body*. Whatever choice the author makes will, by necessity, encode her act of vision as a sign of her own ethical stance toward the event. Similarly, the moral significance of the act of looking places responsibility with the spectator as well. By merely "looking" at a film about abortion, the viewer must mediate between his/her own moral position (imaginary or experiential [pre] conceptions of abortion) and the "objective" filmic interpretation of the event. The problem becomes then what to do with what is among the least malleable, least expressible subjects available to the filmmaker.[8]

Armatage's answer is to avert the camera's gaze altogether. Black leader interrupts the preceding image, and the sound of a storm penetrates the space in between the words of these voices. This blackness (the abruptness of which seems almost violent) punctuates the collusion of narrative and documentary space. It distances the spectator from the cinematic apparatus, insisting on his/her complete absence from the experience—from the very "event" around which the film is structured.

In addition to this, the voices (who) describe the experience of abortion engage us diversely. "No memory," says one; "They anesthetize you so you don't feel the experience," says another; "It was like a four-, four-and-a-half-month miscarriage"; "It was just like a medical procedure"; "It was actually like delivering." Could these individual experiences be more dramatically different?

And yet where do their words take us? What is marked by an absence in the film seems to emphasize what cannot be articulated by the voice either. While these voices signify subjectively in the film's penumbra of spaces, we seem constantly to be reminded of a space which is "extra-discursive," forever resisting interpretation. These negative spaces (including the minimalist representation of the female body and the complete "lack" of a masculine body/voice within the film) become structural absences in *Speak Body*—as crucial to its construction as what is included both aurally and visually.

Space, Subjectivity, and Desire

The conception of extra-discursive space has often been linked to femininity. As Julia Kristeva states:

> Cells fuse, split, and proliferate; volumes grow, tissues stretch, and body fluids change rhythm, speeding up or slowing down. Within the body, growing as a graft, indomitable, there is an other. And no one is present, within that simultaneously dual and alien space, to signify what is going on. "It happens, but I'm not there"; "I cannot realize it, but it goes on." Motherhood's impossible syllogism.[9]

Although Kristeva goes on to position the site of the maternal as the threshold where nature confronts culture, and the female body as a locus of "jouissance," this conception of femininity is particularly useful here in that it situates the "negative," extra-discursive space of the body within the space of desire. What becomes problematic is where to locate this rejection of the maternal body (through abortion) within desire.

While it is clearly not within the scope of this essay to attempt a psychoanalytic reading of the film and of abortion, the layering of subjectivity within *Speak Body* and its emphasis on a space beyond language/vision seem to point toward desire and the unconscious. The abortion experience (through the intervention of memory and the censorship of language) is described as a dream. One voice says: "The dream started there" (in the operating room). Another voice comments on how drugs blur the experience. The images before and after the black leader are similarly obscure, abstracted pictures. Of what, we wonder? They seem to have the spatial, computerized look of video images (a different subjective dimension?) compared to the other images in the film. A voice says during this sequence: "I'm not bleeding or anything but I'm in complete shock."

Further, while the motivating factors which urge these "voices" to have abortions have a definitive socioeconomic link ("Money was running out and I was really confused and I was all alone"; "I couldn't possibly deal with my parents"), there is clearly a psychological/subjective motivation (desire?) which enters into the abortion decision as well. ("There was a phone call saying: 'Come home. We'll work it out; we'll have the kid; I'll get a job and it'll be okay.' And I just couldn't be convinced.")

Yet if the maternal body is the site of jouissance, is the feminine body which rejects this "splitting of the self" necessarily melancholic? (One voice, the same one who will later describe her abortion as a "procedure," says of her visit to the doctor's office: "They write down on a form that you're depressed, and you get depressed.") In other words, does this focus on the unspoken/unknown not fall into the essentialist trap of constantly equating femininity with difference itself? Indeed, "what does woman (really) want?"

Conversely, if we reject given social definitions of women or femininity as mere indicators of social construction at work, what are we left with? Christine Gledhill summarizes this dilemma:

> Assertion of our social difference—maternity, feeling, irrationality—seems only to make patriarchal equations: women as earth mother, woman as other. On the other hand, construction of our cultural heroines as strong and powerful brings charges of male identification, or substitution. We seem trapped. However we try to cast our potential feminine identifications, all available positions are already constructed from the place of the patriarchal order so as to repress our "real" difference.[10]

Gledhill goes on to say that the way of avoiding this trap is not to close our eyes to what is going on in the patriarchal "camps," but to continually explore these socially constructed discourses as sites where women can (and do) resist. Since it would be naive (some have tried) to downplay difference as a way in which women and men are positioned in patriarchy, Gledhill advocates solving the difficulty of difference *through* difference.[11] After all, in deconstructing gender there is a certain construction involved.

Speak Body addresses this polemic remarkably well. While exploring issues (social constructions) surrounding abortion through images and language, this film mediates between (narrativized) patriarchal discourses and the (anti-narrative) realm of the desiring body itself, which (as many feminist deconstructions of Freud have shown) is simultaneously beyond narrativization and within stereotype. *Speak Body*'s innovative form emphasizes not only differences produced for women, but differences produced *by* them as well in their articulation of different rational/emotional/sexual modes of operation.

Conclusion

The unreliability of any single discourse (or voice) to justify/explain abortion becomes the focal point of *Speak Body*. Armatage emphasizes this by providing the viewer with a number of perspectives, without positioning one as the "right" or "most honest" account of the experience. The images, instead of reinforcing one particular point of view, alternately correspond with and run counter to the aural text. For example, in the shot following the abortion sequence, the camera is panned over a bouquet of flowers (paradoxically associated with both life and death), settling on a close-up of baby's breath (the flower) just as a voice says of her abortion experience: "It's something I feel totally fine about."

While Armatage refuses to promote the pro-choice or anti-abortion stand (she emphasizes how the issue is much broader than this), neither is her position a neutral one. The manipulation of image-text relationships in *Speak Body* indicates how no language, even (perhaps especially) the medical terminology, can get at the meaning of the experience. The filmmaker indicates how this "therapeutic" language is dangerous for feminists (black leader is hardly neutral!). This discourse mistakenly thinks it can comfort and pacify the subjective self by trying to denature some unmistakable realities which are constantly redressed in the film. By trying to harden itself against the moral uncertainty of abortion decisions, Armatage would argue, this language strongly weakens the pro-choice position. The emotional, moral self is as central to the abortion issue as the social self.

The penultimate shot of *Speak Body* echoes the first, tilting down across the body of the woman. This time, however, her gaze confronts the camera and the chorus of voices (the only sound accompanying the first shot) is counterbalanced with voice-over narration:

> This is over and these are the images I remember. But the dilemma continues . . . IUD, pills, watching the moon, celibacy; abortion laws and abor-

tion practices; raising children alone, jobs for women, not having children. All are unsatisfactory.

Could this be her interior monologue, we wonder? In the next shot a black image reappears; the words "This is 1979" flash before us. This invokes the same urgency as the flashing words "Speak Body" to which it refers back.

Even though the voices of *Speak Body* recount experiences which, for them, have taken place in the historical past, the mediation of their memories onto these past events transforms them into an historical present. For the spectator of the film these voices take on the immediacy of the filmic experience. The words "This is 1979" convey new meaning. Years have passed, but this issue is no closer to being resolved now (1987) than then.

As we witness the defeat of the ERA [Equal Rights Amendment] movement in the United States, attempts to dismantle abortion (and other rights) in Canada, and a resurgence of ultra-rightist male ideology with, for example, "REAL" women (and many other feminine-ist groupings), the film takes on an added dimension—one which, perhaps even more than in the time in which it was made, asserts that we explore this conjuncture between the "micro-politics" of experience and the "macro-politics" discourse. Only when women work through and between the discourses that oppress them can they begin to make use of these discourses by reworking and manipulating them.

Notes

1. Daniel Callahan, "How Technology Is Reframing the Abortion Debate," *Hastings Center Report* 16, no. 1 (February 1986): 41.

2. Julia Lesage, "The Political Aesthetics of the Feminist Documentary Film," *Quarterly Review of Film Studies* 3, no. 4 (1978): 519.

3. Eileen McGarry, "Documentary, Realism, and Women's Cinema," *Women and Film* 2, no. 7 (1975): 50.

4. Claire Johnston, "Women's Cinema as Counter Cinema," in *Movies and Methods I*, edited by Bill Nichols (Berkeley: University of California Press, 1976), 215.

5. Brian Henderson, "The Long Take," in Nichols, *Movies and Methods I*, 321.

6. Mary Ann Doane, "The Voice in the Cinema: The Articulation of Body and Space," in *Movies and Methods II*, edited by Bill Nichols (Berkeley: University of California Press, 1985), 565.

7. Bill Nichols, "History, Myth, and Narrative in Documentary," *Film Quarterly* 41, no. 1 (Fall 1987): 15.

8. This paragraph, and perhaps part of the motivation to write this essay, is inspired by an essay discussing the ethical dimension of death in documentary. See

Vivian Sobchack, "Inscribing Ethical Space: Ten Propositions on Death, Representation, and Documentary," *Quarterly Review of Film Studies* 9, no. 4 (Fall 1984): 283–300.

9. Julia Kristeva, "Motherhood According to Giovanni Bellini," in *Desire in Language* (New York: Columbia University Press, 1981), 237.

10. Christine Gledhill, "Developments in Feminist Film Criticism," in *Re-Vision: Essays in Feminist Film Criticism*, edited by Mary Ann Doane, Patricia Mellencamp, and Linda Williams (Los Angeles: University Publications of America, 1984), 42.

11. Ibid.

SEVEN

"I Kinda Prefer to Be a Human Being"

Roseanne Barr and Defining Working-Class Feminism and Authorship

MELISSA WILLIAMS

NO LONGER WISHING TO SPEAK IN ACADEMIC LANGUAGE, OR EVEN IN A FEMINIST LANGUAGE, BECAUSE IT ALL SEEMED DEAD TO ME, I BEGAN TO SPEAK AS A WORKING-CLASS WOMAN WHO IS A MOTHER, A WOMAN WHO NO LONGER BELIEVED IN CHANGE, PROGRESS, GROWTH, OR HOPE. THIS WAS THE LANGUAGE THAT ALL THE WOMEN ON THE STREET SPOKE.

ROSEANNE BARR, *MY LIFE AS A WOMAN*[1]

In a 1990 article for *The New Republic*, journalist and public scholar Barbara Ehrenreich stated, "If middle-class feminism can't claim Roseanne, maybe it's gotten a little too dainty for its own good." Predicting a forthcoming "Roseanneology" in academic women's studies in which scholars would attempt to assimilate working-class women into their perspectives on feminism, Ehrenreich likened this move to liberal feminists' "add women and stir" approaches to institutional and legal rights for women within American culture and politics.[2] As an intellectual whose work appeals both to academic and nonacademic audiences, Ehrenreich is one of the few feminist writers[3] who seemed to understand from the beginning of the ABC television sitcom *Roseanne* (1988–1997) that Roseanne Barr's message was at once working-class *and* feminist—in ways that made both the industry and the academy uncomfortable. Barr's experience of being catapulted to fame after her comedy act led to a starring role in her hugely popu-

Figure 7.1. *Roseanne* (1988–1997)

lar television program is, of course, not an experience shared by most other working-class women. However, Barr continued (and continues) to identify as a working-class woman, and her experiences as such inspired her to do something rare, if not unprecedented, with her newly found fame: serve as a public and outspoken voice for working-class women in television.

Visibility of working-class feminism in the public arena was both sorely needed and badly neglected in the late 1980s. According to Ehrenreich, at the height of Barr's popularity as a media personality, the relationship between American women's self-identification as feminists and income were inversely proportionate. In other words, the lower their income, the more likely it was that American women would identify as feminists.[4] Despite that fact, the television images of women that were hailed as "feminist" at that time were almost exclusively middle-class or elite.[5] Most feminists in the United States, then, saw nothing in the mass media to suggest that they were part of a larger community (of working-class women) that both shared their life experiences and held the same concerns and political values. The immense popularity of *Roseanne*[6] and the subsequent attention paid to Roseanne Barr,[7] then, had enormous potential to play a key role in public understandings of working-class women and their lives and needs.

The divergence from the typical practice of depicting women with feminist awareness as middle-class in the mass media that Barr represented, however, did not come without consequences. Barr's authorship of her own working-class character was and continues to be contested for its "authenticity," as liberal feminists in the television industry and feminist media theorists in the academy struggle for control over the definition of "feminism"—and especially "working-class feminism"—in public discourse. Moreover, feminists in positions of power in the industry imposed their narratives and behavioral norms on working-class female personalities like Barr, while feminist media theorists seemed so intent on claiming Barr for their theoretical framework for working-class feminism that they appeared incapable of hearing what she had to say. Thus, Barr's struggle for authorship of her television program and her persona hinged upon her refusal to serve as a working-class "mascot" or to portray working-class women in terms controlled by either the entertainment industry's or feminist media studies' more palatable conceptions of feminism.

The Politics of Defining Working-Class Feminism

IT'S A SHOW ABOUT CLASS AND WOMEN.

ROSEANNE BARR, INTERVIEW WITH TERRY GROSS[8]

Asked in 1992 whether she could still be considered "working-class" after her rise to fame, Barr tried to define what "working-class" meant to her:

> Well, does working-class just mean how much money you make? See, that's part of the whole class issue that I want to talk about and address, because that is not true. . . . It is a culture, and that is the culture I was raised in and that is the culture I portrayed and will always be a part of no matter what, because that's where I come from and it's who I am.[9]

Feminist scholars have long struggled with the intersections of gender and class and how to define those intersections. In the 1970s, these struggles evidenced themselves in critiques of feminism for the way it rendered class invisible. Arguing for the importance of class to the women's movement, famed author and lesbian feminist Rita Mae Brown, who left the National Organization of Women because of their liberal feminist positions in the 1970s, claimed in 1974 that "class is much more than Marx's definition of relationship to the means of production. Class involves your behavior, what you expect from yourself and from others, your concept of a future, how you understand problems and solve them, how you think, feel, act."[10] As bell hooks argued sixteen years later, although the issue of class was at least being discussed within feminist analyses, "well-educated leftist straight women writing about class often remained trapped in academic jargon that kept them from sharing their message with the female masses."[11] In more recent years, feminist studies in general have begun to reexamine the issue of class; scholars engaging in this kind of work include, but are of course not limited to, Julie Bettie, Ann Ferguson, Rosemary Hennessy, bell hooks, Ellen Riordan, and Lisa McLaughlin.

Feminist media scholars in particular, however, are still grappling with how to approach and define class in their analyses. "Class" as a concept within media and cultural scholarship has historically been gendered as a male domain. The field of British cultural studies was one of the first places where mass media received strong scholarly attention. Coming out of a Marxist tradition and a largely male-dominated academy, British cultural studies initially received a great deal of criticism for its early, often patriarchal approach to how popular culture operates within society. As this approach was exported to the United States, its focus on hegemonic structures of power and the role of popular culture's reception in that process combined with a more American tradition of distance from Marxist analysis to create a divide between political economists, whose work more strongly relied on an economic framework of analysis, and cultural studies adherents, whose work tended to focus on the reception of the "masses" to media content. Lisa McLaughlin, whose work spans both political economy and feminist media studies, argues that the split between feminist cultural studies and political economy scholarship has resulted in a kind of "gender apartheid," in which working across these two approaches is increasingly rare.[12]

Because of the emphasis on class and class structure within political economy approaches, this aspect of feminist media studies has been neglected (or perhaps even avoided). Ellen Riordan, who also falls into that small group of scholars who work across this divide, states that this split must be resolved in order for both sides of this divide to be accessible to a wider audience. She sees feminist media studies as having a unique opportunity to open up both sides of this split, by applying the political economy approach to women's personal lives: "Feminist political economists should be concerned with demystifying political economy and making it resonate with women, which means looking to personalized and privatized capitalist moments in addition to looking at institutions, the state, and labor."[13]

More popular treatments of working-class visibility in scholarship concur that "demystifying" academic approaches to class would help resolve this divide. For example, in her 1990 book *Fear of Falling,* Barbara Ehrenreich specifically addresses the ways that middle-class fears of not emulating the "American Dream" myth of upward class mobility serve as motivation for denigrating working-class thinking and practice as undesirable. Critical of the inaccessibility of academic working-class studies, she writes:

> Relative to the vernacular, critical discourse operates at a high level of abstraction, always seeking to absorb the particular into the general, the personal into the impersonal. This is its strength. But the rudely undemocratic consequence is that individual statements from "below" come to seem almost weightless, fragmentary, unprocessed. Since ordinary speech does not aspire to universality and does not hide the speaker in a gauze of rhetoric, it is easily dismissed as "limited" and "anecdotal." Meanwhile, even a truly "limited" idea, when expressed in the impersonal mode common to the middle class, becomes grander than the utterance of an individual person—larger in implication, more consequential.[14]

However, while the acknowledgment in recent years that feminist media studies have virtually ignored the visibility and agency of working-class women in the media is nothing new, attempts to remedy this paucity of recognition and material have been handled badly, at best. There are two primary problems with feminist media scholarship on working-class feminism and women. First, it tends to reduce working-class women to their physical bodies and economic status, ignoring their intellectual contributions to feminism. Rather than allowing space for the language and thought of working-class women, feminist media scholarship focuses on how the literal appearance and actions of working-class women—and their representations in the mass media—destabilize notions of femininity and gender roles for women within *middle-class* culture. Secondly, feminist media scholarship attempts to define and control understandings of working-class feminism within narrowly defined methodologies and language, established not by working-class women themselves, but by an academy dominated by middle-class and elite values, standards, and intellectual practices. If and when working-class feminist rhetoric makes its way into scholarly writing, it is often either criticized for not following the "rules" of discourse within the academy dictated by rigorous intellectual theories and methodologies, or it is rendered imperceptible by just such language. In short, Ehrenreich's assessment of lesser ideas expressed in the "impersonal mode common to the middle class" receiving more attention than stronger ideas expressed in the vernacular is the main culprit in overshadowing the words of working-class feminists within feminist media scholarship.

One such example is Kathleen Rowe's 1995 book *The Unruly Woman*, which contains perhaps the best-known scholarly work on Roseanne Barr. Rowe wrote that "one of the most intriguing phenomena about Arnold[15] is the drive she elicits among critics to 'place' her"[16] into stable and easily definable categories, be it "working-class mother," "feminist," or "television superstar"—three of many categories into which Barr falls and that, to media critics and scholars, seem mutually exclusive. While Rowe attempts to step outside this artificial "placing," she nevertheless falls into that same trap of wanting to "place" Barr by appropriating "Roseanne" the persona into feminist media studies paradigms and rhetoric. Rowe's scholarship addresses, as her title would suggest, the "unruly woman" of popular culture, focusing on Miss Piggy, Roseanne Arnold, and a slew of "unruly" women in film history. Rowe reviews a mélange of Bakhtin, Freud, and Foucault—all male theorists with problematic relationships to feminism—and argues that the body of the unruly woman violates the paradigms these thinkers set up for the importance of, respectively, the "carnivalesque," laughter as aggression, and the discipline of the body as a means of social control.[17] Rowe then lists the (primarily physical) qualities of her "unruly woman," which are, in short: domination of men, excessive bodies (fatness or other demonstration of appetite), excessive speech, jokes, or laughter, androgyny, age or masculinization, "loose" sexuality, and association with the dirty, marginal, or taboo.[18] According to these parameters, then, Barr *can* "fit" within Rowe's categorization of her as an "unruly woman."

Through this categorization, however, Barr is, perhaps unwittingly, reduced to a body rather than a mind. Barr's class identification is only significant to Rowe via physical signifiers, rather than via Barr's thoughts on gender and feminism. This is problematic primarily because Barr was one of the most prolific and outspoken working-class feminists in the United States in the early 1990s; she wrote two autobiographies (no ghostwriters), put out several original comedy albums, and made a number of public statements via her comedy tour, print interviews, and media appearances on talk shows (late night, daytime, cable, network, etc.). She also explicitly discussed her public output as an intentionally political act, stating, "I wanted to create a real woman/mother on TV—for political reasons, as an activist."[19] Barr's use of her body, both in her act and in her public appearances as "herself," was often intended in the "negative" sense—to disrupt the association of women exclusively with their bodies and with patriarchal control of those bodies, so that her words would be heard.[20]

In fact, one of the biggest disagreements Barr had with Matt Williams, the original head writer of *Roseanne*, was his attempt to focus the program almost exclusively around stereotypes of the "gross" body as a signifier of class. Again, although Barr very specifically wanted to illuminate the lived experiences of working-class women, she did not see the method for doing so as one of simply showing physical differentiation from middle-class standards for female behavior. "There was just a ton of snot and shit jokes [when Williams was writing]," she wrote in 1994, "stuff you'll never see on my show now because I hate that sort of thing."[21] Such a rejection of the exclusive use of bodily humor to convey class would seem to contradict Rowe's characterization of Barr's purported affinity for "darkness, dirt, and liminality,"[22] as the unifying characteristic of her comedy.

Moreover, when Barr's public behavior and appearance—the key to Rowe's assertion of Barr as an "unruly woman"—began to change dramatically, her "place" in the pantheon of unruly bodies became less easy to discern. In the conclusion of *The Unruly Woman*, Rowe attempts to reconcile Barr's plastic surgery with the book's earlier assessment of Barr as a transgressive working-class feminist: "I believe we must resist the temptation for closure, for a critical practice that would subject her to a logic of either/or. Why not both/and?" In other words, she sees Barr's lack of "place-ability" as another indicator of her transgression of traditional gender roles. She goes on, however, to attempt to place Barr's act (changing her body via plastic surgery) into a feminist critique, likening her to Orlan, a French performance artist who was at the time reconstructing her face to look like classic examples in Western art of female beauty, and suggesting that Barr was participating in "another variation of masquerade, or 'putting on the feminine.'"[23]

Barr, on the other hand, talks about her choice to employ plastic surgery—and her later gastric bypass surgery—as ways to deal with the emotional and physical damage done to her body by years of abuse.[24] Rowe does address this claim, but rejects Barr's rationale for surgery, claiming that it contradicts Barr's previous "vindication of fatness" and therefore makes her public presentation of her body less transgressive.[25] Ultimately unable to resist explaining away the choices of a human being in rigorous academic terms and concepts, Rowe seems to need to "place" Barr within academic feminist standards, which leaves the impression that she refuses to acknowledge that working-class feminists can, and often do, have different standards for their assertions of rights as women. In other words, because Roseanne's plastic surgery does not fit into a middle-class feminist paradigm of appropriate behavior, it needs to be "explained."

Working-Class Feminism Meets Hollywood

> USING BAD LANGUAGE AND BLUE-COLLAR SYNTAX WAS MORE THAN JUST A HABIT WITH ME (ASIDE FROM BEING PURELY POLITICAL—I LOVE WOODY GUTHRIE). I WANTED TO SEE IF I COULD GET THESE PEOPLE TO FLINCH.
>
> **ROSEANNE BARR, 1994**[26]

In other circumstances, Roseanne Barr and Marcy Carsey might have found themselves on the same side of many issues. Both embrace progressive positions on a myriad of issues, both focus their social awareness around family and motherhood, and both consider themselves feminists. But Carsey's personal history and career affiliations place her squarely within the white, middle-class conception of feminism that Hollywood has embraced, while Barr's feminism is uniquely shaped by her personal experiences as a working-class woman and lifelong "outsider." This conflict, which reached epic proportions by the second season of *Roseanne*, represents a microcosm of how the television industry has rendered working-class women invisible by attempting to control what can and can't be presented as "working-class" on television. Carsey's privileging of "research" on working-class women's lives over Barr's personal experience at the outset of the program; her characterization of Barr as inherently incapable of working within the industry because of her class background; and her eventual decision to distance herself from *Roseanne* can be understood both as resulting from her understanding of feminism from a different class perspective and as paralleling academic efforts to define working-class feminism publicly.

Although Barr's and Carsey's backgrounds do have interesting parallels in terms of generational experiences and encounters with feminism, their class differences produced markedly different conceptions of feminism (subsequently determining their approaches to presenting feminism on television). Roseanne Barr was born in 1952 in Salt Lake City, Utah, to Jewish working-class parents in a predominantly Mormon and middle-class community,[27] while Marcy (Peterson) Carsey was born in the Boston suburb of Weymouth, Massachusetts, in 1944, to a WASP shipbuilder father and a housewife mother. Perhaps unaware of the potential restrictions of patriarchy on her future, Carsey graduated cum laude from the University of New Hampshire with a major in English literature[28] and played in New England summer stock productions until she and a friend decided to pursue life and adventure in New York City.[29] Unlike Carsey's, Barr's youth did not culminate in a college education; she spent her childhood years with the *limits* of class staring her in the face. She treasured television appearances of comedians like Lenny Bruce and Jackie Gleason as examples of "people like me" who found laughter as a means of escaping class and ethnic marginalization.[30] Barr spent much of her childhood trying to hide her family's working-class status and Jewishness, until a near-fatal car accident at sixteen changed her outlook; she began going out of her way to rub her "difference" in people's faces. After eight months in a mental hospital at her panicked parents' behest, a pregnancy, and a wrenching decision to give her daughter up for adoption, Barr left Utah looking for a place where she would no longer be an outsider.[31]

She ended up in what she recalls as a "hippie community" in the Colorado mountains, where she met and married her first husband. They moved to the Denver suburbs and had three children in quick succession, while Barr became a severely depressed housewife and her husband plodded along as a postal worker.[32] Meanwhile, Carsey remembers enjoying New York in her early twenties, landing a few jobs in television and advertising, marrying one of her bosses ("I would have kept my name if I'd known I could!" she states), and moving out to Los Angeles with her new husband.

As adults, Carsey and Barr encountered feminism in very different ways. Carsey characterized 1970s Los Angeles as having "a great progressive feeling in the air," despite the fact that her first job was doing commercials that called for a "young, perky whatever."[33] Displaying a liberal feminist awareness of opportunities made available to her by the 1970s era of second wave feminism, Carsey recounts, "ABC was actively trying to hire women." She was hired by Michael Eisner (then ABC's Vice President of Daytime Programming) as a program executive in 1974, despite the fact that she was pregnant and female in a male-dominated industry. Carsey's primary lessons from her time at ABC were, according to her, about the ethical responsibilities of broadcasting. "You program with respect for the audience, with the knowledge that you have entrusted to you the public airwaves, which belong to the public, so you are in service to the public," Carsey states, crediting Fred Silverman—the only person ever to hold an executive position at ABC, NBC, and CBS—and others with instilling this sense of obligation within her.[34] Carsey branched out on her own in 1980 to form her own production company; her fellow ABC executive and close friend, Tom Werner, followed her a year later, and the now-famous Carsey-Werner Productions was formed. Carsey and Werner had a progressive bent to their programming choices from the beginning, based on their philosophy of industry responsibility to the viewing public. Specifically, the lessons learned about broadcasters' responsibilities to the public influenced their decisions to create *The Cosby Show* and, later, *Roseanne*, as mirroring their liberal political views about race and gender relations in the United States.[35]

Barr's encounter with feminism occurred much later in life and was much more politically charged than Carsey's. After substituting anorexia for agoraphobia, she finally got out of the house and took a job working as a cocktail waitress at a local restaurant . . . and also stumbled into a women's bookstore in downtown Denver, where a feminist collective changed her life forever.[36] There, Barr encountered a type of feminism that especially appealed to her identity as a working-class woman and to her rage at a patriarchal, middle-class, and Christian culture that had always excluded her:

> We [Barr's feminist collective] did not agree anymore with Betty Friedan, Gloria Steinem, or party politics within the woman's movement . . . we began to take to the streets in guerilla theater, disrupting conclave after conclave of women's meetings on Women's History, Feminist Ethics, the International Year of the Woman—all of the circles of the women's intelligentsia and the state of the State which were within our reach.[37]

But Barr still struggled with the disconnect between her old life and her newfound feminism: she was still a suburban "housewife" with an inattentive husband and a side job waiting tables; she was acting out sexually, exchanging sex for money from customers at the restaurant; and she was working through her dichotomous life via her new aspiration. Stand-up comedy became the place where she could bring her feminism, her experiences as a wife and mother, and her sexuality all into one dialogue.[38]

After setting Denver on fire with her feminist comedy, she began encountering resistance from largely male comedy club owners, ostensibly because of her sexually explicit material. Although raunchy material from male comics was considered acceptable, Barr addressed such topics as women's sexual and reproductive issues—menstruation, childbirth, and dissatisfaction with their sex lives—in ways that, according to her, made her bosses extremely uncomfortable because of their "sexually explicit" nature. The publicity created by Barr's accusations of sexism during a stint on a regional women's conference circuit opened the door for her again in Denver clubs. A brief period on the regional comedy club circuit culminated in a trip to Los Angeles to play at Mitzi Shore's Comedy Club on the Sunset Strip. Shore, who was known for actively supporting female comics, gave Barr a chance to perform in the main room, where a representative from *The Tonight Show* saw her act and invited her to perform on television. Several appearances for Johnny Carson and a few HBO specials later, Barr was offered the chance to star in *Roseanne*.[39]

Enter Marcy Carsey and Tom Werner, who executive-produced *Roseanne* and would pitch the program to Barr as her own star vehicle. At the time, they had already hired Matt Williams, one of the writers for *The Cosby Show*, to develop the program. Williams went back to his hometown of Evansville, Indiana, to "do research" for an idea about working-class women juggling jobs and home responsibilities. He interviewed approximately fifty working-class women in the area to create the proposed script for a program called *Life and Stuff*, about three working-class women at various points in their lives.[40] Meanwhile, after catching one of her performances on *The Tonight Show*, Carsey and Werner decided Barr would be ideal for the concept Williams had pitched to them.

Carsey's liberal feminist awareness prompted her to want to address the "double shift" phenomenon of working women in the 1980s, particularly because she as an upper-middle-class career woman was experiencing it herself. "Nothing had changed really at home," she stated, explaining her reasons for pursuing the program's development. "Nobody was doing what the woman used to do. She was just doing eight hours of something else as well now. So to talk about that phenomenon was something that was, you know, near and dear to my heart."[41]

Despite her acknowledgment of this phenomenon, which has always been an aspect of working-class women's lives, however, Carsey thought of its inclusion in her program as a *feminist* statement, rather than a specifically *working-class feminist* statement. She had her doubts about Barr's ability to perform as they wished. Characterizing Barr as a "rube," Carsey later explained that the producers surrounded Barr with an ensemble of respected theater actors to temper any lack of acting ability she might display.[42] In fact, the producers gave more lip service to class inequity in the United States than they did actual *service*: the program was produced in a nonunion studio, which enabled them to start taping well ahead of other programs for the 1988 season, since union sets were held up by the Teamsters' strike that summer.[43]

At the same time, according to Barr, they pitched the program to her as *her* show.[44] The inevitable clash of wills emerged between the college-educated, male head writer and the working-class feminist star who saw her message to the American public as coming from a working-class feminist perspective that gave a voice to the real experiences of real women. Much like the academics who later couldn't "place" Barr, head writer Williams argued constantly with her about what "Roseanne" would or wouldn't do. According to Barr, she would reply, "*She* would do that, Matt, and you know how I know she would? Because *I'm* she, you dumb bastard."[45] Williams, who was also credited with the creation of the program, saw this conflict as merely creative; Barr, in contrast, saw the conflict as a struggle to fashion a public voice for working-class women. Williams stated, "The problem was who was going to have the final say on stories, scripts and the over-all thrust of the show. As the creator and executive producer, I automatically assumed, rightly or wrongly, that I would have the final say. And, obviously, Roseanne thought she had the final say. And that, in essence, was the central conflict."[46] Much like an academic, Williams seemed to think that his systematic "research" of working-class women left him better qualified to speak for them than did Barr's thirty-five years of experience as a working-class woman. But Barr wanted desperately to speak for herself as a working-class feminist, and she knew *exactly* what she wanted to say: "It's about housework being a political thing. It's about never being included in the gross national product, it's about the segregation and apartheid of women's work, and women's energy. . . . I knock myself against a wall saying, 'This is what I mean by female point of view.' I say the same thing about 3,000 times, and nobody hears it. It drives me berserk."[47]

Although Barr eventually won the war over representation on *Roseanne*, she never completely won control over her depiction in the mass media and scholarly literature. In 1989, Barr was on more magazine covers than anyone in history.[48] She was also hounded by the media, hailed by media critics as the representative of various communities, and repeatedly being accused of being "unprofessional" because of her insistence on control over her character on *Roseanne*. Barr fought back the best she could, writing a witty op-ed piece in the *New York Times* that garnered much attention. In the piece, which was entitled "Feminism: What Am I, a Zoo?" she criticized industry, media, and the academy for the way they had characterized her as a surface on which to project stereotypical notions and anxieties about working-class women rather than a working-class woman with something to say:

> Mr. McLuhan, does mass media equal mass unconscious, or does mass unconscious beget mass media, or does mass media belong only to those quasi-elitist folk who feel compelled to be apologists for and/or defend some status quo and/or personal agenda? And what about this Madonna/whore thing? Hmmm? . . . Geez, all these critics can make a gal so nervous![49]

After a long list of the ways she'd been "placed," Barr ended her commentary by observing, "I've stood for so many things this year I need to sit down a while and catch my breath."[50] The national attention she got for this statement garnered her an interview on the first episode of ABC's *Primetime Live*, where she further elaborated on her unwillingness to be claimed by others as a "mascot": "I sorta became a symbol this year, and I kinda prefer to be a human being."[51]

According to Barr, this critique prompted Carsey to try to "manage" the star's protests as one would a spoiled child: "Marcy tried to defuse the situation by not only giving her words a kind of foretelling tone, but subtly putting them in the form of a command."[52] She and Barr waged a war in the press, in which Barr accused Carsey and Werner of trying to steal the character she had created over years of stand-up comedy performances, and they characterized Barr as an ignorant working-class person incapable of navigating the complexities of Hollywood. In their interview with the *Washington Post* in 1990, they hinted that Roseanne's working-class roots made her difficult to handle. With "a pained look on her face," Carsey was quoted as saying, "We just keep saying to ourselves, whatever it is that makes life difficult for her within herself also makes her be what she is. . . . It's where, I guess, a lot of comedy comes from, in performers like Roseanne. It comes out of difficulty and anger and stuff like that. We have to keep realizing that that's who she is, and we can't change it."[53] Years after the show had ended, Carsey made her point more clearly: "She didn't understand. She came out of a trailer . . . in the recent past. And she didn't understand how you behave and what your job is as a professional on a set. So she was difficult to work with."[54] Barr, on the other hand, did everything she could to leverage her star power against what she argued was class privilege. Barr suggested in 1994 that, since ABC had signed on with Carsey-Werner to do three more years without talking to her, the show might end up being "about a couple of—HA!—white people in Cape Cod."[55] For both, the program had political purpose. For Roseanne, however, the show's politics had a personal dimension that did not quite jibe with Carsey's experiences with the "double shift." This disjuncture made Roseanne's status as stand-in for liberal feminism untenable.

Carsey then moved on to what would be her final *modus operandi* for dealing with Roseanne Barr. When Barr married Tom Arnold in 1991 and the two of them leveraged enough power to take over as executive producers of *Roseanne*, Carsey and Werner decided to quietly step back. Their third partner, Caryn Mandabach, took over duties in association with the program for Carsey-Werner Productions, and Carsey ceased to have regular contact with Barr herself. As *Roseanne* was ending, Carsey and Barr were saying at least cautiously nice things about each other, with Barr stating, "Marcy and Tom were the people who got me to television when nobody else wanted to risk putting a woman's story on television. I will always remember that," and Carsey responding, "Roseanne's sheer talent and her voice became so much a part of the show."[56] But while the niceties of retrospective governed the ending of the program, statements in an interview with Carsey and Werner six years later reveal that Carsey still didn't understand Barr's anger from a working-class woman's perspective and that she still saw *Roseanne* as a show about feminism within a liberal paradigm rather than working-class women's visibility. When asked whether their involvement with *Roseanne* and *Grace Under Fire* (ABC, 1993–1998) was because of a desire to reach working-class audiences, Carsey grouped these programs in with *The Cosby Show*, claiming that they all had "universal themes" designed to appeal to a "broad-based audience." She insisted, once more, that Barr's was not the voice of the program, which indicates not only her lack of understanding of Barr's politics, but also of Barr's stand-up routine. Although Barr always strove to highlight the struggles of working-class women *as workers* in the home and outside of it, according to Carsey,

[Barr] had developed a persona in her stand-up comedy . . . where she wasn't a working mother at all. She stayed home. She was lazy. It was a funny persona, you know, 'And hey, if my husband comes home and the kids are still alive, I've done my job.' . . . It wasn't anything like the working-class heroine that we kind of turned her into. You know, we took it 180 degrees around. Still with that great voice, but just turning it around to another way of life and another character. The script was written. The intention of the show was there. We just—we cast her.[57]

"There's a Place for Us": Possibilities for Discussing Class in Feminist Media Studies

A recent posting by Michael Frank on SCREEN-L, a film and television studies listserv, underscored the stakes of a project like mine. Lamenting the inaccessibility of feminist media theory for otherwise bright undergraduates, Frank emphasized the political and cultural implications for those of us looking to create academic work that "matters." After pointing out the anger that many voters in the presidential election expressed against "east coast elite telling us what's good for us and who to vote for," he suggested that "despite the importance of contemporary Marxist thought in the university, we still have not figured out a way to make our most challenging and important work actually seem important to those whose lives and destinies we are programmatically engaged with."[58] Frank highlights the importance of not only making *language* more accessible within feminist media studies, but also expanding definitions of feminism to include the real experiences of those we are trying to reach.

When feminist media scholars participate in the project of increasing the visibility of working-class feminism, we must take great care not to appropriate it within mainstream or academic paradigms of feminism. This appropriation strips authorship—and authority—from, and thereby renders invisible, the very people whose words and ideas we are trying to illuminate. Through the lens of Roseanne Barr's experiences and choices, feminist media scholars might find new ways to bring their own insights to bear on working-class feminism without obscuring working-class voices. Until feminist media scholars learn to talk about working-class feminists as "human beings" rather than "mascots" or "texts," however, working-class feminists like Roseanne Barr will continue to find themselves marginalized in the mass media.

Notes

1. Roseanne Barr, *My Life as a Woman* (New York: Harper & Row, 1989), 161.

2. Barbara Ehrenreich, "The Wretched of the Hearth: The Undainty Feminism of Roseanne Barr," *The New Republic*, April 2, 1990, 29, 31.

3. Ehrenreich is a journalist who, in the tradition of Susan Faludi, has breached the seemingly unassailable gap between the ivory tower and the "real world" (although she does, in fact, have a PhD in biology).

4. Barbara Ehrenreich, *Fear of Falling: The Inner Life of the Middle Class* (New York: HarperPerennial, 1990), 222–223.

5. Examples of programming that could fit into this characterization and were airing the season of *Roseanne*'s premiere include *Murphy Brown* (1988–1998), *Designing Women* (1986–1993), *Who's the Boss?* (1984–1992), *Moonlighting* (1985–1989), *Thirtysomething* (1987–1991), *China Beach* (1988–1991), *Annie McGuire* (1988), *Baby Boom* (1988–1989), *227* (1985–1990), and *Golden Girls* (1985–1992). Only *227* might be considered a working-class sitcom, but its high visibility as a program about black women tended to focus commentary on race rather than class in treatments of the show. See also Bonnie Dow's treatment of the public representation of "third wave" feminism in the early 1990s as a white, middle-class phenomenon. Bonnie Dow, *Primetime Feminism: Television, Media Culture, and the Women's Movement Since 1970* (Philadelphia: University of Pennsylvania Press, 1996), 204–217.

6. *Roseanne* was the number-two show (behind only *The Cosby Show* [1984–1992]) in the Nielsen ratings after its first year; it beat *Cosby* its second year and stayed in the top five until 1994. Alex McNeil, *Total Television* (New York: Penguin Books, 1996), 1158–1161.

7. David Plotz, "Domestic Goddess Dethroned: How Roseanne Lost It," *Slate*, May 18, 1997, http://slate.msn.com/id/1820 [Addendum 2017: URL no longer active].

8. Interview with Terry Gross, March 3, 1994, National Public Radio; as quoted in Julie Bettie, "Class Dismissed? Roseanne and the Changing Face of Working-Class Iconography," *Social Text*, no. 45 (Winter 1995): 134.

9. Ibid.

10. Rita Mae Brown, "The Last Straw," in *Class and Feminism*, edited by Charlotte Bunch and Nancy Myron (Baltimore: Diana Press, 1974), 13–23.

11. bell hooks, *Where We Stand: Class Matters* (New York: Routledge, 2000), 103.

12. Lisa McLaughlin, "Something Old, Something New: Lingering Moments in the Unhappy Marriage of Marxism and Feminism," in *Sex and Money: Feminism and Political Economy in the Media*, edited by Eileen R. Meehan and Ellen Riordan (Minneapolis: University of Minnesota Press, 2002), 30–37.

13. Ellen Riordan, "Intersections and New Directions: On Feminism and Political Economy," in Meehan and Riordan, *Sex and Money*, 12.

14. Ehrenreich, *Fear of Falling*, 222–223.

15. At the time of Rowe's publication, Barr had married Tom Arnold and changed her professional name to Roseanne Arnold; consequently, Rowe refers to her as "Arnold" throughout the book.

16. Kathleen Rowe, *The Unruly Woman: Gender and the Genres of Laughter* (Austin: University of Texas Press, 1995), 217.

17. Ibid., 8–12.

18. Rowe's full list, which appears on page 31, and which I have rather brutally condensed, is as follows:

"1) The unruly woman creates disorder by dominating, or attempting to dominate, men. She is unable or unwilling to confine herself to her proper place.
2) Her body is excessive or fat, suggesting her unwillingness or inability to control her physical appetites.
3) Her speech is excessive, in quantity, content, or tone.
4) She makes jokes, or laughs herself.
5) She may be androgynous or hermaphroditic, drawing attention to the social construction of gender.
6) She may be old or a masculinized crone. For old women who refuse to become invisible in our culture are often considered grotesque.
7) Her behavior is associated with looseness, and occasionally whorishness. But, her sexuality is less narrowly and negatively defined than is that of the femme fatale. She may be pregnant.
8) She is associated with dirt, liminality (thresholds, borders, or margins), and taboo, rendering her above all a figure of ambivalence."

19. Roseanne Arnold, *My Lives* (New York: Ballantine Books, 1994), 6.

20. When Barr does speak about her body, it tends to be a statement dissociating her with patriarchal attempts to identify women exclusively with their physical appearances.

21. Arnold, *My Lives*, 11.

22. Rowe, *Unruly Woman*, 217.

23. Ibid., 218.

24. Roseanne Barr, "I Am an Incest Survivor: A Star Cries Incest," *People*, October 7, 1991, 87. Although Barr has since recanted her claims of incest, she has no obligation to the public (or to other feminists) to explain her rationale for changing her body.

25. Rowe, *Unruly Woman*, 216, 218.

26. Arnold, *My Lives*, 93.

27. Geraldine Barr with Ted Schwarz, *My Sister Roseanne: The True Story of Roseanne Barr Arnold* (New York: Birch Lane Press, 1994), 26.

28. Carsey and Werner, "Who's Who," Carsey-Werner, http://www.cwm.com/bio-carsey.html [Addendum 2017: URL no longer active].

29. Marcy Carsey and Tom Werner, interview with the Academy of Television Arts and Sciences (ATAS), Archive of American Television, March 10, 2003, Los Angeles, California. Because it contains Carsey's own unmediated words, this highly informative interview forms the foundation of my arguments about Carsey's approach to class, feminism, and liberal politics. Many thanks to the Archive of American Television, and to Karen Herman in particular, for their generosity and help on this project.

30. She also cited Gleason's autonomy and voice as informing her own authorship:

"I loved Jackie Gleason, of course, because, you know, the whole author/performer thing is so awesome. You knew that these people were his own creations that he gave birth to and not what somebody wrote and he copied. His message said, 'take a minute to laugh at what's wrong, rather than attack it.' It's really a beautiful thing." "Comedian's Choice: Acts and Influences: Roseanne Barr; All in the Family; The Honeymooners," [interview at] Museum of Broadcasting, 1990.

31. Arnold, *My Lives*, 21–23, 27.

32. Barr, *My Life as a Woman*, 101–146.

33. Carsey and Werner, interview with ATAS.

34. Ibid.

35. Ibid.

36. Arnold, *My Lives*, 33–49.

37. Barr, *My Life as a Woman*, 161.

38. Arnold, *My Lives*, 48.

39. Barr, *My Life as a Woman*, 168–185.

40. Judith Mayerle, "*Roseanne*—How Did You Get Inside My House?: A Case Study of a Hit Blue-Collar Situation Comedy." *Journal of Popular Culture* 24 (1992): 72.

41. Carsey and Werner, interview with ATAS.

42. Ibid.

43. Mayerle, "*Roseanne*," 84.

44. Arnold, *My Lives*, 2.

45. Ibid., 4.

46. Marc Gunther, "What's Bugging Roseanne Barr?" *Toronto Star*, August 17, 1989.

47. Liz Lufkin, "No Holds Barred: Roseanne Lives Like a Reckless Train," *San Francisco Chronicle*, Sunday Datebook, December 10, 1989.

48. Plotz, "Domestic Goddess Dethroned."

49. Roseanne Barr, "Feminism; What Am I, a Zoo?" *New York Times*, July 31, 1989.

50. Ibid.

51. "Roseanne," *Primetime Live*, Diane Sawyer, interviewer, ABC, August 3, 1989.

52. Arnold, *My Lives*, 5.

53. Tom Shales, "Glum in the Grim Factory: The Worries of Hit Producers Carsey-Werner," *Washington Post*, February 8, 1990.

54. Carsey and Werner, interview with ATAS.

55. "Museum of Television and Radio's Eleventh Annual Television Festival: Roseanne," March 12, 1994, Beverly Hills, California.

56. Lynette Rice, "Wrapping It Up with Roseanne," *Broadcasting & Cable* 127, no. 16 (April 14, 1997): 28.

57. Carsey and Werner, interview with ATAS.

58. Michael Frank, "Do We Have to Talk to Each Other This Way?" SCREEN-L, November 9, 2004, http://bama.ua.edu/cgi-bin/wa?A2=ind0411b&L=screen-l&T=0&P=150 [Addendum 2017: URL no longer active].

EIGHT

Riot Grrrl

It's Not Just Music, It's Not Just Punk

MARY CELESTE KEARNEY

IF YOU DISSECT IT YOU CAN CONTROL IT
IF YOU CAN NAME IT YOU CAN OWN IT . . .
YOU WANT TO DIAGRAM MY HEART
IS IT SO THAT YOU WILL KNOW HOW TO TAKE IT APART

HEAVENS TO BETSY, "DONATING MY BODY TO SCIENCE"[1]

In one of the first mainstream articles written about the burgeoning female youth culture known as "riot grrrl," Ann Japenga argues,

> To call herself a Riot Grrrl, a woman need only rally to the slogan "Revolution Girl Style Now" and appreciate bands like Bikini Kill and Bratmobile, whose aggressive, unpolished sound has much in common with the early punk rockers. . . . Indeed, the movement is above all a triumph of punk, a genre not normally noted for its enlightened attitude toward women. Riot Grrrls say they owe their existence to punk's do-it-yourself ethic: if you have something to say, pick up a guitar, write a song and say it.[2]

Since the members of punk bands such as Heavens to Betsy, Bikini Kill, and Bratmobile were the first to bond together as "riot grrrls," Japenga's privileging of punk in the hierarchy of alternative cultural practices relevant to this community is certainly compelling.[3] But what is *not* said here about riot grrrl's roots is just as, if not more, significant. Situating punk as a father figure for riot grrrls, Japenga not only dismisses the other elements that make this community such a powerful force for female youth today, but, more importantly, ignores the connections riot grrrl has with other anti-hegemonic cultures and forms of political resistance, especially feminism, the mother figure obscured in this skewed genealogy.

Unlike Japenga's and other media representations of this group, riot grrrl is not just a subgenre of punk, nor is it simply the newest chapter in the history of girl cultures formed through musical fandom. Therefore, to consider riot grrrl only in relation to such music cultures stymies any discussion of the relevancy of radical politics to this revolutionary community. To consider riot grrrl in relation to *feminism*, however, allows us to explore the various political ideologies and practices which inform this group, as well as to rethink the place of female youth in the fight to end oppressions based on gender and generation.

With a critical view of power and its misuses, riot grrrls often refuse to talk with academics interested in analyzing their culture and question the status of professional intellectuals who have the cultural access and authority denied to grrrls by virtue of their marginalized identity as female adolescents. Aware that my speaking *about* riot grrrls can be easily confused with my speaking *for* them, I acknowledge that my work and my commitment to riot grrrl's objectives are seriously compromised by my exploitation of this community as an object of academic analysis. Rather than feeling disempowered to act in this conflicted situation, however, I believe that, as Teresa de Lauretis argues, feminist critical writing can function "as a variation of consciousness raising or better, its transformation into a significant form of feminist cultural practice, and one not always reducible to 'academic' activity."[4] With this goal in mind, I hope my appropriation of riot grrrl will be seen as an attempt to elicit dialogue about the relationship of age, gender, and political agency.

Revolution Girl-Style Now: Riot Grrrl's Counterculture

Coming to critical consciousness about their doubly subordinated position as female adolescents at a time when MTV ruled mainstream youth culture and Madonna the "Material Girl" seemed the only role model for female youth, some girls began to speak out about their complicated relationship to the patriarchy, adultism, and heterocentrism perpetuated by dominant ideology and often reproduced in the alternative cultures to which they belonged. Enraged by our largely misogynist culture which leaves many girls victims of both child abuse (for example, rape, assault, child neglect) and self-abuse (for example, drug addiction, bulimia, anorexia, alcoholism), they decided that the only way to survive was to unite with others like themselves in order to fight the oppressions girls experience each day. They began to meet, they began to organize, and soon they formed a community that had spread internationally via their self-made cultural products and in-your-face political activism.[5] The year was 1991, and the bottom line was "Revolution Girl-Style Now."[6]

When right-wing and fundamentalist agendas speak of "family values" while girls continue to be violated and abused by brothers, fathers, boyfriends, and other men who feel they have a right to enter a girl's room and possess her body as well as her space, riot grrrls have broken the code of silence normally associated with victims of abuse by challenging female youth to stand up for themselves, for their rights, and for each other. As Misty, creator of the riot grrrl zines *Just Like a Girl* and *I Can't Get Far Enough Away*, writes,

> Wimmin need to learn that power is not given, we have to take it. We need to realize that we don't have to stand around and be treated like this. Don't let anyone control you or dictate your life to you. . . . No one can save you from your oppression except yourself. GIRLS UNITE![7]

With the knowledge that "growing up" and "becoming a woman" means leaving the self-confidence and homosocial bonds of youth behind, riot grrrls have redefined girlhood as a powerful space of sociopolitical agency by appropriating the word "girl" from its dominant connotations and reformulating it as "riot grrrl" to represent their revolutionary spirit.[8] Creating such new forms of collective identification and political agency for female youth, riot grrrls seriously challenge the popular understanding of female youth cultures as "bedroom cultures" where boys are considered girls' primary fantasy/identification figures and romance and marriage are thought to be their only goals for the future. Indeed, riot grrrls have created an all-grrrl community where boys are not "on the side" (as the recent movie by that title would have it); they are removed from the equation altogether.

As feminist theorists and activists continue to debate the effectiveness of separatist strategies, riot grrrls contextualize the exclusion of boys and men from many of their gatherings as an issue of empowerment as well as an issue of safety. Though their "grrrls only" stance is often misinterpreted as "male bashing," an early riot grrrl manifesto powerfully foregrounds safety as a primary reason such separatism exists:

> BECAUSE we need to acknowledge that our blood is being spilt, that right now a girl is being raped or battered and it might be me or you or your mom or the girl you sat next to on the bus last Tuesday, and she might be dead by the time you finish reading this. . . . BECAUSE a safe space needs to be created for girls where we can open our eyes and reach out to each other without being threatened by this sexist society and our day-to-day shit.[9]

Temporarily appropriating spaces for their grrrl-only meetings and annual conventions in order to create a supportive environment for the discussion of personal/political concerns and the empowerment of a collective political agency, riot grrrls are also known for creating spaces for themselves in places where they feel marginalized by their status as female youth (for example, at political events and concerts).

This mobile community, which transgresses local, regional, and national boundaries and moves between schools, concert halls, and political rallies, demonstrates a profound understanding of the impossibility today for girls to have a "room of one's own" and signals the formation of what Benedict Anderson refers to as an "imagined community."[10] Such an imagined identification with other like-minded female youth exists primarily due to the circulation within their community of self-produced cultural products, products which signal a rebellion against not only their subordinated sociopolitical position as female adolescents, but also their complicated economic position as teenage girls (a primary target group for the fashion, beauty, and culture industries).

Perhaps in reaction to the rampant materialism of the 1980s, which created conservative yuppies instead of leftist radicals, riot grrrls have created a counterculture for themselves outside and independent of patriarchal corporate capitalism. Opting for alternative and less expensive ways of spreading their "grrrl power" message through the production and distribution of music, zines, films, videos, and fashion, the anti-corporate "Do-It-Yourself" (DIY) ethos associated with other alternative cultures has been fully adopted by these female youths who have found it politically necessary to empower themselves rather than to be empowered by corporate profit schemes.

Radically refuting the misogynist messages perpetuated by the fashion and beauty industries that encourage girls and women to believe that we will never look "good enough," riot grrrl's anti-commercialist stance is perhaps most apparent in their recuperation and reformation of the female adolescent body and its accessories. Calling attention to the objectification of female bodies in patriarchal society, riot grrrls embody their politics by marking their hands, arms, stomachs, and faces with provocative political slogans, as well as with words commonly used to denigrate women (for example, "slut," "whore," "cunt"). Additionally, through an uncategorizable amalgam of what were once fashion faux pas—thrift store dresses, barrettes and bobby pins, industrial boots, knee socks, body piercings, and unconventional haircuts and colors—riot grrrls appropriate the accoutrements of girlhood, femininity, and alternative youth culture for an ironic (dis)play of gender and generation.[11]

While riot grrrl's anti-fashion style is the most visible evidence of the formation of a collective identity among these female youth, the circulation of riot grrrl zines—which contain (in varying amounts) poetry, stories, personal "confessions," interviews, drawings, collages, cultural criticism, advice columns, political manifestos, and advertisements for riot grrrl products—remains one of the primary ways of spreading the "Revolution Girl-Style Now" message. Whether individually or collectively created, zines function as an important networking tool for girls who feel isolated within their homes, schools, workplaces, and local communities by establishing a place where they can meet others like themselves, as well as a place where they can discuss their most personal/political concerns without fear of editorializing and censorship.[12] As alternatives to the mainstream teen magazines that privilege consumerism and romance over self-empowerment and critical consciousness, riot grrrl zines provide not only the support system that many female youth lack, but also a means of communal fantasy where riot grrrls can formulate plans of action for the creation of a more just society.

Though riot grrrl zines are a crucial component in the continual, collective critique and redefinition of riot grrrl's community and its objectives, they have been less responsible for communicating riot grrrl's messages beyond girls already involved in this community since, for reasons of privacy, they are usually exchanged only among riot grrrls and other supportive individuals. The music created by riot grrrl bands and performers, however, has been instrumental in spreading the "grrrl power" message due to its wide dissemination outside this community via record sales and concert tours.[13] From Bikini Kill's early "Double Dare Ya" call for girls to "stand up for your rights" to The Tourettes' more recent "Battle

Hymn," which roars "I can't change who I am to fit into your world," the songs of riot grrrl bands courageously model the assertiveness lacking in many adolescent girls and challenge them to speak out and fight back.[14] In addition, band members effectively model riot grrrl's DIY anti-corporatist ethos when not touring by producing their own work and that of other musicians on various grrrl-run labels.

The national (and international) distribution of riot grrrl zines and music has been quite influential in encouraging riot grrrls to create other forms of cultural expression, especially film and video projects. For example, Sadie Benning, a young video artist much celebrated for her pixelated Fisher-Price visions of lesbian youth, has indicated that the inspiration for her video *Girl Power* came from her contact with riot grrrl music and zines:

> When I heard Bikini Kill and when I read these zines, it was so much what I had wanted when I was in high school. It really creates a break in the chain, you know, being able to have words to put upon things that are happening to you and knowing that we all exist and finding one another.[15]

In addition, a riot grrrl in the Pacific Northwest has created a video zine that distributes collections of material by female filmmakers and video artists who work outside the mainstream systems of production, distribution, and exhibition. On the other coast, the collaborative spirit of riot grrrl inspired the making of the lesbian fantasy film *Frenzy*.[16]

While separatist practices inspired by the DIY ethos have helped create this radical community, what remains unique and innovative about riot grrrl in comparison with other female youth cultures is that its focus goes far beyond the imagined identification elicited by these cultural creations. Indeed, it is the in-your-face political activism of riot grrrls—whether marching in feminist rallies, boycotting psychiatric institutions, volunteering at Rock for Choice concerts, sponsoring self-defense workshops, or organizing gay youth groups—that signals the ruptural difference of this community. Formed to express rage and ignite action in female youth, riot grrrl's coalition-building with other groups of resistance such as the Feminist Majority, the National Children's Rights Alliance, and Students Organized Against Racism (SOAR) refutes popular representations of this community as an exclusive club for elitist white girls.

But riot grrrl activism does not manifest itself only in the more public arenas of political activism; many riot grrrls incorporate resistance in their personal lives via politicized practices such as vegetarianism, environmentalism, and a "straight-edged" body ethic (no cigarettes, no alcohol, no drugs). As suggested in an early riot grrrl manifesto, a leftist "personal is political" ethos guides the revolutionary praxis of this community and signals its importance in the history of youth and feminist activism:[17]

> BECAUSE we seek to create revolution in our own lives every single day by envisioning and creating alternatives to the status quo . . . BECAUSE every time we pick up a pen, or an instrument, or get anything done, we are creating the revolution. We *are* the revolution.[18]

Women-in-Rock or Punkettes?: Riot Grrrl as a Musical Phenomenon

In his highly influential work *Subculture: The Meaning of Style*, Dick Hebdige employs theories of deviance in order to explore how innovative cultural formations such as youth cultures become diffused (and often defused) by dominant ideology and culture. As he notes, the media hysteria which accompanies the emergence of new styles signals that the commercial and ideological processes of recuperation have already begun, as the new cultural phenomenon is "codified, made comprehensible, rendered at once public property and profitable merchandise" at the same time that its potential threat to social order is denied or placed beyond analysis.[19]

From an offer by MTV to tape one of their meetings to invitations to publish their writings in texts such as *Girl Power: Young Women Speak Out!*, riot grrrls have been approached by journalists wanting to tell (and sell) the story of this revolutionary female youth culture.[20] By now, five years after its initial emergence, much has been written about this community . . . and riot grrrls have rejected most of it as incompatible with their experiences. Following what they saw as the repeated exploitation and misrepresentation of their culture by prominent newspapers and magazines such as the *New York Times* and *Newsweek*, riot grrrls initiated a press blackout in 1993 and now refuse to speak with or be photographed by anyone associated with the mainstream media (and academic, as noted above).[21]

As their blackout suggests, riot grrrls are profoundly aware of how easy it is for those in control of representational discourse to exploit and commodify marginalized cultures, and how difficult it is for young people today to resist such misrepresentation, co-optation, and containment. This community's relation to the recuperative processes described by Hebdige, therefore, seems unique since its blackout helped prevent the massive exploitation normally associated with emergent youth styles. Riot grrrl's countercultural products have, for the most part, successfully resisted corporate exploitation by being self-produced in small quantities and sold cheaply or traded primarily within the alternative community. However, it is important to note that this blackout was not initiated until riot grrrls realized their culture was tasty bait in the massive feeding frenzy for commodifiable information. By then, riot grrrls had been photographed, interviewed, and narrativized by almost all of the major US newspapers and magazines.

Riot grrrl culture is diverse and dynamic, but it is also unique in the way it has reformulated adolescent girlhood into a powerful location of political identity. Because of that ruptural difference, riot grrrl's challenge to dominant notions of adolescence, youth culture, femininity, and political activism has resulted in repeated attempts to contain its threat to the semblance of societal order. Such attempts have most often resorted to contextualizing this community within our dominant frameworks for understanding youth cultures, namely by representing riot grrrl as a musical phenomenon.[22]

Although the media's focus on riot grrrl's music is, as I noted above, primarily due to the fact that this community's philosophy and practices have been most widely disseminated by riot grrrl bands, this limited perspective also results from several simultaneous phenomena which have redirected corporate marketers' gaze towards alternative music culture, primarily: (1) the recent increase of female musicians and all-female bands as spotlighted in the media as the "women in rock" phenomenon; and (2) the overwhelming mainstream success of many bands recorded on "indie" labels. Because both of these phenomena occurred alongside, and not independent of, the emergence of riot grrrl, this community is more easily understood as a chapter in one or both of these larger musical narratives and thereby more quickly recuperated through purchasable products such as CDs and music reviews.[23]

By focusing on the sex of riot grrrl musicians, many journalists have problematically reduced this diverse community to a few grrrl bands in a seamless narrative that conflates them with all other female musicians or, more specifically, with all "women in rock."[24] In this historical mapping, older female rock musicians like Joan Jett and Chrissie Hynde have been dubbed the "original Riot Grrrls."[25] Other writers, attempting to update this musical "herstory," connect riot grrrl bands with contemporary "angry women" / "foxcore" bands like Hole, L7, and Babes in Toyland.[26] Since several of these female musicians have stated publicly their uneasiness with labeling themselves and their art "feminist," and most of them have struggled for and earned recognition and success within the mainstream corporate music industry riot grrrls so rigorously oppose, the construction of these women as the matron saints of grrrl bands further obscures riot grrrl's status as a countercultural political community. In addition, several other problems result from these misguided genealogies: (1) riot grrrl music which is not categorizable within rock genres is ignored; (2) the nonmusical components of riot grrrl culture are subordinated to music (if not dismissed outright); (3) the history of female/feminist musicians outside the realm of rock is effaced; and (4) individuals and groups who have influenced riot grrrl but are not involved in music are obscured.

On the other hand, many writers attempt to situate riot grrrl within the history of the alternative music community by referring to riot grrrls as "punks" or "punkettes."[27] While the representation of the riot grrrl community as a group of "girl punks" is no doubt due to the emergence of riot grrrl bands from the male-dominated punk scenes of Washington, DC, and Olympia, Washington, journalists who contextualize riot grrrls as punks often fail to define the (boy) bands against which the grrrl bands are reacting so strongly.[28] In addition to those problems resulting from riot grrrl's contextualization within the "women in rock" narrative, comparisons of riot grrrl music to "boy punk": (1) conflate this community with a few punk riot grrrl bands (namely Bikini Kill and Bratmobile, who are mentioned in every mainstream article on riot grrrl); (2) construct riot grrrl musicians as appropriating "masculine" forms of music without problematizing how these female artists (like other female punk musicians before them) use masculine-coded genres such as punk to foreground the social construction of gender; and (3) reduce the punk movement to music by ignoring all its nonmusical components.[29]

Since the DIY ethos advocated within the riot grrrl community is consistently linked to the alternative production ethic of punk music, it is often assumed that riot grrrls are either punk musicians or punk fans and nothing else. By extension, riot grrrl zines—which frequently contain artistic expressions and information unrelated to music—are most often discussed as *fan*zines, a genre of publications which is usually traced back only as far as the alternative press created to celebrate punk bands in the late 1970s, in spite of its connections to a variety of alternative groups such as the popular science fiction press of the late 1930s, beat poets of the 1950s, and French leftist radicals of the 1960s.[30]

The unproblematized conflation of riot grrrl's countercultural community with punk music obscures many of the ideological, political, and economic motivations behind the DIY ethos and, thus, effaces much of its history as an anti-hegemonic philosophy of production and distribution.[31] Outside the alternative community, however, such reductive representations make it easier to contain the rage of riot grrrl's radical political community by commodifying it as just another anarchic youth pose like that made purchasable by master punk promoter Malcolm McLaren.

Grrrl Power: Theorizing the Place of a Radical Female Youth Culture

Because popular notions of female youth cultures rely on the "teenybopper" stereotype, media descriptions of riot grrrl zines as fanzines imply an equation of this community not only with punk, but also with girl cultures formed by fans of specific musicians (for example, the hysterical female fans of Elvis in the 1950s, the "Beatlemaniacs" in the '60s, the Madonna "wannabes" in the '80s, etc.). Since mainstream representations of girl fans as irrational, boy-crazy (not to mention white and middle-class) consumers have played an important role in the ideological construction and social treatment of female youth, we do well to question how this construction informs the emergence of riot grrrl as a countercultural community.[32]

While I do not mean to imply that these previous girl fan cultures did not serve a function for the female youth who were involved in them, when riot grrrl is conflated with other girl cultures formed through musical fandom, the complexity of its community is obscured and the potential threat of its sociopolitical power is displaced. Unlike the female adolescents involved in such fan groups whose cultural identity was connected to the consumption of commodities produced by the dominant culture industries, riot grrrls attempt to exist outside the corporations which support mainstream culture by creating the music, zines, and other creative products they consume. Riot grrrl's countercultural community indicates the extent of its interests beyond the boundaries of music and, more significantly, signals an important shift in female youth cultures from the level of consumption to the level of production.

Furthermore, while riot grrrls value the centrality of homosocial bonds found in youth cultures, they often move far afield from the heterosexual fantasies of romance reproduced in previous girl cultures. Since "girl love" is advocated continuously in riot grrrl music, zines, videos, and drawings, it is important to consider why its more obvious meaning—lesbianism—has been downplayed, if not outright ignored, in mainstream accounts of this all-grrrl culture. For example, some writers, in an attempt to situate this community within the larger narrative of homosocial girl cultures, contextualize riot grrrl's notion of "girl love" as childish play rather than adult sexuality.[33] Other journalists efface the possibility of any homosexual desire or activity amongst riot grrrls by foregrounding the place of boys in this grrrl-only culture. For instance, Lauren Spencer asserts, "And make no mistake: Most Riot Grrrls still find boys useful for the usual teenage things."[34] In using such rhetorical strategies, these writers efface the lesbian subjectivity and desire many riot grrrls are learning to embrace assertively as their own.

While the contextualization of riot grrrl as a musical phenomenon reflects an attempt to incorporate riot grrrl within popular notions of female youth cultures, such representations more significantly reveal the desire to not speak about riot grrrl as a radical political community. For example, if riot grrrl is represented as a girl culture, it can be equated with other fan cultures and recuperated as a new consumer fad for girls.[35] Similarly, if riot grrrl is represented as a (sub)genre of punk music (an alternative genre of rock commercialized since its emergence in the 1970s) or "women in rock" (a musical category exploited since the "girl group" phenomenon of the 1950s), its difference is naturalized and commodified through purchasable products. Considered as a political community, however, riot grrrl is not easily recoupable since radical political movements are rarely absorbed in consumerist forms. Riot grrrl becomes threatening, therefore, when its members refute such mainstream representations by insisting that they be taken seriously as political activists who demand that the rest of us rethink the social, cultural, economic, and political power of female youth.

In 1980 Angela McRobbie articulated her prediction for future female youth cultures:

> To the extent that all-girl subcultures, where the commitment to the gang comes first, might forestall [the search for boyfriends] and provide their members with a collective confidence which would transcend the need for "boys," they could well signal an important progression in the politics of youth culture.[36]

In spite of the heterocentrism inherent in her statement, it would seem that riot grrrl has become the culture McRobbie dreamed of over fifteen years ago. By providing female youth with a collective confidence, riot grrrl's revolutionary counterculture and radical political activism empowers girls to liberate themselves from the misogyny, ageism, and, for some, homophobia they experience in their everyday lives. Thus, unlike previous female youth cultures which were formed and sustained by a patriarchal ideology of dependence which kept girls tied to the feminized spheres of consumption and domesticity, riot grrrl signals an important moment not only in the politics of youth, as McRobbie predicted, but in the politics of feminism as well.

No Future?: Youth Identity, Youth Culture, Youth Activism

In her street-smart analysis of contemporary American adolescents *Teenage Wasteland*, Donna Gaines speaks of the colonization of youth by adults (that is, the surveillance, regulation, and containment of their movements through time and space), a process which has resulted in the decreasing status of young people in our society since the emergence of youth as a new social category and consumer class.[37] As she makes clear, the spaces of youth (for example, streets, bedrooms, etc.) and the forms of youth identification (for example, fashion, music, etc.) have become battlegrounds in the cultural processes of identification that often leave young people feeling disconnected and powerless as adults continuously deny youth their political agency while exploiting their forms of cultural expression and selling them back via the corporate consumer industries.

While Gaines is specifically referring to youth in the 1980s, and while much of what she says remains true for youth today, she concludes *Teenage Wasteland* by noting that youth activism is on the rise in the 1990s. Since scholars are now theorizing the social category of youth to be less connected with age than affective experience or attitude, I believe that the impetus for young people to unite politically *as youth* has occurred precisely because that category, *their* category, no longer belongs to just them. In the United States youth culture *is* mainstream culture, but *whose* youth culture it is remains difficult to tell. As Andrew Ross notes,

> It is not just Mick Jagger and Tina Turner who imagine themselves still to be eighteen years old and steppin' out; a significant mass of baby boomers partially acts out this belief in their daily lives. . . . On the other hand, it is also

true that many kids listen obsessively to exactly the same music that their parents did.[38]

At a time when many individuals are bemoaning the inability of the Left to effectuate sociopolitical action, politicized youth groups such as riot grrrl indicate that the very concept of youth is in crisis.

What remains to be seen, therefore, is how well theories of youth's cultural expressions ("style") can be used to adequately understand riot grrrl as a political community. Since many studies of youth have focused on the leisure-based social cultures of working-class adolescents formed to negotiate adult authority and dominant ideology, it is important to note that these localized working-class youth cultures are often far less politically active than the diffuse "countercultures" of disaffiliated middle-class youth, which form in direct opposition to those institutions which reproduce hegemonic roles, practices, and relations.[39] Because riot grrrl's opposition of dominant ideology is strongly resonant of previous anti-hegemonic cultures such as the hippies whose position *within* hegemonic culture (that is, as part of the middle class) afforded them greater political agency, theories of middle-class countercultures may be more useful in understanding riot grrrl's political significance.

Unlike working-class youth, riot grrrls are privileged with more education, greater access to the means of cultural production and advanced forms of communication (for example, camcorders, computers, etc.), and a longer transitional stage between adolescence and adulthood, which allows them more time (especially for those who attend college) to experiment with new identities, relationships, forms of work, etc. In turn, the middle-class sensibility of riot grrrls appears in their ability to blur the boundaries between work and nonwork time as they incorporate their "personal is political" philosophy in every aspect of their daily lives, not just in the cultural activities associated with leisure time.

While riot grrrl's DIY ethos and separatist practices recall many of the radical political movements of the late 1960s which advocated a non-integrationist approach of resistance through the formation of separate cultures and communities, it is important to note that many of the anti-hegemonic values of those movements are traceable to the middle-class hippie counterculture of the mid-1960s, whose oppositional stance emerged via a generational crisis caused, in part, by youth's increasing critical consciousness of their powerlessness in relation to dominant ideology and mainstream society.[40] Though encompassing a vast array of cultures, the hippie counterculture eventually fragmented into distinct strands: (1) the "mystics" who avoided direct political activism and practiced individual revolution in their daily lives and alternative communities; and (2) the "politicos" who believed social revolution could only come from community action and, thus, became involved in New Left politics and the various civil rights movements of the 1960s and '70s.[41]

Sisters Doing It for Themselves: Riot Grrrl and Feminist Stratagem

Of those political movements that developed from the hippie counterculture, riot grrrl most strongly echoes the pro-woman/consciousness-raising radical feminist community of the late 1960s which insisted upon separatism from men and the mainstream along with the politicization of personal life for women's liberation from patriarchy and misogyny. (It is no coincidence, therefore, that, just like the young women who became active in the New Left and the women's movement, many riot grrrls are or have been college students.[42]) Though radical feminism was dominant in the early years of the women's liberation movement, its philosophies and practices have been consistently criticized as politically ineffectual in terms of long-term social transformation, except by the lesbian-feminist community which grew out of feminism's radical wing and continues to assert the necessity of separatist politics, alternative institutions, and an autonomous "womyn's culture" free from patriarchal and heterocentric domination.

While the connections between riot grrrl and the culture-oriented lesbian-specialist community are fairly obvious, Val Phoenix is one of the few journalists to explicitly relate these two groups by noting their similar forms of cultural and political expression: (1) an assertive pro-female stance; (2) resistance to patriarchy, misogyny, and homophobia; (3) grassroots organizing strategies; (4) alternative practices informed by the DIY ethos; and (5) the creation of safe havens for females to gather and express themselves in personal, political, and sexual ways.[43]

Considering the tremendous influence music has had on the formation and popular understanding of both riot grrrl and the lesbian-separatist community, it is interesting that Phoenix frames her comparison of these diverse groups through descriptions of their musical styles and interviews with their musical "leaders" (Kathleen Hanna of Bikini Kill and Alex Dobkin, respectively). Why Phoenix constructs her argument this way has less to do with the recuperative processes of the media discussed above than with the predominance of a cultural form of feminism in the United States in the last twenty years. Indeed, I would argue that, despite Phoenix's accurate comparisons, we might understand the emergence of riot grrrl, at least in part, as a reaction to the culture-oriented politics advocated by feminists since the mid-1970s.

As Alice Echols notes in her comprehensive history of radical feminism *Daring to Be Bad*, since 1975 the feminist movement has moved away from what was seen as a male-dominated leftist emphasis on political activism and has shifted its focus to the creation of an alternative culture for women.[44] Although such a separate counterculture continues to be theorized as a place of active resistance to patriarchy, misogyny, and homophobia, many feminists feel that, when women withdraw from political resistance and the mainstream in order to celebrate female difference and form separate communities, relationships, and practices, feminism risks becoming little more than a marginalized lifestyle practiced by individuals interested in personal rather than social transformation. (These same criticisms were made of "mystic" hippies, who allegedly gave rise to the "me generation.") Whether individual forms of resistance preclude social transformation is highly debatable, yet concerns over the relative decrease in feminist activism and the long-term effectiveness of women's separatism continue today.

Since its emergence five years ago, many criticisms have been made against riot grrrl which echo those made of separatist/cultural feminism: it is essentialist, it does not appeal to the mainstream, it is elitist, it is nothing more than an apolitical lifestyle. With evidence for such allegations presumably at hand, many journalists have rung the death knell of riot grrrl and, in so doing, have demonstrated mainstream society's unwillingness to see riot grrrl as a lasting, important youth culture, not to mention an innovative form of radical political activism. While riot grrrl may be accused of reifying youth culture through its countercultural practices or "reinventing the wheel" of radical politics by relying on essentialized notions of girlhood and separatism for political agency, its adamant refusal to be reduced to a commodifiable cultural phenomenon reveals a unique ability to incorporate the strengths of other cultural and political movements without succumbing to the recuperative processes of dominant ideology and the rampant commercialism of late-twentieth-century capitalism. Riot grrrl may very well operate within the dialectic created by youth culture and radical politics; however, its recuperation of girlhood as a structure of political investment has initiated a profound rupture in our understanding of adolescence, femininity, youth culture, and political agency.

My thanks to the riot grrrls who shared with me their zines, music, and videos and talked with me about their community. Thanks also to Ellen Strain, who provided many useful suggestions for this essay.

Notes

1. Heavens to Betsy, "Donating My Body to Science," *Calculated* (Kill Rock Stars, 1993).

2. Ann Japenga, "Punk's Girl Groups Are Putting the Self Back in Self-esteem," *New York Times*, November 15, 1992, H30.

3. The female members of Heavens to Betsy, Bikini Kill, Bratmobile, Kreviss, Tiger Trap, 7 Year Bitch, and Mecca Normal united as "riot grrrls" during Girls' Night at the International Pop Underground convention held in Olympia, Washington, during the summer of 1991. Emily White, "Revolution Girl Style Now," *LA Weekly* (July 10–16, 1992): 21.

4. Teresa de Lauretis, "The Essence of the Triangle, or Taking the Risk of Essentialism Seriously," in *The Essential Difference*, edited by Naomi Schor and Elizabeth Weed (Bloomington: Indiana University Press, 1994), 34.

5. Riot grrrls exist in almost every major city in the United States, as well as some cities in Canada and Britain. I have also heard that the riot grrrl community has now spread to Japan.

6. Introducing the song "Double Dare Ya," Kathleen Hanna screams, "We're Bikini Kill, and we want REVOLUTION GIRL-STYLE NOW!" *Bikini Kill* (Kill Rock Stars, 1991).

7. Misty quoted by Hillary Carlip, *Girl Power: Young Women Speak Out!* (New York: Warner Books, 1995), 58. In order to make this essay less exploitative than it already is, I have purposely included only those statements made by riot grrrls which appear in material circulating within mainstream culture (for example, song lyrics and quotations used in newspaper and magazine articles) rather than those statements made in conversations with me or in grrrl zines I have collected. In addition, except in the case of musicians and visual artists who have more public personas, I have not used the last names of grrrls in order to respect their privacy.

8. While one grrrl has informed me that twenty-five is the maximum age for riot grrrls, there seems to be a lack of consensus as to the "official" age boundaries of this community, which is composed of both teenage girls and young women.

9. Erika quoted by Lauren Spencer, "Grrrls Only," *Washington Post*, January 3, 1993, C2.

10. Benedict Anderson, *Imagined Communities: Reflections on the Origin and Spread of Nationalism* (London: Verso, 1991).

11. Riot grrrls also create various anti-corporatist fashions. For example, several

grrrls have started a "girl run and powered" mail-order catalog, which they describe as an anti-corporate service designed to promote pro-girl messages.

12. A middle-class version of grrrl zines appears on the Internet in the form of private grrrl-only user groups.

13. Contrary to popular conceptions of this community, riot grrrl concerts are not only for punk bands; folk singers and spoken-word performers also spread the "grrrl power" message through their art. In addition, riot grrrl concerts function as alternative marketplaces for the selling and trading of records, tapes, zines, books, clothing, etc. Reviews of riot grrrl bands and performers by both alternative and mainstream music critics have also disseminated knowledge about riot grrrl music and this community.

14. Bikini Kill, "Double Dare Ya"; The Tourettes, "Battle Hymn," *Hidden Keys to Loving Relationships* (Lookout! Records, 1994).

15. Sadie Benning quoted by Val C. Phoenix, "From Womyn to Grrrls: Finding Sisterhood in Girl Style Revolution," *Deneuve* (January–February 1994): 41–42. Benning has commissioned Bikini Kill, whose music appears on the video, for the soundtrack of her longer 16-mm film version of *Girl Power.*

16. *Frenzy*, dir. Jill Reiter, noted in Phoenix, "From Womyn to Grrrls," 41.

17. I define *praxis* as any politically informed action which, unlike *labor*, does not involve the processes of exploitation, reification, and alienation experienced by individuals in capitalist economies.

18. Erika quoted by Spencer, "Grrrls Only," C2 (also quoted by Carlip, *Girl Power*, 32 and 35).

19. Dick Hebdige, *Subculture: The Meaning of Style* (London: Routledge, 1979), 96. For an excellent analysis of haute couture's appropriation of youth culture, see Janice Gore's "Bringing the 'Masses' to Culture: Thrift Shopping, Use(d) Value, and the Aesthetic of Poverty," *Spectator* 15, no. 2 (Spring 1995): 34–35.

20. Carlip, *Girl Power*, 30–63.

21. Some riot grrrls have willingly dialogued with journalists of alternative publications. See, for example, Melissa Klein's "Riot Grrrls GoGo," *off our backs* 23, no. 2 (February 1993): 6–12, and Angela Johnson's "Start a Fucking Riot," *off our backs* 23, no. 5 (May 1993): 6–10. Riot grrrls have also participated in Carlip's text, as well as *Listen Up: Voices from the Next Feminist Generation*, edited by Barbara Findlen (Seattle: Seal Press, 1995).

22. The contextualization of riot grrrl as a cultural phenomenon is most apparent in the placement of articles about this community in the "lifestyle" sections of mainstream newspapers and magazines, which are popularly coded as feminized spaces of cultural trends, gossip, and consumerism (as opposed to the "news" sections, which are widely thought to contain "real" politics and "serious" information). See Japenga, "Punk's Girl Groups Are Putting the Self Back in Self-esteem"; Farai Chideya with Melissa Rossi and Hannah Dogen, "Revolution, Girl Style," *Newsweek*, November 23, 1992, 84–86; Elizabeth Snead, "Feminist Riot Grrrls Don't Just Wanna Have Fun," *USA Today*, August 7, 1992, 5D.

23. This tendency to situate riot grrrl within the "women in rock" phenomenon at the expense of understanding this community as a political counterculture has ex-

tended to scholarly studies of riot grrrl. For example, see Joanne Gottlieb and Gayle Wald, "Smells Like Teen Spirit: Riot Grrrls, Revolution, and Women in Independent Rock," in *Microphone Fiends: Youth Music and Youth Culture*, edited by Andrew Ross and Tricia Rose (London: Routledge, 1994), 250–274; and Simon Reynolds and Joy Press, "There's a Riot Going On: Grrrls Against Boy-Rock," in *The Sex Revolts: Gender, Rebellion, and Rock 'n' Roll* (Cambridge, MA: Harvard University Press, 1995), 323–331.

24. See Christopher Napolitano, "Rock Girls," *Playboy* 41, no. 11 (November 1994): 102, 104.

25. BMG Music Service catalogs, 1994. See also Lorraine Ali's "The Grrrl Who Heads the Jett Set" and "More Grrrl Talk" (about Chrissie Hynde), *Los Angeles Times*, June 18, 1994, F1, F12.

26. Elizabeth Wurtzel, "Girl Trouble," *The New Yorker* 68, no. 19 (June 29, 1992): 63–70; and Kim France, "Angry Young Women," *Utne Reader* 53 (September–October 1992): 24, 26.

27. Snead, "Feminist Riot Grrrls Don't Just Wanna Have Fun," 5D.

28. This is perhaps most evident (and most egregious) in Gottlieb and Wald ("Smells Like Teen Spirit") and Reynolds and Press ("There's a Riot Going On"), who repeatedly emphasize riot grrrl's reactionary stance to the male-dominated punk and hard-core scenes yet fail to name the "boy bands" riot grrrls oppose.

29. Spencer describes punk as "high testosterone." Spencer, "Grrrls Only," C1.

30. For example, Reynolds and Press argue, "The Grrrl-zines' biggest preoccupation is with the need to break down 'boy-rock,' the homosocial camaraderie of the alternative and hardcore music scenes which shun(t)s girls (to the sidelines)." Reynolds and Press, "There's a Riot Going On," 325. For a history of fanzines, see Frederic Wertham, *The World of Fanzines: A Special Form of Communication* (Carbondale: Southern Illinois University Press, 1973).

31. As Greil Marcus has brilliantly demonstrated, the roots of DIY as an alternative, countercultural, and anti-corporate/-commercial ethos are not in punk, but in the French leftist intellectuals of the 1950s and '60s who advocated individual responsibility for revolution. See Marcus, *Lipstick Traces: A Secret History of the Twentieth Century* (Cambridge, MA: Harvard University Press, 1989). I would argue that the DIY ethos is also connected to what the French call *la perruque*, an anti-industrial practice in which a worker appropriates company resources (for example, work time, materials, postage, etc.) for the creation of personal work. See Michel de Certeau, *The Practice of Everyday Life*, translated by Steven Randall (Berkeley: University of California Press, 1984), 25–26.

32. Several feminist scholars have recuperated the female adolescent fan from dominant representations of her as a clueless dupe of the culture and consumer industries. See Angela McRobbie, *Feminism and Youth Culture: From* Jackie *to* Just Seventeen (Boston: UnqinHyman, 1991); Lisa A. Lewis, *Gender Politics and MTV: Voicing the Difference* (Philadelphia: Temple University Press, 1990); Barbara Ehrenreich, Elizabeth Hess, and Gloria Jacobs, "Beatlemania: Girls Just Want to Have Fun," in *The Adoring Audience: Fan Culture and Popular Media*, edited by Lisa A. Lewis (London: Routledge, 1992), 84–106; and Wini Breines, *Young, White, and Miserable: Growing Up Female in the Fifties* (Boston: Beacon Press, 1992).

33. For example, see Gottlieb and Wald, "Smells Like Teen Spirit," 266–267.

34. Spencer, "Grrrls Only," C2.

35. This contextualization is perhaps most attributable to *Sassy*, a mainstream magazine for teenage girls that was, for a period, heavily influenced by feminism and helped spread knowledge about riot grrrl outside the alternative community.

36. Angela McRobbie, "Settling Accounts with Subcultures: A Feminist Critique," in *On Record: Rock, Pop, and the Written Word*, edited by Simon Frith and Andrew Goodwin (New York: Pantheon Books, 1990), 80. Originally published in *Screen Education* 39 (Spring 1980).

37. Donna Gaines, *Teenage Wasteland: Suburbia's Dead End Kids* (New York: Harper Perennial, 1991), 86.

38. Andrew Ross, "Introduction," in Ross and Rose, *Microphone Fiends*, 8–9.

39. John Clarke, Stuart Hall, Tony Jefferson, and Brian Roberts, "Subcultures, Cultures, and Class: A Theoretical Overview," in *Resistance through Rituals: Youth Subcultures in Post-War Britain*, edited by Stuart Hall and Tony Jefferson (London: Harper Collins, 1976), 57–71.

40. Michael Brake, *Comparative Youth Culture: The Sociology of Youth Culture and Youth Subcultures in America, Britain, and Canada* (London: Routledge & Kegan Paul, 1985), 90–102.

41. Clarke et al., "Subcultures, Cultures, and Class," 61.

42. Indeed, of the riot grrrl groups on the Internet, I know of two that are (or were) tied to student accounts.

43. Phoenix, "From Womyn to Grrrls," 40–43.

44. Alice Echols, *Daring to Be Bad: Radical Feminism in America, 1967–1975* (Minneapolis: University of Minnesota Press, 1989), 5.

PART III Queering Media

NINE

Soap Slash

Gay Men Rewrite the World of Daytime Television Drama

HOLLIS GRIFFIN

On *Days of Our Lives*, Philip Kiriakis and Shawn-Douglas Brady are two points in a hotly contested love triangle with female character Belle Black. Philip and Shawn make up, fight, and make up again as they struggle for Belle's attention and affections. But on the Internet, many slash fiction authors refer to Philip and Shawn as "Phawn," combining their names to denote the fact that they have recast them as two halves of a highly romantic, erotic, even pornographic pair. In the slash story "Salem High," one author has appropriated the two characters for a narrative in which they leave their girlfriends waiting for them outside of the locker room after a big basketball win in order to celebrate by engaging in mutual masturbation in the showers. In other words: "Too Hot for Daytime TV."

While there is a considerable amount of scholarship on female authors slashing traditionally "male" television genres, particularly science fiction, there is almost no scholarship on slash written about traditionally "female" television genres, nor is there any substantive literature on gay male slash fiction authors. Though this particular fan practice from this particular subject position is definitely a minority among a wider slash community, its authors constitute a vibrant presence within that community. Gay male–authored slash fiction of soap operas features fairly prominently on slash fiction websites, and I have examined a fairly large sample from slashcity.com, squidge.org, and nifty.org. This fan practice raises interesting questions about issues of gay male representation within the genre, gay male audiences of soap operas, what makes soap operas and their characters "slashable," and how original soap opera texts are appropriated and used by these particular gay male soap fans.

Gender, Genre, and Slash Fiction

Constance Penley and Henry Jenkins have both written extensively on slash fiction, though neither examines the fan practice in any depth outside of heterosexual female writers slashing Captain Kirk and Commander Spock [K/S] from *Star Trek*. Nevertheless, their work provides a useful starting point for this discussion. Penley uses a psychoanalytic framework in her examination of K/S slash fiction to argue that the fan practice offers a diverse range of identifications and object-choices to female slash authors.[1] Furthermore, she identifies one impulse to write slash fiction in the instance when fans are invested in a text as a whole but are dissatisfied with the quality of representations of their identity categories in that text:

> As loyal as the women fans of *Star Trek* have been, they have always been vocal about their disappointment with the women characters. . . . There is bitter disappointment that these women of the twenty-third century are still behind the switchboard, at the doctor's side, or in miniskirts serving coffee to the men. . . . It was, then, in large part, women fans' abiding love for the *Star Trek* universe . . . and their disappointment [with] everything they felt was missing from *Star Trek* that pushed them to begin elaborating on the *Star Trek* universe.[2]

She also locates what I call "slashability" at the level of genre, contending that the science fiction convention of alternate or mirror universes gives authors a highly effective way to mobilize the fantasy lives of their characters in a way that carefully and explicitly delineates imagination and reality.[3]

Yet Penley posits that while female slash authors who write K/S slash stories write narratives wherein the characters engage in homosexual sex, they don't necessarily narrativize these encounters as the basis for a sexual identity. Rather, for the slashed characters, "The whole issue of . . . sexual orientation gets resolved in an idea of cosmic destiny: the two men are somehow meant for each other and homosexuality has nothing to do with it."[4] I would argue that for gay men writing slash fiction, questions of sexual identity are foregrounded by the very nature of the subject positions they occupy, as well as the long history of gay male under- and misrepresentation in television programming. This isn't to suggest that women have not also been under- and misrepresented in television programming, but that the act of narrativizing male-male sex acts is more likely to be attended by an investment in identity politics for gay male slash fiction authors than for female slash fiction authors.

Like Penley, Jenkins argues that slash fiction writing is a fan practice that allows women to reclaim texts in which female characters are underrepresented or in which traditionally feminine interests in relationships and romance go unaddressed. Yet he engages in problematic essentialism in trying to account for the fact that K/S and other fan fiction is a fan practice dominated by heterosexual women. He asserts that reader interest in character development and taking narratives beyond original texts is necessarily the realm of the female, yet never considers the reasons why male writers engage in the same practice.[5]

In his work with John Tulloch, Jenkins directly addresses the issue of gay-authored *Star Trek* slash fiction. They explore gay fans' frustrations with a lack of gay representation in the series' various incarnations even though it is firmly in line with the *Star Trek* ethos of "Infinite Diversity in Infinite Combinations." Yet they do so by charging that writing slash narratives involving homosexual relationships between characters is not necessarily an "adequate" fan response to a lack of representation on a program.

> The circulation of slash within [the gay] subcultural community cannot adequately substitute for their lack of access to the media, since the aired episodes, even within fandom, enjoy an authority which cannot be matched by any subcultural production and since [gay *Star Trek* fan organizations'] push for a gay character on the aired episodes is intended as much for the consumption of closeted gay teenagers or straight parents, friends and coworkers as for the group itself. . . . Resistant reading is an important survival skill in a hostile atmosphere where most of us can do little to alter social conditions and where many of the important stories that matter to us can't be told on network television. It is, however, no substitute for other forms of media criticism and activism.[6]

While Tulloch and Jenkins do admit that writing slash fiction can be a pleasurable fan activity for television viewers in and of itself, they seem nonetheless to set up a hierarchy of worthy fan activities in the face of inadequate representation in original show texts. Surely there are many possible reasons why slash fiction authors engage in this particular fan practice, but Tulloch and Jenkins leave little room to consider how slash fiction authors, of various genders and sexual orientations, might consider this fan practice an effective political response to underrepresentation in mainstream media texts.

The extent to which gay slash fiction authors rework soap opera story lines in fiction highlights the paradoxical nature of their fandom: a heavy investment in this programming even though they very rarely see themselves represented in it. In the next section, I trace the history of gay male representation in daytime television melodramas and examine the means by which gay men have been relegated to the margins of soap opera. In looking at how gay men have been under- and misrepresented here, the practice of gay men slashing soap operas comes into sharper focus as one with both liberatory and resistant potential.

Gay Male Representation in Soap Operas

Soap operas have historically dealt with a variety of taboo social issues (for example, rape, abortion, alcoholism, mental illness, and domestic violence), but homosexuality has been largely disregarded by daytime melodramas. Tania Modleski contends that "only those issues which can be tolerated and ultimately pardoned are introduced on soap operas. . . . An issue like homosexuality, which could explode the family structure rather than temporarily disrupt it, is simply ignored."[7] C. Lee Harrington attributes this underrepresentation to a combination of generic restrictions, network constraints, and assumptions about soap opera audiences.[8] Because this programming deals so overwhelmingly with romance in general, and heterosexual romance specifically, it is very difficult to fully integrate gay characters into a soap opera landscape when all of the other characters are foreclosed as romantic possibilities. In addition, like so many television texts, story lines and characters are written into soap operas with economics in mind, and the broadcast medium operates on the premise that stories will not alienate audiences and advertisers. The genre is predicated on the industrial assumption that heterosexual women watch these shows for the romantic story lines and that gay male characters—and whatever romantic involvements that might involve them—lie squarely outside what is perceived to be the key audience's primary reason for watching the programs in the first place.

Historically, gay male representation has been relegated to the margins on soap operas, when it has been dealt with at all. Soap operas generally use marginal characters to introduce taboo social issues like homosexuality so that they can be "embodied" by a single character. Joy Fuqua states that either this character can be written out of the program with little disruption to the main story lines or the problematic issue can be "detached" from the marginal character, after which he/she can be made a permanent part of the soap opera community. One example is the "wanton woman," the taboo issue being her illicit sexuality, from which she is detached by marrying into a program's core family. But because homosexuality is so tied to a character's identity, the "problem" of his/her sexuality can never be detached from the character.[9] In the 1980s and 1990s, the few gay male soap opera characters that were introduced were marginal and narrativized at the level of "social problem," and were then dispensed with when they could not be incorporated into the soap opera universe. Gay clothing designer Hank Eliot appeared sporadically on *As the World Turns*, but the character was written out of the show to care for a boyfriend with AIDS who, conveniently, lived in another city. Billy Douglas came out of the closet and was disowned by his father on *One Life to Live*, but the character was tangential to the core narratives and the story line disappeared from the program quickly and neatly.

Fuqua indicates that "it is the representation of the 'everyday' in relation to gay characters which causes the difficulty for soap opera. Gay characters can be represented, but only in terms of the sexuality-as-problem paradigm."[10] This begs a larger question regarding the pleasure of these texts for gay male audiences if their only representations on soap operas read like overly earnest, completely asexual public service announcements. In the next section, I examine some of the historical and theoretical implications of gay men's historic identification with and appreciation for melodramas in an attempt to locate a capacity for gay male pleasure in soap opera texts.

Soap Operas and Gay Male Fandom

Gay male camp aesthetics and readings have usually been studied in terms of the actresses with whom gay male audiences most identify. However, in gay-authored soap slash fiction, the characters appropriated from the original texts are male. Furthermore, the highly erotic nature of gay-authored soap slash points to a spectatorial involvement with soap operas beyond simply making fun of them, which is what camp implies. For this reason, it is useful to examine gay male spectatorial involvement with melodramas as a generic form. Linda Williams casts melodrama as a "body genre" because "the body of the spectator is caught up in . . . the emotion or sensation of the body on the screen."[11] Williams locates this spectatorial overinvolvement in the Freudian fantasy of origin, whereby the melodramatic genre is structured around the child's memory of wholeness with the mother. She also highlights how melodrama, as a genre, is marked by a related temporal fantasy wherein "the quest for connection is always tinged with melancholy or loss."[12]

While Williams deals largely with female subject positions and female characters, Michael DeAngelis extends her framework to argue that the melodramatic form offers ample possibility for gay male identification with, and erotic desire for, male melodramatic characters and the male stars who portray these roles. DeAngelis discusses the appeal of mainstream film stars and the roles they play in filmic melodramas geared (arguably) for heterosexual audiences. However, because soap opera actors frequently perform a kind of excessive hegemonic masculinity on daytime television, his argument can be extended here. He posits that because melodrama is so participatory, it enables and accommodates fantasies of same-sex desire among gay male spectators—even in texts or at historical moments that would seem to preclude them.[13] DeAngelis states that this occurs because the fantasy of origin operates at two different sites in melodramas: between a character and a spectator as well as between characters in a text. The gay male spectator has an affective investment in the male actor "in an attempt to forge and maintain a bond with [him]."[14] At the same time, this spectatorial fantasy of reunion and reconnection can take place when two characters are united on-screen.

Of course the character unions as imagined in the slash fiction here are not going to be realized in the original soap opera texts as they air on daytime television anytime soon. Yet as DeAngelis states, ultimate return to a state of oneness with the mother is always impossible but "poses no definitive obstacle in the realm of fantasy. What remains crucial is the continuous dynamic—offered by melodrama and the notion of genre itself, with its emphasis on formulas and repetitions—that allows the audience to keep experiencing . . . pleasure."[15] Moreover, the seeming conflict between subject-choice and object-choice in this theoretical model, what DeAngelis calls "the being and the having," can be explained by the fact that people inhabiting subject positions frequently engage in these activities simultaneously.[16]

> While identification is based on likeness or similarity between subject and object, . . . desire is based on a perceived difference. . . .The perception of likeness helps to construct a subject position for both the viewer and the narrative protagonist's entry into the fantasy scenario, offering a necessary first step for placement within a scene. At the same time, the perception of difference between self and other provides a required distance between subject and object that activates the dynamic of desire, spurring the fantasy of contracting distance and overcoming spatial boundaries.[17]

The melodramatic origin of fantasy opens up a variety of different subject positions with access to identification and desire. As such, soap operas address the gay male spectator even if, at face value, the texts seem to offer little potential for gay male identification or erotic desire.

Nevertheless, all of this takes place at the level of connotation and is easily denied by the obvious, preferred readings of soap opera texts. As Alexander Doty states, "Conventional heterocentrist paradigms [have already] decided that expressions of queerness are sub-textual, subcultural, alternative readings, or pathetic and delusional attempts to see something that isn't there."[18] Yet gay-authored soap slash moves queerness[19] from the connotative to the denotative level by appropriating characters, story lines, and generic conventions to rewrite the world of daytime television. In the next section, I will examine how the generic form of the soap opera offers slash writers the potential to make a soap opera's queerness extant and not just latent.

Locating "Slashability" in the Soap Opera

A soap opera can never be discussed teleologically; scholars have characterized these texts as having "an infinitely expanding middle" with constant interruptions from both inside and outside the diegesis. Characters are interrupted by various intrusions in individual scenes, story lines are broken up as programs cut between story lines or cut to commercials within individual episodes, and narratives cut across episodes as story lines are dropped for days, weeks, and years and are then reintroduced at some later point in time. Robert Allen has stated that soap opera writers take advantage of these gaps by leaving narrative questions unanswered in order to constantly draw viewers back to programs by prolonging suspense and preventing an ultimate telos.[20]

Tania Modleski argues that these interruptions should be seen as the means by which women who work in the home, their attention constantly diverted by household and familial duties, can enjoy soap operas:

> The flow within soap operas . . . reinforces the very principle of interruptability crucial to the proper functioning of women in the home. . . . The formal properties of daytime television thus accord closely with the rhythms of women's work in the home. Individual soap operas as well as the various programs and commercials tend to make repetition, interruption, and distraction pleasurable.[21]

She also states that the narrative conventions common to the genre, those that "[place] ever more complex obstacles between desire and fulfillment makes expectation an end in itself," thereby investing the "waiting" that is characteristic of work traditionally done in the home by women with pleasure.[22] This, however, points to the widely assumed gendered homogeneity of soap opera audiences, an assumption troubled by the very existence of gay male–authored soap opera slash fiction.

I contend that the net effect of these gaps and prolongings is that the characters in the diegesis never achieve the moment of happiness and closure that is supposed to attend a male-female coupling. While scholars have identified a distinctly feminine pleasure in this prolonged yearning for heterosexual closure, my argument is that by never fully resolving romantic tensions, making them constantly open to new controversies and clashes, the soap opera form is rife with opportunities for the gay male slash author to mine it for material and queer the narrative. Yet this is not the only place where the unstable codes employed by soap operas can be used to queer narratives. In catering to what is perceived to be (by both the television industry and academics) an overwhelmingly female audience, soap opera narratives deliberately put the bodies of male soap opera actors on display.[23] The taut physiques of these actors are featured prominently, in various states of dress and undress. This excessive performance of hypermasculinity invites queer interpretations of the roles they portray.

In his work on male pinups, Richard Dyer states that the spectacle of unclothed male muscularity attempts to naturalize and legitimize the model's male power and dominance while helping to avert the castrating gaze that attends male-as-spectacle.[24] While the penis and the phallus are conflated in the popular consciousness, they are not at all one and the same. Because the penis can only suggest phallic power, Dyer locates an excessive quality in male imagery that attempts to bolster what it can never really achieve with a cloak of muscle and performed virility so as not to imply passivity, and by extension, homosexuality.[25]

But because sexualized male imagery and gay visibility have increased to such a large extent in both popular culture and society at large, I would argue that a soap opera actor's performance of hypermasculinity calls into question the very heterosexual identity it is intended to signify; it can read as a kind of gay macho drag. Judith Butler calls such a gender performance

> a repetition of the law into hyperbole. . . . Interpellation thus loses its status as a simple performative, an act of discourse with the power to create that to which it refers, and creates more than it ever meant to, signifying in excess of any intended referent. It is this constitutive failure of the performative, this slippage between discursive command and its appropriated effect, which provides the linguistic occasion and index for a consequential disobedience.[26]

In her conceptualization of drag, Butler leaves room for an ambivalent drag, a performance that both denaturalizes and reidealizes heterosexual gender norms.[27] Thus, a male can displace notions of heterosexuality even via a performance of masculinity.

Moreover, within gay male subculture a taut physique is idealized to such a large extent that it troubles any connection between musculature and heterosexuality. Macho drag can also be read as an excessive performance of masculinity wherein those who perform it are doing so in order to disprove the belief that homosexual identity is necessarily achieved via an effeminate gender performance. As Butler charges, "hegemonic heterosexuality is itself a constant and repeated effort to imitate its own idealizations. . . . [It] is beset by an anxiety that it can never be finally or fully achieved, and . . . is consistently haunted by [the] domain of sexual possibility."[28] As a result, male soap opera characters frequently resemble roles performed by men in gay male subcultures, and their placement in various gay romantic and erotic scenarios within slash narratives is not much of a stretch of the imagination.

Gay-Authored Soap Slash Fiction: Resistance, Liberation, Porn?

Jenkins outlines a number of different narrative devices utilized by slash authors that provide a good practical foundation for the discussion of how original soap opera texts are appropriated and reconstructed in gay male–authored soap slash fiction. His list includes personalization, eroticization, refocalization, crossovers, and moral realignment.[29] As I have stated, personalization and eroticization figure prominently in gay male–authored soap slash. Personalization is a narrative device used by slash authors to rework narratives so that they are more reflective of the author's personal experiences.[30] Eroticization allows slash writers to explore the erotic dimensions of characters' lives and to transform censored television texts into narratives that explore sexuality and sexual themes.[31] Gay male slash authors employ these narrative techniques to rewrite daytime melodramas according to the needs and desires that have gone unrepresented in the genre for so long, capitalizing on the genre's mode of address and the gay erotic potential that exists—sometimes quite blatantly—in the original show texts.

Jenkins defines refocalization as the device some writers use in order to bring secondary characters to the foreground of slash fiction and shift attention away from the programs' central figures.[32] In "Days of Our Summer, Part II," based on male characters from *Days of Our Lives*, the author focuses attention on Jason, a teen character who goes to high school with children from the program's core families but remains on the periphery of the main story lines. In "Gay General Hospital," a long-running gay-authored slash series, the author constantly focuses attention on peripheral characters. The nameless male characters who act as villain Lorenzo Alcazar's bodyguards and henchmen on the program are featured as main characters in the first installment. In the third and fourth installments, the butler of the core family on *General Hospital* is the main character even though he is rarely a figure in main story lines in the original program text.

A crossover story is a single slash story that features characters from different programs. An example is "Soap Chat," a five-part slash serial where the author uses characters from nearly every soap opera on television. While the series revolves around Dr. Colin MacIver from *One Life to Live*, the stories also feature a number of other characters, including J. T. Hellstrom from *The Young and the Restless*, Joey Buchanan also from *One Life to Live*, Ryan Lavery from *All My Children*, and Thorne Forrester from *The Bold and the Beautiful*. The author appropriates these characters in order to place them in different sexual pairings throughout the series' five installments in what is truly a testament to the breadth of the author's knowledge of different programs, but also the depth of his investment in daytime television.

Moral realignment is a narrative device whereby slash authors "invert or question the moral universe of the primary text, taking the villains and transforming them into protagonists."[33] Perennial villain Stefan Cassadine is the main character in the second installment of the "Gay General Hospital" series. Throughout the course of the story, the author explores the sense of loss Stefan feels as a result of his rocky relationships with family members Lucky and Nikolas in the original show text.

Yet I don't want to discount the profound pornographic quality of nearly all of these slash stories. Many of these stories create a kind of "gay pornographic utopia" whereby sexual encounters between male characters are used to solve the problems presented in original show texts. For instance, the "Gay General Hospital" story that features Stefan and Nikolas Cassadine and Lucky Spencer resolves the characters' conflicts with a highly graphic ménage à trois. On the show, they are bitter enemies, but in the slash narrative they resolve their differences via a sexual encounter. On *Days of Our Lives*, stepbrothers Austin Reed and Lucas Roberts fought for Carrie Brady's affections in a story line that stretched across several years in "real" time and featured Lucas plotting and scheming to keep his brother and Carrie from achieving happiness as a couple. Yet in slash stories like "Samesex: Lucas' Master" and "Austin and Lucas," the authors resolve the heated conflict between the two stepsiblings by featuring the pair in erotic narratives. In "Austin and Lucas," Lucas tells Austin, "You see, it's been a long time since I've had sex, and I am offering to leave Carrie alone if you'll screw me over good." And because this is a slash story written by a gay male fan who has probably imagined this situation while watching the program on many different occasions, Austin eagerly complies.

Another common attribute of these slash narratives is a borrowing of generic conventions in creating seriality. Things like surprise intruders, hostage taking, blackmail, and secret electronic surveillance all figure prominently in these stories, though they all result in further sexual pairings between the "poached" male characters. In a slash series based on *The Young and the Restless* called "Young & Restless Men," Victor Newman imprisons and rapes Bradley Carlton in a dungeon in his mansion to get revenge on Bradley for having an affair with his wife and trying to take over his business. While they are having sex, Victor's son Nick watches and tapes them on the Newman mansion's intricate surveillance system. In the second installment of "Young & Restless Men," Nick blackmails

Bradley with the tape in order to convince Bradley to sleep with him. But at the end of the second installment, the author reveals that a fourth character had been watching Bradley and Nick's encounter through a window. True to the form on which it is based, the interloper isn't introduced until midway through "Young & Restless Men, Part III," and Nick, Bradley, and Victor (who by this point in the series has even had sex with his son) can't imagine what he'll do with this information.

As gay male slash authors rewrite the soap opera according to their own interests and fantasies, they do so by using the excessive style and generic conventions that are characteristic of the genre. But unlike the case of *Star Trek*, where there is a religiosity about the dogma attending the program among its slash-writing fans, soap slash authors often make fun of soap opera style and conventions even as they adopt them in their narratives. For example, in "Days of Our Summer, Part I," the author pokes fun at the soap opera's history as a lowbrow form of entertainment and makes several tongue-in-cheek references to various narrative devices used in the original *Days of Our Lives* text. This includes several send-ups of the show's dependence on mysterious villain Stefano DiMera and suspension of realism via narrative events like brainwashing and kidnapping. The author of the "Gay General Hospital" series pokes fun at earnest moments in soap opera by including lines like "He could take anything but a goddamn afterschool special" in the narrative. The dialogue of the "Gay General Hospital" series also includes ironic, humorous statements that point to the camp wit present in a lot of gay male–authored soap slash: "Hey, let's not forget the real reason we're here. Sex, and lots of it!" and "Enough of this soap opera detritus! Just kiss already!"

Richard Dyer has noted the centrality of this camp aesthetic to gay men's identity formation, and its championing of kitsch highlights how gay male soap slash authors differ from the slash authors that have been studied to date.[34] Jenkins and Penley state that science fiction slash generally contains a high level of editorial professionalism, but the particular slash writing I am looking at involves less of that policing. One reason for this could be that I examined slash fiction published on the Internet while Jenkins and Penley examined print slash. Also, *Star Trek* fandom is characterized as one famously devoted to the dogma of the show, as well as one that is famous for the culture of consumption built around that fandom. The playfulness and valorization of "bad art" so central to the gay male camp aesthetic raise the possibility of a more flippant involvement with soap operas and slash fiction among gay men.

Related to Dyer's notion of camp as being at the heart of gay identity formation, the gay soap slash I examined contains an element of dialogism as many of the writers include notes at the bottom of stories encouraging readers to send notes and story ideas for inclusion in future series and narratives. This appears to be a way for this fan community to forge adequate gay male representation in secondary texts since the original show texts have historically failed to do so. Also, these stories frequently begin with disclaimers akin to "this is what might happen if we actually got our way," denoting the fact that the soap slash authors are frequently engaging in this particular fan activity as a form of liberation and resistance to a dominant system of representation that has left their desires hidden at the level of connotation for so long.

Conclusion

Being a gay male soap opera fan myself, I have to admit a more than passing interest in how other gay male fans negotiate identification and desire in a television genre that has all but erased gay men from their texts even as they prominently feature ostensibly heterosexual male characters that are so infinitely queerable. Being that the organization of television as an institutionalized communications medium precludes much viewer involvement with texts beyond reading strategies and various fan practices, slash fiction appears to be a powerful means by which some fans can act out resistance to dominant systems of meaning. Nevertheless, I do not wish to valorize one form of viewer resistance and liberation over another. As such, I see this as part of a larger project in which interviews with actual gay male soap slash authors could shed some light on the pleasure they find in writing slash fiction. To what extent do they see the act of writing as an end in and of itself?

Still, the very presence of gay male–authored slash fiction complicates current conceptualizations of slash fiction writers as a group. Further analysis of who is reading this slash fiction and why is necessarily rooted in a discussion of how fans enjoy slash fiction in relation to their viewings of the shows on which the stories are based. Does one replace the other? Do fans see writing and/or reading soap slash as something distinct from watching the show?

At the same time, gay male–authored soap slash also complicates notions of soap opera audiences. The level of affective investment implied by the many long-running gay-authored soap slash serials published on the Internet troubles common conceptualizations of the typical soap opera viewer as a heterosexual housewife. As daytime audiences continue to shrink and television networks face stiffer competition from cable programming than ever before, the soap opera industry may benefit from taking note of their vital gay male fan base. Of course, even if this were to happen, the pornographic content of gay male–authored soap slash would still never find its way to daytime television. As a result of this, the practice of writing slash fiction will always contain a significant amount of resistant, liberatory potential.

A Note on Methodology

In using the Internet as a source for gay male–authored soap slash fiction, I was faced with the difficulty of determining authorship in a medium notorious for its anonymity. As such, my sample includes fiction written by self-identified gay men. This was easier to determine in some cases than in others. I want to highlight the fact that the Nifty Web Archive is a website wholly devoted to the publication of erotica written by gay men. As such, their many pages on gay male slash fiction provided a valuable resource. When using websites linked to slashcity.com and squidge.org, I only included slash fiction when I was able to determine that the author was in fact a gay male.

Slash Fiction Used in This Analysis

From nifty.org: "Austin and Lucas," "Days of Our Summer, Parts 1–3," "Daytime, Dark and Dangerous," "Dudes of Our Lives, 1–2," "Gay General Hospital, 1–6," "Salem High," "Soap Chat, 1–5," "Young & Restless Men, 1–6."

From other archives: "Days of Revenge," "A Days of Our Lives Sex Story: Lucas' Master."

Notes

1. Constance Penley, "Feminism, Psychoanalysis, and a Study of Popular Culture," in *Cultural Studies*, edited by Lawrence Grossberg, Cary Nelson, and Paula A. Treichler (New York: Routledge, 1992), 488.

2. Ibid., 489.

3. Ibid., 491.

4. Ibid., 487.

5. Henry Jenkins, "*Star Trek* Rerun, Reread, Rewritten: Fan Writing as Textual Poaching," in *Television: The Critical View*, 6th ed., edited by Horace Newcomb (New York: Oxford University Press, 2000), 476–477.

6. John Tulloch and Henry Jenkins, *Science Fiction Audiences: Watching* Doctor Who *and* Star Trek (New York: Routledge, 1995), 264–265.

7. Tania Modleski, *Loving with a Vengeance: Mass-Produced Fantasies for Women* (Hamden, CT: Archon Books/Shoestring Press, 1982), 93.

8. C. Lee Harrington, "Homosexuality on *All My Children*: Transforming the Daytime Landscape," *Journal of Broadcasting and Electronic Media* 47, no. 2 (2003): 221.

9. Joy V. Fuqua, "There's a Queer in My Soap!: The Homophobia/AIDS Story-Line of *One Life to Live*," in *To Be Continued . . . : Soap Operas around the World*, edited by Robert C. Allen (New York: Routledge, 1995), 201.

10. Ibid., 209.

11. Linda Williams, "Film Bodies: Gender, Genre, and Excess," *Film Quarterly* 44, no. 4 (1991): 4.

12. Ibid., 11.

13. Michael DeAngelis, *Gay Fandom and Crossover Stardom: James Dean, Mel Gibson, and Keanu Reeves* (Durham, NC: Duke University Press, 2001), 10.

14. Ibid., 6.

15. Ibid., 6–7.

16. Ibid., 9.

17. Ibid., 16.

18. Alexander Doty, *Making Things Perfectly Queer: Interpreting Mass Culture* (Minneapolis: University of Minnesota Press, 1993), xii.

19. My intention here is not to conflate "gay man" with "queer," but to adopt Doty's terminology in placing gay male readings both within and adjacent to queer readings as something different from though not completely unrelated to identity categories and their labels.

20. Robert C. Allen, *Speaking of Soap Operas* (Chapel Hill: University of North Carolina Press, 1985), 78–79.

21. Modleski, *Loving with a Vengeance*, 100.

22. Ibid., 88.

23. Bradley S. Greenberg and Mark G. Woods, "The Soaps: Their Sex, Gratification, and Outcomes," *Journal of Sex Research* (August 1999): 253.

24. Richard Dyer, "Don't Look Now: Instabilities of the Male Pin-Up," *Only Entertainment*, 2nd ed. (New York: Routledge, 2002), 128.

25. Ibid., 134.

26. Judith Butler, "Gender Is Burning: Questions of Appropriation and Subversion," *Feminist Film Theory: A Reader*, edited by Sue Thornham (New York: New York University Press, 1999), 337.

27. Ibid., 338.

28. Ibid., 338–339.

29. Henry Jenkins, *Textual Poachers: Television Fans and Participatory Culture* (New York: Routledge, 1992), 162.

30. Ibid., 171.

31. Ibid., 175.

32. Ibid., 167.

33. Ibid., 168.

34. Richard Dyer, "In Defense of Disco," in *Only Entertainment* (New York: Routledge, 2002), 153–154.

TEN From Excess to Access

Televising the Subculture

ERIC FREEDMAN

CAMP IS ESOTERIC—SOMETHING OF A PRIVATE CODE, A BADGE OF IDENTITY EVEN, AMONG SMALL URBAN CLIQUES. I AM STRONGLY DRAWN TO CAMP, AND ALMOST AS STRONGLY OFFENDED BY IT. THAT IS WHY I WANT TO TALK ABOUT IT, AND WHY I CAN. FOR NO ONE WHO WHOLEHEARTEDLY SHARES IN A GIVEN SENSIBILITY CAN ANALYZE IT; HE CAN ONLY, WHATEVER HIS INTENTION, EXHIBIT IT. TO NAME A SENSIBILITY, TO DRAW ITS CONTOURS AND TO RECOUNT ITS HISTORY, REQUIRES A DEEP SYMPATHY MODIFIED BY REVULSION.

SUSAN SONTAG, "NOTES ON 'CAMP,'" *AGAINST INTERPRETATION AND OTHER ESSAYS*

While Susan Sontag's 1964 essay "Notes on 'Camp'" has proven to be a seminal text in the study of camp as a phenomenon, it has, as with most canonized works, not aged very well; it has gone through much-needed rethinking and revision by numerous scholars, as well as by Sontag herself, since its publication. Routledge's recently published anthology *The Gay and Lesbian Studies Reader* includes a piece by D. A. Miller that, through a close textual analysis of such essays as "AIDS and Its Metaphors" and "Notes on 'Camp,'" takes Sontag's work to task for its authoritativeness and, more importantly, for its homophobia.[1] As Miller observes, Sontag concludes her "Notes" with a remark that attempts to sever any inherent ties between camp and gayness.

> Camp taste is much more than homosexual taste. Obviously, its metaphor of life as theater is peculiarly suited as a justification and projection of a certain aspect of the situation of homosexuals. (The Camp insistence on not being "serious," on playing, also connects with the homosexual's desire to remain youthful.) Yet one feels that if homosexuals hadn't more or less invented Camp, someone else would.[2]

Could the "gayness" of this sensibility be the source of Sontag's revulsion? By positioning those who share in a given sensibility (members of an unidentified urban clique) as analysands (as subjects of analysis) and herself as analyst (as arbiter of the camp aesthetic), it is Sontag who disempowers, who depoliticizes her subject. She seriously believes that: "It goes without saying that the camp sensibility is disengaged, depoliticized—or at least apolitical."[3]

Whatever "goes without saying" is indeed something that bears need of enunciation. In one grand gesture, Sontag attempts to excise queers, along with "exhibitors" (any clique will do), from the active process of writing history. Indeed, several recent political battles involving the media clearly illustrate the value of the position of history (and/or policymaker):

- On October 12, 1987, Senator Jesse Helms passed an amendment through the Senate as part of a Health and Human Services bill that would eliminate any federal funding for AIDS educational material that promotes or encourages homosexual behavior.
- In mid-August of 1993, Colorado Springs Cable Vision (located in Colorado Springs, home of numerous right-wing religious groups and a population that overwhelmingly voted in favor of Amendment 2, a ban on gay rights laws) refused to air *Sacred Lies, Civil Truths*, a pro-gay video.
- On August 16, 1993, the American Civil Liberties Union filed a lawsuit against Denver Community Television, a cable television firm, for violating the free-speech rights of the host and producer of the public access program *Magazine* by refusing to air one of its programs. (The company contended that the program contained obscene footage that suggested a man was performing fellatio.)
- On August 26, 1993, the producer and host of the Austin, Texas, public access program *Infosex* was indicted on charges of promoting obscenity and exposing minors to prurient material for airing a program that included footage from a safer-sex video (Source: GLAAD's Media Watch).

Whether it be a senate or a cable company, the body in charge of policy is in direct control of cultural production, and thus relegated to the position of determining what artifacts can and will constitute the history of a governed civilization. While it may be problematic for some to position the products of television alongside other cultural achievements, the value of such a correlation may become more obvious if one considers the importance of mass media in general.

The mass media is a core system for the construction and distribution of ideology; it serves as a linchpin in the construction of fantasy, for we are constantly mediating, or negotiating, between our desires and images provided to us in culture. By extension it is apparent that the insertion of otherwise marginalized (underrepresented) bodies into the flow of mass media is a critical process for their legitimation. Only by inserting our own bodies into the flow of representations, into the discourse of the media, can we take control of our desire. If fantasy lies at the intersection of desire and image, we must attempt to reconsider and enlarge the lexicon of images rather than limit the realm of desire. Thus, access to the media can be equated with access to history, for representations provide a site for negotiating a position within a continuous discursive flow. This is not to suggest a desire for the creation of an archive, a testament to the diversity of human experience as evidenced by a warehouse of images and assorted by-products, whatever those would be. Rather, it is to suggest that individuals do indeed negotiate positions in relation to the images that surround them as part of an active social process.

This essay will address issues of marginality made manifest through cable access programming and consider public access as a performative space for subcultural work, investigating both the politics and aesthetics of activist production (linking program content with program form). In particular, the focus here will be to examine the use of access programming in the queer community, activity that simultaneously functions (as a tool) to negotiate cultural difference, to edify a polymorphous sexuality, to visualize coalition politics, and to formulate new histories. Ideally, the methodology incorporated in this study can be used to investigate the manner in which other forms of cultural difference (for example, difference based on race, class, nationality, or gender) are negotiated through specialized and localized access programming.

"Amateur" video productions provide a means of access (to power) for those interest groups who both create and consume them. On a fundamental level, the videos serve to counteract increasing censorship and, more specifically, to provide positive representations of alternative cultural identities seemingly at odds with and therefore absent from the familial moralism of the mass media, functioning outside and therefore against the entire structure of "official" representations afforded by Western society. "Access" implies not only access to the resources needed to produce programming, but also access to the same civil rights heretofore restricted to the prevailing hegemony.

Access programming is necessarily politicized through its alternative modes of production (low-end production values can be equated with a subversion of the broadcast medium itself and the production standards of network programming), distribution, exhibition, and reception. Many of these programs circulate outside of the traditional channels of broadcast television, achieving international recognition through closed-circuit distribution among localized interest groups, far from their points of origin. Live shows are taped for distribution and are made readily available by their producers for distribution or "bicycling" (an informal distribution system among fellow viewers) at a nominal fee (normally the cost of a blank videotape).

In the history of alternative modes of independent access, cable access is only one form of access, existing within an absolute boundary of the era of televisual practices. The introduction of cable television in the early 1970s was accompanied by a Federal Communications Commission (FCC) mandate for new (cable) systems in the 100 largest television markets to include provisions for public, education, and government (PEG) access channels. While the mandate was not precise in defining the contours of these provisions, "public access" itself was construed to mean that the cable company should not only make available airtime, but also make available equipment so that literally anybody could make use of the access channel on a first-come, first-served basis, with a freedom of speech and action subject only to standard obscenity and libel laws.[4] In some cases, a local organization was set up to manage the access system, while in others the cable operator itself assumed these duties.

The availability of access channels depends, for the most part, on the political savvy and/or clout of committed community groups and local government.[5] The privately owned cable company must make a bid to each region that it intends to service, and as part of its franchise agreement it must pay a franchise fee to the city (in effect, to justify its monopoly over a given geographic radius). A percentage of this fee can then be used to fund PEG channels; the extent to which fees are used for public access as opposed to more general community services is determined by the city itself. In addition to a public access channel, most cable operators also offer leased access channels (that are made available for a programming fee) and local origination channels (that are run by the cable company itself typically for its own community affairs programs or other in-house productions). Although a 1979 Supreme Court decision struck down the aforementioned 1972 FCC mandate (construed to be a violation of freedom of speech, for cable companies claimed they were "forced" to air programming over which they had little or no editorial control), by this time cable had expanded so rapidly and become such a competitive industry that city governments were besieged by companies making lucrative offers and thus were able to negotiate for access channels as well as financial support to maintain and operate public access systems, which continued to grow significantly throughout the 1980s.[6]

As part of its development through the late 1980s and early 1990s, access programming has become increasingly stratified; current community-based programs are developed by and for rather specialized interest groups within quite restricted geographic radii. Despite the emergence of programs with a unique community focus ("community" in this sense refers to a particular geographic boundary and demographic constituency), there are numerous examples of fairly similar programming developments in rather diverse areas of the nation.

Access programming is currently being used in the queer community as a vehicle for the distribution of information (on public affairs broadcasts and through community-based coverage of newsworthy events) as well as a forum for media analysis and intervention; both processes are fundamental parts of a coalition-based politics.

As one of several activist media strategies, public access is being used as a tool to take control of the discourse surrounding AIDS and to empower those populations who aim to redefine their relationship to the disease through the acquisition of scientific knowledge. Since the early days of ACT UP, a video collective called Testing the Limits (formed in 1987) has been documenting demonstrations and creating a public archive. Its six members produced the twenty-eight-minute documentary *Testing the Limits: NY* in 1989 as well as several programs for the weekly New York cable network show *Living with AIDS*. There are, indeed, many educational aspects of AIDS activist video production, and these can be related to the Brechtian notion of radio communication, the prime objective of which is "turning the audience not only into pupils but into teachers."[7] The New York–based program on AIDS is in fact only one of several community-based productions providing support for local communities affected by the disease (productions that include the Los Angeles–based Being Alive *Medical Update* as well as AIDS Project Los Angeles's *AIDS Vision*).

Developing alongside these more politically engaged or information-based programs, there are numerous access productions created by and for the queer community that, though certainly not disengaged or apolitical, are first and foremost entertaining—including a trio of shows produced as part of the New York–based Gay Entertainment Network (*Party Talk*, *Makostyle*, and *Inside/Out*). Recent queer work in access also includes a number of programs which incorporate cross-dressing or drag, among them *Decoupage* (produced in Los Angeles), *Dish* (produced in Los Angeles), *The Brenda and Glennda Show* (produced in New York), and *DeAundra Peek Live from Odum's* (produced in Atlanta). Although all of these shows have drag hostesses, each show is distinct in its format and style.

DeAundra Peek Live from Odum's is hosted by DeAundra herself from Odum's double-wide mobile home park. Each show is comprised of a variety of segments including, but not limited to, fan mail, music videos, and live performance. As part of "DeAundra's Nitetime Soiree Partie" and "DeAundra's Teenage Music Club," DeAundra performs interpretive renditions of newly released pop songs by artists such as REM, The B52s, and Deeelite. *Decoupage* follows a more traditional interview talk-show format as the hostess Summer Caprice chats with celebrities after performing her opening monologue. *Drag Talk* (which appears on leased access channels outside of New York) follows a similar format as the hostess Hedda Lettuce opens with a monologue, banters with other local drag divas, and closes with a solo performance. *Dish* departs from the interview format, being a combination of both talk show and cooking show; the show's hostess, Madame Dish (Steven J. McCarthy), chats with and exchanges recipes with various celebrities from the local community. In a more overtly politicized gesture, *The Brenda and Glennda Show* takes drag to the streets as the two hostesses, Brenda Sexual and Glennda Orgasm, bring drag into a number of diverse public arenas such as the Taj Mahal casino and the Circle Line cruise.

MANIPULATION—ETYMOLOGICALLY, "HANDLING"—MEANS TECHNICAL TREATMENT OF A GIVEN MATERIAL WITH A PARTICULAR GOAL IN MIND. WHEN THE TECHNICAL INTERVENTION IS OF IMMEDIATE SOCIAL RELE-

VANCE, THEN MANIPULATION IS A POLITICAL ACT. IN THE CASE OF THE MEDIA INDUSTRY, THAT IS BY DEFINITION THE CASE. . . . A REVOLUTIONARY PLAN SHOULD NOT REQUIRE THE MANIPULATORS TO DISAPPEAR; ON THE CONTRARY, IT MUST MAKE EVERYONE A MANIPULATOR.

HANS MAGNUS ENZENSBERGER,
"CONSTITUENTS OF A THEORY OF THE MEDIA"

The producers of many access programs are unapologetic users of cheap media, with a commitment to making alternative media which directly counter and interfere with dominant media assumptions. The access programs identified in this analysis (and, for that matter, most access programs) adhere to a number of identifiable aesthetic principles, foremost among them "showing the seams." Using a relatively unpolished style (an aesthetic dictated by its limiting conditions), these programs, in effect, demystify the processes of live television and suggest that making shows need not be prohibitively expensive.

The "style" of these shows is commonly marked by a simplicity of design and lighting, a single stationary camera and a static wide-angle shot, in-camera effects (rather than studio mastering), a minimum of editing, and a raw sound quality. By virtue of their departure from network standards, most of these programs have an immediately discernible visual quality, and by using improvisation (with a minimum of scripting), many have an immediacy in their narrative format akin to a guerrilla-vérité style (and agitprop theater). A homology can be drawn between the formal properties of these tapes and their mode of production; the mode of production determines the physical characteristics of the work, while at the same time a "reading" of the tapes necessarily reveals the traces by which they came into being.

Drag lays bare the elements of its production—makeup and costuming (typically excessive or hypernormal)—in a manner similar to how cheap media proceeds, laying bare the theatricality of broadcast production. Both drag and cheap media are potential mechanisms for what Dick Hebdige defines as "semantic disorder": drag provides an interruption in conventional constructions of sexuality while countermedia production provides an interruption in conventional conceptions of production values.

The apparatus of gender production and the apparatus of media production are both subject to interrogation, thus both drag and public access can function as performative spaces for subcultural work. Hebdige suggests that as possible sites of "interference" in the orderly sequence which leads from real events and phenomena to their representation in the media, subcultural activities, of which drag can be considered a part, are not only metaphors for potential anarchy but actual mechanisms of semantic disorder—deviations which can briefly expose the arbitrary nature of the codes which underlie and shape all forms of discourse. Yet, as Hebdige relates, the challenge posed by the subculture to the symbolic order can be effectively incorporated in two ways:

1) The conversion of subcultural signs (dress, music, etc.) into mass-produced objects (that is, the commodity form)
2) The "labeling" and redefinition of deviant behavior by dominant groups—the police, the media, the judiciary (that is, the ideological form)[8]

The ideological form of incorporation is itself composed of two strategies: First the Other can be trivialized, naturalized, or domesticated. Here, the difference is simply denied. Alternatively, the Other can be transformed into meaningless erotica, a "pure object, a spectacle, a clown (Barthes, 1972)." In this case, the difference is consigned to a place beyond analysis (the spectacular subculture).[9]

Can drag, as one of various subcultural activities, be effectively incorporated into the symbolic order?[10] Certainly the performances of network figures such as Milton Berle and Benny Hill exemplify the first strategy of incorporation, in the actors' method of naturalizing drag (by virtue of its becoming simply one of many comedic routines and one of a series of personalities that the performer can assume, ultimately retreating to the safety of a more conventional [straight] masculine persona) and in the networks' method of subsequently domesticating their activity (by virtue of being listed on the network schedule, these performers are broadcast into people's homes on a regular and determinable basis—no surprise visits here).[11]

What, however, can be said of the activity of "full-time" drag performers such as DeAundra Peek, Summer Caprice, Madame Dish, Hedda Lettuce, and Brenda and Glennda? Certainly, by existing on the margins (being queer, being on cable), their actions can be consigned to that "place beyond analysis." But by virtue of their active dialogue with the space of access, and their reflexive acknowledgment of the sphere of network television (both in the content of their work and in their method of presentation), these performers appear not to be "consigned" to a place, but to actively adopt and appropriate it, marking it as their own. Brenda and

Glennda appropriate public space, literally defining the body of their program as they move through the city of New York; their shows are site-specific and dependent upon their interaction with the public sphere (the results of which are often unpredictable). Summer Caprice marks the surfaces of her studio with the accoutrements of decoupage (and refers warmly to her audience as fellow "decoupers"); likewise, her monologues are themselves littered with references to popular culture. In a markedly similar strategy, DeAundra, too, draws from the world of popular culture; broadcasting from her trailer park at Odum's (and often featuring local entertainers and celebrities from surrounding lots), DeAundra appropriates pop melodies as her own. In each case, the "real" and the "fictive" are circumscribed by the unlimited domain of performance.

These drag programs can be viewed in light of a more generalized or larger evolution of camp activity, emerging from an intelligent body of sociocultural analysis; all of these shows manage to be simultaneously populist and avant-garde in both their text and their stylistic trappings. In each, drag operates not simply as a survivalist ethic, but more importantly as an oppositional critique; by incorporating camp humor each hostess uses drag in a manner that allows it to operate above and beyond the need for an essentialized goal as validation.[12]

Artist and activist Gregg Bordowitz has noted that television is a "situation" that can be used in directed pragmatic ways as a means of defensive action; yet, if made in the interests of community, it can also be proactive. The fact that the programs used in this analysis are engaged in a critique of the media is in part the result of the inherent character of queer-aligned drag strategies, and not necessarily the result of any directed political action. First and foremost, these programs are made in the interest of a particular audience, an audience of which its producers and performers are also a part.

> A CAMP APPRECIATION OF ART AND THE MEDIA CAN KEEP US ON GUARD AGAINST THEM.
>
> **RICHARD DYER**

The increased use of electronic transmission and recording has brought with it a multitude of contradictions. With the advent of affordable camcorders, community video has found its place not only on public access and at local media centers, but also on every block (as evidenced by the growing number of visual documents of police brutality). Not only has the more widespread use of video raised certain problems for the state at large, it has also proven troublesome for the regulatory agencies and corporations that own and control the several thousand cable systems in this country.

Community video and, in particular, public access channels have found themselves at the center of a debate about censorship and the scope of First Amendment rights in the information age. As information has become a profitable commodity, access to it for free has become considerably more difficult. The cable corporations have attempted to use the First Amendment as a means of protecting their corporate profits and to reclaim channels that are devoted to access so that they may be used for profitable ventures.

While the cable industry was in fact deregulated with the introduction of the 1984 Cable Act (an act which, nevertheless, contained strong language in support of PEG access channels, although it changed their funding base), Congress finally acted to reregulate the industry in 1992 as frustrated consumers began to voice concern over skyrocketing cable rates. Yet the 1992 Cable Act does not only include provisions for standardizing rates; more critical is the fact that this act also contains censorship provisions for PEG and leased access channels and, furthermore, makes cable companies liable for the programming carried on their access channels, shifting the liability for program content from producers to cable operators (and presumably the access organization from which programs are distributed). Although public access has not had the same FCC content restrictions that other channels have had, public access stations have always opted to have restrictions on presenting "unprotected speech," that is, anything that is not free speech under the First Amendment, such as invasion of privacy, libel, slander, obscenity, and pornography, which are usually defined by "community standards." The 1992 Cable Act, however, reworded the obscenity standard as an indecency standard, a new area whose limits have not yet been clearly defined. In addition to the issue of obscenity, the new Cable Act also includes provisions for the prohibition of "material soliciting or promoting unlawful conduct," which will prove problematic for access programming depending on the specificity of, for example, drug laws, abortion laws, and sodomy laws in particular states.[13] The reregulation of access systems by the government simply enhances the control private business has over free speech—the systems themselves have always been "owned" by private business (the cable companies).

The "community standards" under which local access stations have been operating are perhaps the last holdout of an ever-shrinking "public sphere," a social realm of community-based communications systems.

Defining a "constructive political televisual aesthetic" is indeed a difficult task, but one that must address the importance of politically integrated opposition, of a hegemonic resistance by marginalized groups against mainstream broadcast television. Yet it is problematic to visualize such an aesthetic solely in relation to mainstream broadcast television, for, as John Downing notes:

> Even though TV critiques are fine and necessary, we should not risk having our ground defined for us by broadcast TV. Our media politics should strive to be autonomous, influenced more by political movements than by the hegemony of dominant ideology. It should be creating alternative public spheres and be organized in self-managed structures. . . . It is urgent that media politics, video politics, should not confine itself to a discourse internal to media or TV.[14]

Indeed, the expansion of the number of broadcast channels has not resulted in a correlative expansion of the diversity of available programs. Most examples of narrowcasting have amounted to little more than extensions of specific preexisting programming categories into entire channels, and access programming may itself be interpreted as the most extreme manifestation of narrowcasting—serving up shows that cater to a very select (and localized) demographic.[15] Furthermore, many access programs rely on generic formulas derived from network television (though their production values are quite distinct).[16]

The future role of access stations is dependent, in part, upon the future of communication technologies, keeping in mind the questionable structure of a predicted 500-channel cable system (which suggests at once the possibility for expanding the localized public sphere of the community as well as simply being another symptom of ever-increasing privatization). Will local access stations be provided, through satellite linkage or other forms of networking, with a larger national or international audience? Will the number of stations allotted to access increase, given the increase in the number of viable broadcast channels? With the scenario still left open to question, we must at this time consider how we will negotiate free speech within the context of a public sphere which is itself in flux.

A media politics that engages solely with a discourse of the media is indeed an empty strategy, for the only way to challenge mainstream media is to consider the ideological underpinnings of the institutions that dictate the use of the apparatus in a particular historical moment. Community-based programming should not simply follow the lead of network television, but rather should serve as a forum for envisioning the future of the medium. Indeed, we cannot wait for television to fall into our hands; we need to take it with whatever force is necessary, and with the aid of a few fierce drag queens, we will certainly do so in style. "Go on, girls!"

Notes

1. D. A. Miller, "Sontag's Urbanity," in *The Lesbian and Gay Reader*, edited by Henry Abelove, Michele Aina Barale, and David M. Halperin (New York: Routledge, 1993), 212–220.

2. Susan Sontag, "Notes on 'Camp,'" in *Against Interpretation and Other Essays* (New York: Anchor Books, 1966), 290–291.

3. Ibid., 277.

4. Douglas Kellner, "Public Access Television: Alternative Views," in *American Media and Mass Culture: Left Perspectives*, edited by Donald Lazere (Berkeley: University of California Press, 1987), 610.

5. Ibid., 611.

6. Ibid. For a more detailed critical history of cable access and activist video production, refer to Martha Rosler's essay "Video: Shedding the Utopian Moment," and Deirdre Boyle's "A Brief History of American Documentary Video," both of which can be found in *Illuminating Video: An Essential Guide to Video Art*, edited by Doug Hall and Sally Jo Fifer (New York: Aperture Foundation, Inc., and the Bay Area Video Coalition, 1990). Other resources include Daniel Marcus, ed., *Roar! The Paper Tiger Television Guide to Media Activism* (New York: Paper Tiger Television Collective, 1991); Michael Shamberg, *Guerilla Television* (New York: Holt, Rinehart and Winston, 1971); and Monroe E. Price and John Wicklein, *Cable Television: A Guide to Citizen Action* (Philadelphia: Pilgrim Press, 1971).

7. Bertolt Brecht, "The Radio as an Apparatus of Communication," in *Video Culture: A Critical Investigation*, edited by John Hanhardt (New York: Visual Studies Workshop, 1986), 54.

8. Dick Hebdige, *Subculture: The Meaning of Style* (London: Routledge, 1979), 94.

9. Ibid., 97.

10. Not to be overlooked is the fact that *Wayne's World* has successfully commodified public access itself.

11. The element of sexual play employed by a straight male performer in drag is quite distinct from that employed by his queer counterpart. While the punch line of a straight male drag is the awkwardness of being mistaken for a woman (resulting in same-sex desire), for the gay male performer this is commonly a source of great pleasure. The straight male's fear of loss of self is quite unfounded and markedly homophobic. While both players indeed possess a penis, it is only the gay male performer that maintains an active dialogue with it (a heightened phallic awareness) throughout his performance. (Hedda Lettuce often speaks of engaging in ass play with other men,

and although she wears a dress, she usually finds herself on top.) A drag queen is only as good as her tuck (and her tape).

12. For a further discussion of the performative dimension of gender, and the manner in which drag exposes the constructedness of all gendered positions, see Judith Butler's essay "Imitation and Gender Insubordination" in *Inside/Out: Lesbian Theories, Gay Theories*, edited by Diana Fuss (New York: Routledge, 1991), 13–31. In her essay, Butler constructs an analytic framework that attempts to leave the domain of a Freudian/Lacanian psychoanalysis (the masterful Oedipal narrative and its subsequent manifestations and rearticulations) to reposit or reinstate the points of origin that serve to construct sexual identity: an identity structured through actual praxis. What she proposes is a model that understands sexual identity as a construction. Despite its liberatory prospects, and perhaps against her will, Butler's theory has itself been canonized within academic discourse, becoming more prescriptive than descriptive. Originally acting as a corrective to biological determinism, Butler's theory has itself become deterministic. What is most important here, however, is the manner in which Butler's all-inclusive conception of performativity (all gender is performed) upstages Sontag's theater of homosexuals; the camp insistence on play is uniquely connected with "the homosexual's desire to remain youthful," for, as evidenced by the broad range of styles and costumes, drag itself embodies much more than traditional conceptions of beauty would allow. (Hedda Lettuce's Hasidic drag does not qualify as a conventional pursuit; as for DeAundra Peek, she is simply an old-fashioned yet vociferous southern belle wrapped in layers of foundation, eyeshadow, and rouge.) This is not to suggest that I am in agreement with Sontag's dismissal of the inherent link between camp and homosexuality; rather, it is to suggest that her assumptions are problematic on several grounds, including what she assumes to be the role of play in the gay community. While Sontag does consider both male and female drag, her invocation of the androgyne suggests a commitment to the traditional binary of male and female.

13. Given this context, and in light of the chaos caused by certain recent political actions, including Colorado's virulently homophobic Amendment Two and President Clinton's ruling over homosexuals in the military, programming produced by and for the queer community may be construed within an ever-increasing number of communities as "promoting unlawful conduct." It should be noted that the indecency clause is currently under contestation and will most likely be struck from the 1992 Cable Act.

14. John Downing, "Political Video in the United States: A Statement for the 1990s," in *At Arm's Length: (Taking a Good Hard Look at) Artists' Video: Essays by John Wyver, Leslie Fuller, John Downing, and Jon Burris*, edited by Barbara Osborn (1990), 113–114. Available at: http://www.experimentaltvcenter.org/sites/default/files/history/pdf/armslength_2474_master.pdf.

15. John Walden, "Unpacking the Revolution in a Box," in *Roar!: The Paper Tiger Television Guide to a Media Activism*, edited by Daniel Marcus (New York: Paper Tiger Television Collective, 1991), 22–23.

16. Indeed, the most distinguishing feature of these drag shows is also what is most problematic about them: the persona of the hostess. These cable shows are true to form to network talk shows in the credence that each gives to star power, for each show is only as successful as its hostess. The occasional hostility between local drag

queens seems quite antithetical to any notion of coalition building; yet most of these same men and women are vital members of their communities—often bridging the gap between politics and entertainment. In the summer 1993 issue of *Girlfriend*, a zine devoted to the drag scene, Los Angeles drag queen Gender commented: "Nobody puts on a dress to be political, but once the motivation is there, a lot of people answer the call. I mean, how political can a piece of clothing be?"

ELEVEN

Pronoun Trouble

The "Queerness" of Animation

SEAN GRIFFIN

In 1993, a small scandal erupted over rumors that Bert and Ernie, the beloved Muppet characters from PBS's long-running series *Sesame Street*, were a homosexual couple.[1] After all, they were two men who had lived together in the same New York apartment since the show began in 1969—and they were never seen dating women. The outcries were numerous, tending to fall into two categories. The first group declared that public television had conspired to actively (if covertly) promote "perversion" to young children.[2] Conversely, the second group complained that "someone" was defaming the wholesomeness of Bert and Ernie's friendship by suggesting that they were sexually attracted to each other.[3] Although there were those who found the rumor a positive development, in which a same-sex couple had seamlessly been brought into American homes for over twenty years,[4] the Children's Television Workshop, which produces the series, quickly issued a statement which assured viewers that the duo "do not portray a gay couple."[5]

Concerned parents might have figured that this was only one isolated incident. Yet, current children's fare on TV contains many relationships that seem "queer"—Ren and Stimpy, Beavis and Butthead, Mr. Burns and Smithers in *The Simpsons*.[6] A full-scale epidemic of heterosexual parents reading everything as "queer" could have erupted. This possibility was quelled when columnists and late-night talk-show hosts began to joke about the development, framing the whole idea as somehow "ludicrous."[7] One letter writer to *TV Guide* about the incident pointed out that, with the relationship between Kermit the Frog and Miss Piggy, it was far easier to claim that "Oh my gosh, *Sesame Street* is promoting bestiality!"[8]

Although the "Bert and Ernie" affair died away relatively quickly, the incident points out how easy it is to read "queerness" into these texts. Animation, an art form generally conceived as made for children, has always had a history of "queerness." Those who made fun of the commotion caused by "outing" Bert and Ernie used a conventional weapon against "queer" readings—that "too much" was being read into the texts, and that any overt moments were isolated and meant only as "jokes." Yet, many "queer" theorists would classify these readings as divergent, subverting the hegemonic "preferred" subject position that Stuart Hall describes.[9] Furthermore, animation's use of metamorphosis and inanimate objects "brought to life" creates a constant potential for "queerness" to be read by audience members. As Alexander Doty claims in his introduction to *Making Things Perfectly Queer*, "I've got news for straight culture: your readings of texts are usually 'alternative' ones for me, and they often seem like desperate attempts to deny the queerness that is so clearly a part of mass culture."[10] What is remarkable about the "Bert and Ernie" affair was that for a moment the "queerness" was no longer denied by straight culture and threatened to appear everywhere.

This essay's purpose is to examine closely a few animated texts to explore the "queerness" of animation. Although I am focusing on an American studio animation, I do not feel that this phenomenon is peculiar to this one institutionalized form of animation (especially as a number of American-produced cartoons use cels that are actually painted outside of the United States). The work of Czech animators or independent avant-garde filmmakers, for example, could also be rich in substance when examining how "queerness" works in these texts.[11] Yet, the "queerness" of the texts is both culturally and historically specific, and this essay also will examine how to reconcile historical research with the sometimes ahistorical approach that "queer" theorists take towards texts.

Queer Theory and Historical Research

A film archivist can find overt references to homosexuality quite easily in American cartoons. For example, in the Max Fleischer cartoon *Any Rags* (1932), one of the rag-seller's male customers buys a nude statue of a male discus thrower and then sashays offscreen. In the Mickey Mouse cartoon *Shanghaied* (1932), a group of pirates sings, "The Captain's got a girl!"—

including one sailor with a falsetto voice who bats his eyes. At the end of the Bugs Bunny cartoon *What's Cookin', Doc?* (1944), Bugs waxes enthusiastic when he gets a rabbit-shaped Oscar, saying, "I'll even take youse ta bed wit me every night!" The statue comes to life, kisses Bugs on the mouth, and, standing in an effeminate manner, says, "Do you really mean it?" In *Hair-Raising Hare* (1946), Bugs becomes a talkative fey manicurist as he files a monster's nails. Bugs himself has become recognized by many as a constant cross-dresser throughout his long career.[12]

These readings isolate specific moments within cartoons to highlight their representation of homosexuality. Unfortunately, these excessive moments are dissociated from the rest of the texts, and the rest of the animated films under analysis are affirmed as resolutely heterosexual. This type of discussion falls neatly into Eve Sedgwick's "minoritizing" category of sexuality, which views sexuality as an issue of active importance primarily for a small, distinct, relatively fixed homosexual minority, and not needing to be considered by the "normal" heterosexual majority.[13]

A lot of recent scholarly work on animation has begun to discuss how animation creates an "illusion of life" through the illusion of movement. Characters reveal their personality through the rhythm of their walk or the way they manipulate their facial expressions. "Animation thus poses the very questions of life itself, movement itself and their relation . . . suggesting that the two . . . can only be thought through each other."[14] In this exploration of the importance of motion in the creation of identity, recent animation theory ties directly into current social constructionist arguments about sexual identity, that all genders and sexualities (not just homosexuality) are learned and performed. In contrast to Sedgwick's definition of the "minoritizing" viewpoint, her "universalizing" view sees sexuality "on the other hand as an issue of continuing, determinative importance in the lives of people across the spectrum of sexualities."[15] Sedgwick argues from a "universalizing" standpoint, which forces not only homosexuality to come to terms with its construction but heterosexuality as well. If so, all renditions of heterosexuality in animated films are just as performative as any rendition of homosexuality. As a result, isolating Bugs's turns in drag ignores how Bugs performs masculinity the rest of the time.

The image of Bugs in feminine garb raises another issue unique to animation. Whether in or out of a dress, Bugs Bunny is always "in drag" as a human being. Although much of early animation featured human characteristics such as Mutt and Jeff or the Katzenjammer Kids, by the early

1920s, many of the stars of various cartoon series were anthropomorphized animals. (Even Betty Boop began her career as a humanized dog, complete with long floppy ears.) From Felix the Cat to Mickey Mouse and his friends to the menagerie of Warner Bros. characters, these animals only rarely referred to the characteristics of their supposed species. A mouse as large as Mickey or Minnie (standing taller than their dog Pluto) would belong in *The Guinness Book of World Records*. Bugs chomps on his carrot as if it were a cigar. Bugs, Mickey, and Minnie also walk upright rather than on all fours. Furthermore, these animals are never drawn with sexual organs.[16] Many never wear clothing, and those that do tend to wear only tops (such as Donald Duck and his nephews). Yet, the sexual organs of the animals are not visible. Walt Disney's studio was even forced to remove a cow's udder by censors in the early 1930s. Without these signifiers, cartoons must rely on voices and attire to assign gender (and it is also possible to deny the existence of sexuality entirely).

Consequently, to see Bugs wearing lipstick and a wig is to see a drawing of a gender-neutral rabbit acting like a human male pretending to be a human female. The levels of impersonation reach the sublime, to the point where boundaries seem impossible to nail down. This breakdown of categories is precisely what Sedgwick and others have attempted to promote through the reinvestment in the term "queer," which Alexander Doty describes as "an attitude . . . that begins in a place not concerned with, or limited by, notions of a binary opposition of male and female or the homo versus hetero paradigm."[17]

Judith Butler's deconstruction of the categories of identity in *Gender Trouble* proposes as an answer to the material oppression of sexuality not some fantasy overthrow of the system, or impossible "return" to a prehistory that is itself a construction.[18] Rather, Butler sees how the multiple discourses occurring within culture(s) (which attempt to regulate, prohibit, and generate the approved hegemonic discourse) often overlap, complicate, and contradict each other. Hence, possibilities for resistance occur when the complications of these multiple discourses are revealed. The material discourses of power that define identity are subverted by playing them out in such a manner that the various levels reach absurd and parodic extremes, exposing the constructedness of gender, sexuality, and sex itself.

I would argue that a perfect instance of multiple discourses swirling within one text, exposing the constructedness of gender and sexuality through parodic redeployment, is the animated cartoon. For example, the representation of homosexuality in animation as "effeminacy" in male characters (dressed in drag, swishing, etc.) runs through much of American animation (and in American mainstream film in general). Yet, the ability of supposedly male characters to convincingly move or costume themselves as female characters starts to question the stability of gender. After all, without any sexual organs to mark them as different, it only takes a polka dot skirt, some pumps, and long eyelashes to turn Mickey Mouse into Minnie Mouse (and factoring in the breakdown between animal and human further complicates this stability). Also, the tradition in animation that began as early as French animator Émile Cohl of metamorphosis and transmogrification of objects further emphasizes how shaky the boundaries of identity are.[19] Furthermore, animation has conventionally been used for creating comic narratives, usually using the technique of metamorphosis or putting characters into disguise precisely to parody society's norms. In terms of gender and sexuality, cartoons point to the foibles of all points of view—conventional heterosexual coupling as well as homosexual stereotypes, male as well as female—in a chaotic, ever unstable universe.

This is not to say that Sedgwick's universalizing viewpoint is not without its own problems. Since "queer" theory deals with breaking down the various definitions or categories, many self-defined homosexuals worry that "queer" theory might deny them a subject position just at the moment that it begins to become acknowledged in mainstream culture. I would argue that just as constructivist arguments are used in different contexts for divergent purposes (for example, to show that all sexuality is constructed or, conversely, to claim that homosexuality can be unlearned), the term "queer" either can be used progressively to deconstruct the stability of "straightness" or can be used to minimalize specific historical group definitions, depending on the contexts of its use and reception. The purpose here in using the term "queer" is to challenge and subvert the assumed natural order of heterosexuality, "by any means necessary," and not to decenter the lived experience of individuals.

Although "queer" theory began precisely to create a space for the wide spectrum of lived experience, the use of "queer" theory in close textual analysis often creates an aura of ahistoricity—that all texts are already imbued with sexuality. For example, Doty examines mass media texts, such as *Gentlemen Prefer Blondes* (1953), *Sylvia Scarlett* (1937), and the character Pee-Wee Herman, to examine "queerness" in the culture. In doing so, there is an implicit assumption that how Doty reads these texts as "queer" *now* is how they could *always* be read as "queer." To be fair, Doty acknowledges that gay or lesbian viewers (amongst others) "enter cultural history at various times and under differing circumstances, which affect how we make sense of the personalities and products within a culture."[20] But he never analyzes how these differing circumstances might alter how "queerness" is found by these individuals.

A large group of work has been done within the past twenty years reclaiming a history of gay and lesbian lives and cultures, and "queer" readings need to touch on this vital research to ground their concepts. The groundswell of work that has become known as "cultural studies" is an outgrowth of the ahistoricity of much of poststructuralist theory. The importance this work places on material reception rather than an imagined or "ideal" reception to texts must be brought to bear on "queer" readings. "Queerness" attempts to transcend or deconstruct boundaries, but in different eras and cultures; what these boundaries are differs. While a gay man in the 1990s may appreciate the "queer" nature of Bugs Bunny imitating Carmen Miranda on a video screen, that does not necessarily mean that the "queer" reading is the same that a gay man did in a 1940s movie theater when the cartoon was first released. The wealth of gay and lesbian history now makes such distinctions possible and necessary to analyze.

Animation developed under specific cultural conditions, and the techniques and narrative tropes that animation adopted are imbued with the multivalenced (and often contradictory) concepts of sexuality that informed the society that the animators lived and worked in. Animation has consistently represented homosexuality as "effeminacy" in men. Yet, the ways in which these "effeminate" characteristics could be read by individuals and how that related to, enforced, or threatened hegemonic definitions of heterosexuality differed from time to time, as the conception of sexual orientation was redefined. The following discussions of three different American animated films from different time periods are preliminary exercises, examining how the individual texts attempt to draw boundaries between heterosexuality and its other according to the conceptions of each text's time.

Snow White (1933)

Five years before Walt Disney and his studio would produce a feature-length version of the Grimm Brothers fairy tale "Snow White," Max Fleischer's studio refashioned the story to create a surreal, jazz-influenced cartoon starring their most popular character, Betty Boop. In this tale, the beautiful Betty goes to visit the ugly Queen, who jealously orders her killed. After a number of mishaps, she escapes death, but is encased in a coffin-like block of ice which the seven dwarfs find and carry down into the Mystery Cave. The Queen (disguised as a hag) and Betty's friends Koko and Bimbo follow her to the Cave, where a surreal performance of "Saint James Infirmary Blues" takes place before Betty is rescued and the Queen defeated.

Eric Smoodin, in his analysis of the multiple discourses that inflect American cartoons, points out how Fleischer and his studio differentiated their product from their main competitor, Disney, by emphasizing adult humor rather than family entertainment.[21] Betty's overt sexuality stands as a perfect example of this. The fetishized distortion of Betty's body, drawn by Grim Natwick, is readily apparent—in addition to a very oversized head, Betty has a small torso, yet ample hips and thighs. In cartoon after cartoon, Betty's sexuality during the early '30s was on explicit display as she sang in burlesque houses, did the hula, and was chased around by various predators out to "take her boop-oop-a-doop away."[22]

What also must be acknowledged is the uniquely urban outlook of most of the Fleischer cartoons, specifically New York City—the metropolis that Fleischer's studio was situated in up until the end of the 1930s. Fleischer animator Shamus Culhane has commented, "These were East Side Jewish kids or people like me . . . so they had this very vigorous style . . . kind of earthy, certainly crude, but honest."[23] If the Fleischer cartoons exhibit an overt expression of sexuality, it is defined in terms of how the intersecting cultures of New York City's communities comprehended sexuality during the 1920s and 1930s. The Prohibition era created in New York City a vast underground of speakeasies and gin joints that allowed individuals who had considered themselves law-abiding before Prohibition to mix with minorities and outcasts from society. Consequently, the horizon of sexual possibilities was widely broadened in the city during this period.

Tied to the Prohibition era in New York City was the Harlem Renaissance, which brought urban African-American culture in contact with the dominant white American society—in literature, in art, in dance, and especially in music.[24] Fleischer's *Snow White* is obviously indebted to the "Negro Vogue" of New York entertainment. The trip into the Mystery Cave is underground, much like the entrance to a speakeasy, dark and secret. In the Cave, Cab Calloway and His Orchestra perform "Saint James Infirmary Blues," the centerpiece of the short, with Calloway singing for Koko the

Clown after the Queen turns him into a ghost (or, shall we say, "spook"). The song itself refers to gambling and drinking "booze," with the ghostly figure metamorphosing into a bottle during this section of the lyric. The ghost shuffles through the cave using the rotoscoping process invented by Max Fleischer to copy Calloway's movements during the number.[25]

The aura of illicitness that enticed white audiences to go "slumming" in black speakeasies also "encourage[d] middle-class men and women to interact even more casually and to experiment further with the norms governing acceptable public sociability."[26] George Chauncey, in his work on gay life in New York before World War II, finds evidence that speakeasy culture all through New York (not just in Harlem) created a space for lesbians and gay men to exist in public. Nightclub owners noticed that "if whites were intrigued by the 'primitivism' of black culture, heterosexuals were equally intrigued by the 'perversity' of gay culture."[27] Seeing the popularity of drag balls (such as the enormous Hamilton Lodge balls, as well as events held in Madison Square Garden and the Astor Hotel), entrepreneurs began bringing this culture onto their stages. In straight clubs such as the Club Abbey, the Argonaut, the Club Calais, and eventually a place called the Pansy Club, "pansy acts" became the rage of Broadway. According to *Variety*, by the end of 1930, two of Times Square's most successful clubs "depended upon 'pansy personalities' for their main draw."[28]

It should, then, come as no surprise to see the "Pansy Craze" also finding its way into the cartoon—albeit in not so easily read a manner as Calloway's performance. By looking at the Queen as a "queer" figure, one can read the influences of "pansy culture" in the work. The Queen is introduced with a number of signifiers that complicate "her" gender. The film begins with the Queen hidden behind the Magic Mirror, with what looks like cigar puffs emerging from the sides of the Mirror. A side view reveals the visual joke that the puffs are from the Queen powdering the royal nose. Yet, the ugly Queen has no visual signs of makeup—no eyelashes, no lipstick, no rouge—quite unlike the appearance of that paragon of femininity, Betty. When Betty arrives, the Queen literally peers through the Mirror at her, poking "her" head through it. In doing so, the Queen's wig comes off, revealing what appears to be a bald man, who is jealous of Betty's womanly beauty.

It was commonly thought by American society during this period that sexuality was ruled by gender. Homosexual men desired men because they wanted to be women (and, similarly, lesbians wanted to be men). There was no other way to conceive why men would sexually desire other men unless they thought of themselves as women. This definition of homosexuality separated the insertive partner in male-male sex from the label. It was only the man who was in "the woman's position" that was considered homosexual. The drag queens showcased at the Hamilton Lodge balls were reported in New York newspapers with the conception that all the men who watched the show from the balcony were heterosexual, never considering that any of these respectably dressed (that is, respectably gendered) gentlemen could be defined as homosexual.[29] In 1903, German physician and sexologist Dr. Magnus Hirschfeld termed homosexuals as literally "the third sex." Although his organization in Germany that worked for the rights of homosexuals abandoned this term in 1910, it is obvious in many of the popular representations of homosexuality at the time that straight culture (and many lesbians and gay men themselves) still conceived of homosexuality in this manner.

Consequently, it comes as no surprise that, in thinking of the Queen as a member of "the third sex," the Queen would be jealous of Betty's femininity. Desiring to be a "real" woman, "the fairest of them all," would seem to be of tantamount concern to a homosexual man during this period. Yet, for the Queen to become jealous of Betty's "natural" femininity begs a viewer to question Betty's naturalness, which bears no resemblance to anatomical plausibility. Furthermore, the manic use of metamorphosis in cartoons from the Fleischer studio always heightens the instability of objects and identities. The shape-shifting of the Queen further establishes "her" as a "queer" figure. When viewing Betty's beauty, the Queen's face turns into a pan with two frying eggs. Later, when entering the Mystery Cave, the Queen passes the Mirror over her body and becomes a hag/goblin. Towards the end of the film, the Queen is once more transformed, this time into a dragon that chases Betty and her friends until Bimbo, in one final moment of shifting, grabs the dragon by its tongue and pulls the monster inside out.

The moments of transmogrification are not limited, though, to the Queen, who uses this power to change the rest of the cast as well, exposing their unstable identities. Betty and her friends are turned into statues, and the Queen also turns Koko into the shape-shifting ghost that sings "Saint James Infirmary Blues." It's almost as if the sheer presence of the Queen in this culture topples the certainty of things. As Chauncey shows, a shift in definition was beginning to occur, complicating the assumed ties between gender and sexuality. As early as the 1910s and 1920s, some men began to "identif[y] . . . themselves as different from other men primarily on the basis of their homosexual interest rather than their womanlike gender status."[30] Gradually, even the persona of the "fairy" came to disturb middle-class men who had previously considered them as a separate gender category. "His womanlike manner challenged the supposed immutability of gender differences by demonstrating that anatomical males did not inevitably become men and were not inevitably different from women."[31] The attempt to "minoritize" the "fairy" had failed, and the "universalizing" view became too apparent and too threatening to the rest of society. After the repeal of Prohibition, the "Pansy Craze" died quickly; seen as part of the widespread degeneracy that contributed to the cause of the Depression, homosexuality was pushed into what now is called "the closet," through arrests, bar closures, and media censorship. It is no wonder that the Queen is pictured as such a threat, and must be vanquished by the trio of protagonists.

Rabbit Fire (1951)

Unlike the culture that *Snow White* was created in, Chuck Jones's *Rabbit Fire* (1951) was made for Warner Bros. under completely different circumstances. There was no "Pansy Craze" to speak of—at least, not the type of "Pansy Craze" that Chauncey describes in *Gay New York*. Rather, after the onset of the Depression and the repeal of Prohibition, homosexual men and women were forced more and more by legal authorities to hide themselves. Furthermore, after World War II, there rose a mass paranoia about homosexuality, its ties to sex crimes (particularly pederasty), and the threat homosexuals could pose to national security.

The beginning of the Cold War in the late 1940s created an air of distrust and fear in the United States, and, as Communism advanced into China and Eastern Europe, many began to fear that a growing internal subversion was out to sabotage the country. The postwar years of McCarthyism made any individual potentially Communist. One wrong opinion expressed, or one misplaced association, and you could be suspect. An accusation was almost as good as proof. Loyalty oaths and Senate investigations proliferated.

It was in this atmosphere that a renewed and heated attack on homosexuality began. John D'Emilio describes how,

> facing sharp interrogation by members of the State Appropriations Committee, Under Secretary John Peurifoy testified on February 28, 1950, that most

of ninety-one employees dismissed for moral turpitude were homosexuals. . . . In the succeeding months, the danger posed by "sexual perverts" became a staple of partisan rhetoric. . . . Finally, in June 1950 the full Senate . . . authorized an investigation into the alleged employment of homosexuals "and other moral perverts" in government.[32]

Thousands would be banned from serving in the government as a result of these investigations, and many more would be dishonorably discharged from the military or barred from employment by major businesses who followed similar screening procedures during this period. Even the Post Office abetted the persecution of homosexuals, deeming it within their rights to open mail of suspected homosexuals in order to tip off the authorities.[33]

Many film historians have noted how the McCarthy era was represented in American film directly (anti-Communist films like *My Son John* [1952]) and indirectly, such as in *High Noon* [1952] and *On the Waterfront* [1954]). No one has analyzed its effect on the animated cartoons of the period. Jones's remarkable series of cartoons with Bugs Bunny, Daffy Duck, and Elmer Fudd have been analyzed by a number of animation aficionados in terms of their comic structure. What hasn't been analyzed is how they replicate the society in which they were produced. In a series of three cartoons—*Rabbit Fire, Rabbit Seasoning* (1952), and *Duck! Rabbit! Duck!* (1953)—Daffy manically attempts to get Elmer to hunt Bugs instead of himself. The initial ploy is to convince Elmer that it is actually Rabbit Season rather than Duck Season. Bugs, through hilarious trips of language, consistently turns the tables on the duck, and Elmer ends up blasting Daffy's bill off in a number of different ways. Albeit in a consistently humorous fashion, all three cartoons replicate the hyperparanoid atmosphere of postwar America. Daffy accuses Bugs in order to keep suspicion from falling on himself. Bugs continuously counters by exposing what Daffy has to hide in the first place. And as an impartial punisher, Elmer is willing to shoot at anything. As he announces at one point in *Rabbit Fire*, Elmer is a vegetarian, and hunts only for the sport of it.

While this would fit quite well into a discussion of McCarthyism, the accusations throughout all three cartoons continually revolve around notions of gender and species. Later in the same cartoon, when Elmer has Bugs cornered, Bugs points out that Elmer has an elephant gun, and it can only be used to shoot elephants. Immediately, Elmer turns to find a large, irate, and very fey elephant with his hands on his hips standing behind him, warning, "You do and I'll give you a pinch!" before pounding him into the ground and flouncing off. In *Rabbit Seasoning*, Daffy ends up fighting with Bugs over who Elmer can "take home," forgetting that the one who accompanies Elmer arm-in-arm to his lodge is about to be filled with gunshot. Daffy eventually terms the slippage in the language tricks that Bugs is using against him as "pronoun trouble!" Consequently, these cartoons also speak of the paranoia about sexuality that was part of this era as well.

The paranoia over homosexuality resulted in a new dominant conception of what a "homosexual" was in American society. In 1948, Alfred Kinsey's *Sexual Behavior in the Human Male* was published, revealing a high incidence of homosexual behavior among white American males. Furthermore, his research showed that individuals engaging in homosexual relations consistently did not fit the prevailing stereotype that society had fashioned—the "pansy." Any individual could potentially be homosexual; it was not possible to tell "just by looking." This shift, from conceiving of sexuality as tied to gender roles to conceiving of sexuality as tied to object choice, made the distinctions between homosexuality and heterosexuality both more distinct and hazier. Now, whether a male was in the dominant insertive role or the receptive role, he was still considered homosexual, making men who were considered masculine in every other conventional way homosexual. The crisis of masculinity that resulted helped fuel the paranoia of the age, reflected in texts such as *Rabbit Fire*.

After Daffy and Bugs accuse and counter-accuse each other of being the "truly" hunted individual, the two begin a round of cross-dressing. First, Daffy and Bugs disguise themselves as each other in order to evade Elmer's bullets. Daffy finds a bunny suit and chomps on a carrot, while Bugs hides his ears in a rubber swimming cap, puts on flippers and a homemade bill. Adding yet another level of impersonation to the "queerness" of animation ("species drag"?), Mel Blanc's vocal performance is stretched to the limits with Bugs trying to imitate Daffy's lisping(!) and Daffy quoting "What's up, Doc?" Then, Bugs rises out of his rabbit hole in drag as a female hunter (complete with Daffy as his/her hunting dog—gender unknown) in order to woo Elmer and escape. Elmer readily falls for Bugs's seduction until a rather erect rabbit ear pops out from under Bugs's blond wig. The ease with which both Daffy and Bugs assume other identities in the cartoon highlights the performativity of their roles. Butler has pointed out that "drag constitutes the mundane way in which genders are appropriated, theatricalized, worn, done; it implies that all gendering is a kind of impersonation and approximation."[34] The constant removal of Daffy's bill from his face by Elmer's gunshot blasts further emphasizes the importance of costuming and accessorizing in order to create a convincing performance.

Yet, as Daffy and Bugs show, costume and performance can be used by an individual to hide what an individual might not want to reveal. How many men were consciously overperforming masculinity to hide their homosexuality? The "queerness" of the levels of impersonation ends up implicating the "straight" man, Elmer, as well. After all other strategies have been exhausted and Bugs and Daffy tear off poster after poster claiming its alternately Rabbit or Duck Season, they reach a poster that proclaims it's actually "Elmer Season." Elmer can easily be read as a gay character, hiding his "queerness" (his own vocal peculiarities, his vegetarian habits) behind the mask of being a big game hunter. In a fitting climax to such paranoia and confusion, the cartoon ends with Daffy and Bugs, now wearing "Elmer drag" (oversized hunting cap, khaki jacket, and boots), being "vewy, vewy quiet" as they "hunt Elmers." Heterosexuality in American society perceived itself under attack by the shifting definition of homosexuality from gender to object choice, and countered this paranoia with homosexual witch hunts. Just as Elmer's status is "compromised" by the end of the short, heterosexuality was in danger of being "compromised" by this new conception of boundaries.

The Lion King (1994)

More than forty years later, day-to-day existence for many lesbians and gay men has changed markedly. Most gay historians describe the Stonewall Riots of 1969 as ushering in a new era in lesbian and gay culture and politics—more outspoken, more explicit, and more confrontational towards the heterosexual community that had oppressed and attempted to ignore lesbians and gay men through much of the century. The 1970s became a decade of liberation as more and more men and women openly acknowledged and celebrated their homosexuality. In the 1980s, as homosexual communities (cultural, political, and otherwise) became aware of the AIDS crisis, the momentum of the 1970s transformed into more direct demands for equality and acceptance, looking on this struggle as not just over the right to live openly, but increasingly the right to live, period.

With the growth of a visible and vibrant lesbian and gay community has come a conception of this community's buying power. In the 1970s, many lesbians and gay men boycotted Florida orange juice to protest the anti-gay statements of spokesperson Anita Bryant (a strategy that was recently reemployed when Florida orange juice hired conservative funnyman Rush Limbaugh as their spokesperson). In 1977, the gay periodical *The Advocate* conducted a survey to create an economic profile of its readers, and repeated the survey in 1980. As Karen Stabiner and Danae Clark have both pointed out, this research interested some businesses in what was now seen as a "gay market." Indicating "that 70% of their readers aged 20–40 earned incomes well above the national median . . . companies such as Paramount, Seagram, Perrier, and Harper & Row [began] to advertise in gay male publications like *Christopher Street* and *The Advocate*."[35] Since Stabiner's article in 1982, this ad trend has only increased, moving out beyond the pages of these specific periodicals. In 1994, for example, the IKEA furniture store began test-marketing a TV spot that showed a gay white male couple shopping for a dining room table. Films have also jumped on the bandwagon. While Stabiner opens her article with an analysis of the ad campaign for the 1981 film *Making Love*,[36] since then, other films with explicit gay subject matter (*Philadelphia*, 1993; *The Adventures of Priscilla, Queen of the Desert*, 1994) or appeal (*Madonna: Truth or Dare*, 1992) have placed articles in gay publications and attempted to position lesbians and gay men as a target group, much like "yuppies" or senior citizens.

It is in this culture that the Disney studio has resurrected its animation department. Having coasted through the 1970s and early '80s on their reputation for and virtual monopoly over animated features, the popularity of non-Disney features—such as *An American Tail* (1986) and *The Land Before Time* (1988)—forced Disney to update its technology, sharpen its storytelling, and include humor that adults would appreciate, even if it was sometimes beyond a child's understanding. Furthermore, the animated features were marketed more towards adults without children. Starting in 1989, with the release of *The Little Mermaid*, Disney's new strategy has consistently resulted in highly profitable animated features, drawing adults with and without children.

It is impossible not to see how gay audiences figure into this new approach. The songwriting team that helped begin this new era of Disney animation included lyricist Howard Ashman, an openly gay man. When Ashman died of an AIDS-related disease in 1991, the release of *Beauty and the Beast* (1991) was turned into a tribute to his creative genius. Jeffrey Katzenberg, Vice President in Charge of Production, was quoted as saying, "We have two guardian angels. One is Walt Disney, who continues to touch every frame of our movies. The other is Howard Ashman, who continues to touch every note of our movies."[37] Even after Ashman's death, such association of the animation with gay figures has continued. Openly gay animator Andreas Deja has been interviewed by various gay journals, and *The Lion King* featured songs written by Elton John, who officially came out as a homosexual while being interviewed by Barbara Walters a few months before the film's premiere. With such attendant publicity, "queer" readings of these films are not only more possible, but specifically marketed.

Yet, this increased target marketing towards lesbian and gay consumers has its problems. The advertisers have selected mainly one small segment of the homosexual population as their target—"the white, single, well-educated, well-paid man who happens to be homosexual."[38] Clark points out that white well-educated lesbians have also begun to be targeted by advertisers (particularly in the fashion industry). Yet, the term "queer" attempts to deal with the wide diversity of lived experience, and to acknowledge that the gay community is actually a number of communities that intersect with each other and various "straight" communities in a number of ways, and advertising to a select group within this diversity, tries to deny this complexity.

Disney has begun to discover this diversity and complexity the hard way. Although their animated features have been extraordinarily successful (*Aladdin* [1992] was the first animated feature to make over $200 million domestically, and *The Lion King* surpassed it to become the sixth most successful film at the time of its release), the studio has encountered protests from various individuals for its stereotypical portrayal of women and race/ethnicity. Women were outraged by the mermaid Ariel's dependency on men in *The Little Mermaid* (1989). The studio attempted to respond to these complaints when working on the character Belle in *Beauty and the Beast*, taking care to show her intelligence and independence (although the narrative still focuses on her selecting a suitor). The enormous outcry by Arab-Americans over *Aladdin* caused the studio to change a few lyrics before the film's release to video. Just as the protests over *The Little Mermaid* probably had an effect on the studio's hiring a woman (Linda Woolverton) to script *Beauty and the Beast*, the complaints of Arab-Americans over *Aladdin* probably influenced the number of Native Americans involved in the production of the studio's 1995 animated feature *Pocahontas*.

The studio might have thought that they would avoid all these problems in *The Lion King* by creating an all-animal cartoon. By hiring many African-Americans as voice artists for this story about animals in the African veldt, Disney attempted to be sensitive to racial issues. Yet, the film caused protests from many groups. Even if Ariel was a problematic character for feminists, at least she was the focus of the narrative. In *The Lion King*, lionesses (not to mention females from other species) are barely present. Many African-Americans were also disturbed that the film actively refused to show any existence of African civilization—and the use of actor Robert Guillaume to create a mystic baboon with an Uncle Tom accent didn't help matters.

With the songs of Elton John and an ad campaign that included cartoon characters saying that the film was "to die for" or that they would "put on a grass skirt and do the hula," there seemed to be plenty for gay audiences to enjoy. Contrary to the complaints of nonvisibility by women and African-Americans, "gay" animals could be found quite easily in the film. The adviser to the Lion King is a fussy and pompous bird, who seems to be modeled after actor Clifton Webb. The two friends that the young lion cub protagonist Simba encounters after he is banished from his tribe can be read as a gay male couple, living together, reveling in their marginalization from the rest of jungle society, and looking askance at Simba's budding heterosexual romance with a lioness. The most obvious gay figure is the villainous lion Scar, voiced by Jeremy Irons, an arch portrayal of a physically weak male who makes up for his lack of sheer strength with catty remarks and invidious plotting. Animated by Deja, the character seems to swish (as much as a lion can), disdaining the concept of the heterosexual family in his attempt to usurp the throne for himself.

While Disney's villains have routinely veered towards camp (Captain Hook, Cruella de Vil, Ursula, Jafar), Scar's homosexual signifiers become disturbing when, after initially enjoying his dry wit, he sings a musical solo that becomes an animated version of the Nuremberg rallies, with Scar at the podium as hyena henchmen goose-step in perfect cadence before him. The color scheme turns black-and-white during this section, furthering the similarities to the Nuremberg documentary *The Triumph of the Will* (1936). Also unlike the other villains, Scar actually kills someone (not even the evil Queen in Disney's *Snow White* [1937] did that). His reign over the kingdom seems to directly cause drought, pestilence, and the general destruction of the ecosystem. It is only with the restoration of Simba to the throne that the land comes back to life, in a dissolve that makes the change seem miraculously immediate.

Scar's unforgivable sin seems to be his refusal to support the heterosexual patriarchy that Simba and his father represent. The other gay figures are not seen as monsters, mainly because they help the young "straight" lion and see him as the rightful ruler of the land. This would fit directly into how the corporations that target "the gay consumer" would like to define homosexual individuals. John D'Emilio's essay on "Capitalism and Gay Identity" and Clark's on "Commodity Lesbianism" discuss a "constant interplay between exploitation and some measure of autonomy," in which lesbians and gay men are constituted as a market but not as a political social group.[39] A dissatisfied individual is encouraged to create change not through protest and revolt, but through consumption, which only reinforces the established system which made the individual dissatisfied initially. By buying into the society, "the gay consumer" effectively supports the hegemonic order, much as Simba's gay friends aid his return to power. "Queer" activism and theory counters this notion of "the gay consumer" with the recognition that not all homosexuals are white upscale men with the money or the inclination to support Disney's product; indeed, this is rather poignantly pointed out in an article in the West Hollywood gay zine *Planet Homo* (in which the author lambastes the film's portrayal of women and its handling of racial issues).[40] In trying to attract "the gay consumer," *The Lion King* works against the "queerness" that animation often displays.

Conclusion

Snow White, *Rabbit Fire*, and *The Lion King* all posit a specific historical formation of gender and sexuality in American culture, attempting to establish specific boundaries that keep heterosexuality separated from its other. Yet, the "queerness" that has become a dominant characteristic of animation continually begins to break down those boundaries just as they are being erected within the texts. The metamorphoses, transmogrifications, disguises, and levels of impersonation (animal/human, male/female, masculine/feminine, gay/straight) turn the established boundaries into a chaotic playhouse of signification. Even as *The Lion King* tries to establish heterosexual patriarchy as the natural "Circle of Life" (to quote one of the songs from the film), the presence of interspecies couples, such as Simba's friends the meerkat and warthog, show that all is not "straight" in the "natural" world.

As Alan Cholodenko points out in his introduction to *The Illusion of Life*, conceiving of animation as some subcategory of film is to deny its importance in understanding the workings of all cinema—that cinema was derived from animation, not the other way around, and that live-action film is just another form of animation.[41] In this age when Bob Hoskins interacts with an animated rabbit, Sam Neill and two teenagers run from computerized dinosaurs, and Michael Jackson electronically "morphs" his face into a number of other extras of varying races and ethnicities, the boundaries between animation and film are growing more and more tenuous, creating even more levels of categorical slippage. Consequently, to argue animation from a universalizing "queer" viewpoint is to argue against "minoritizing" animation and to implicate all cinema. Yet, just as the move towards cultural studies has made it imperative to become aware of the modes of reception that were possible when doing textual analysis, it is important to read texts "queerly" within these same modes.

Notes

1. "Cheers 'n' Jeers," *TV Guide* 41, no. 52 (December 25, 1993): 6.

2. Ricky L. Hart, from Huntsville, Alabama, wrote in a letter to *TV Guide* (42, no. 3 [January 15, 1994]: 45), "We don't want a gay lifestyle portrayed as normal and acceptable to impressionable children."

3. A letter to *TV Guide* 42, no. 3 (January 15, 1994): 45, from Pamela Shillingburg from Roanoke Rapids, North Carolina, said: "It's ludicrous to believe that two fuzzy puppets are gay, but I definitely do not believe the subject of gay couples has any place on a show for preschoolers."

4. The editors of *TV Guide*, in the December 25, 1993, article ("Cheers 'n' Jeers"), had the opinion that "kids—and parents—need to learn that a person's sexual orientation really shouldn't matter."

5. "Cheers 'n' Jeers," 6.

6. Also worth mentioning are Grandpa Simpson's flashbacks to his cross-dressing days in World War II.

7. See Shillingburg, letter to *TV Guide*, January 15, 1994.

8. Steven C. Rich, Riverside, California, letter to *TV Guide*, January 15, 1994.

9. Stuart Hall, "Culture, Media, and the 'Ideological Effect,'" in *Mass Communication and Society*, edited by James Curran, Michael Gurevitch, and Janet Woolacott (London: Edward Arnold, 1977), 344–346.

10. Alexander Doty, *Making Things Perfectly Queer: Interpreting Mass Culture* (Minneapolis: University of Minnesota Press, 1993), xii.

11. For example, Amy Lawrence's essay "Masculinity in Eastern European Animation" (*Animation Journal* 3, no. 1 [Fall 1994]: 32–43), although not explicitly addressing "queer" readings, examines the crisis in masculinity in post–Cold War Eastern Europe as it is manifested in their highly regarded animation.

12. Hank Sartin, "Bugs Bunny: Queer as a Three-Dollar Bill," *Windy City Times*, June 24, 1993, section 2, 79.

13. Eve Kosofsky Sedgwick, *Epistemology of the Closet* (Berkeley: University of California Press, 1990), 1.

14. Alan Cholodenko, "Introduction" to *The Illusion of Life: Essays on Animation*, edited by Alan Cholodenko (Sydney: Power Publications, 1991), 15–16.

15. Sedgwick, *Epistemology of the Closet*, 1.

16. In regards to the "Bert and Ernie" affair, the characters conceivably have no sexual organs since they are never shown below the waist. In this regard, the scandal could easily be read as the introduction of the possibility of sexuality itself.

17. Doty, *Making Things Perfectly Queer*, xv. Activist groups such as Queer Nation began to use the term in the late 1980s to be more inclusive of gay men, lesbians, bisexuals, transsexuals—in short, the wife variety of sexualities (and, hopefully, the diverse racial/ethnic and class identities) which are created by the matrices of social discourse. Soon, academics began to use the term to discuss theories of sexuality, specifically the slippage, breakdown, or deconstruction of attempts to categorize individuals according to a gender or sexuality. Lisa Duggan, "Making It Perfectly Queer" (*Socialist Review* [April 1992]: 11–31) provides a good survey of the development of the term "queer" as it is used by activists and theorists in the late 1980s and 1990s.

18. Judith Butler, *Gender Trouble: Feminism and the Subversion of Identity* (New York: Routledge, 1990).

19. For a history of Cohl's work, see Donald Crafton, *Before Mickey: The Animated Film (1898–1928)* (Chicago: University of Chicago Press, 1993), 59–88.

20. Doty, *Making Things Perfectly Queer*, 21.

21. Eric Smoodin, *Animating Culture: Hollywood Cartoons from the Sound Era* (New Brunswick, NJ: Rutgers University Press, 1993). His first chapter, "Studio Strategies: Sexuality, the Law, and Corporate Competition," deals directly with Fleischer's and Warner Bros.' attempts to differentiate their product from Disney.

22. The quote is from the short *Boop-Oop-a-Doop* (1932), when circus performer Betty is sexually menaced by her ringleader boss.

23. Quoted in Leonard Maltin, *Of Mice and Magic: A History of American Animated Cartoons* (New York: McGraw-Hill, 1980), 98.

24. Amongst the sources for a history of the Harlem Renaissance, see Jervis Anderson, *This Was Harlem* (New York: Farrar, Straus & Giroux, 1982); Nathan Irvin Huggins, *Harlem Renaissance* (New York: Oxford University Press, 1971); Bruce Kellner, *The Harlem Renaissance: A Historical Dictionary of the Era* (Westport, CT: Greenwood, 1984); and David Levering Lewis, *When Harlem Was in Vogue* (New York: Knopf, 1981).

25. On Fleischer's invention of the rotoscope, see Crafton, *Before Mickey*, 169–170.

26. George Chauncey, *Gay New York* (New York: Basic Books, 1994), 307–308.

27. Ibid., 310.

28. "'Pansy' Stuff Slipping," *Variety*, December 31, 1930, 31.

29. For example, "Masquerade Ball Draws 5,000 People: As Usual, Feministic Males Turn Out in Gorgeous Costumes," *Amsterdam News*, February 20, 1929, 2; "Mere Male Blossoms Out in Garb of Milady at Big Hamilton Lodge Ball: Coy Imitators Simper Sweetly at Affair Attended by 7,000," *Amsterdam News*, February 19, 1930, 3; and "Snow and Ice Cover Streets as Pansies Blossom Out at Hamilton Lodge's Dance," *Amsterdam News*, February 28, 1934, 1.

30. Chauncey, *Gay New York*, 101.

31. Ibid., 115.

32. John D'Emilio, *Sexual Politics, Sexual Communities: The Making of a Homosexual Minority in the United States, 1940–1970* (Chicago: University of Chicago Press, 1983), 41–42.

33. Ibid., 47.

34. Judith Butler, "Imitation and Gender Insubordination," in *Inside/Out: Lesbian Theories, Gay Theories*, edited by Diana Fuss (New York: Routledge, 1991), 21.

35. Danae Clark, "Commodity Lesbianism," *Camera Obscura*, nos. 25–26 (January–May 1991): 182. The data in this quote come from Karen Stabiner, "Tapping the Homosexual Market," *New York Times Magazine*, May 2, 1980, 34–36, 74–85.

36. Stabiner, "Tapping the Homosexual Market," 34.

37. Quoted in Mimi Avens, "Aladdin Sane," *Premiere* 6, no. 4 (December 1992): 67.

38. Stabiner, "Tapping the Homosexual Market," 34.

39. John D'Emilio, "Capitalism and Gay Identity," in *Powers of Desire: The Politics of Sexuality*, edited by Ann Snitow, Christine Stansell, and Sharon Thompson (New York: Monthly Review Press, 1983), 102.

40. Todd Hayward, "The Lyin' King," *Planet Homo* 69 (September 21, 1994): 16–17.

41. Cholodenko, "Introduction," 9–10.

PART IV Containment and Its Critiques

TWELVE

Of Fleiss and Men

The Transgressions and Containment of a Hollywood Madam

MARY CELESTE KEARNEY

IDEAS ABOUT SEPARATING, PURIFYING, DEMARCATING AND PUNISHING TRANSGRESSIONS HAVE AS THEIR MAIN FUNCTION TO IMPOSE SYSTEM ON AN INHERENTLY UNTIDY EXPERIENCE. IT IS ONLY BY EXAGGERATING THE DIFFERENCE BETWEEN WITHIN AND WITHOUT, ABOVE AND BELOW, MALE AND FEMALE, WITH AND AGAINST, THAT A SEMBLANCE OF ORDER IS CREATED.

MARY DOUGLAS, *PURITY AND DANGER* [1]

Two summers ago, after undergoing major surgery to remove a mass of tissue that threatened my reproductive organs, I lay in bed fascinated by the media frenzy surrounding the arrest and arraignment of Heidi Fleiss, alleged madam to Hollywood movie stars and studio executives. Although the simultaneous attempts to contain the threat of our unruly bodies to the reproductive practices of biology and society now seem more connected than I could have ever imagined, I must confess that, at the time, I was only minimally aware that my obsession to know everything about Heidi was somehow related to my inability to move. Following Hollywood's infamous party girl from section to section in the *Los Angeles Times* and from channel to channel on television, I moved with Heidi as her story traveled from the front pages of "legitimate" newspapers to the sensationalized displays of tabloid papers, magazines, and "infotainment" news programs.[2]

Arrested June 9 and arraigned August 9, 1993, for alleged pandering, Heidi attempted to have the charges against her dismissed due to obvious gender discrimination as the "johns" who used Heidi's services have been neither identified nor arrested.[3] A Superior Court judge rejected this argument, noting that it was Heidi's "flamboyant behavior," not her gender, which brought her to the attention of the police.[4] Despite the obvious illogic of this judgment (it was Shawn Hubler who publicized Heidi's boastful statements about the success of her prostitution business in the *Los Angeles Times*), I would like to pursue this coding of Heidi as a "flamboyant" and, therefore, dangerous woman in relation to dominant notions of commercial and sexual propriety in contemporary US society, notions which have categorized both female ambition and prostitution as marginal and pathological, if not criminal.

As Patricia Mellencamp argues in *High Anxiety*, often the only "crime" of the unruly women reported on by the media is their transgression into the male-defined and -dominated public space of narratable news and commerce.[5] Indeed, when a scandalous woman such as Heidi enters the public sphere through the *mediation* of her improperly "flamboyant" actions, her embodiment of a transgressive, deviant ideology and lifestyle signifies a serious threat to the very boundaries—private/public, propriety/deviance, ordinariness/celebrity, information/entertainment, truth/secrets, mind/body—constructed for her categorization and criminalization, and causes the official powers of social regulation, containment, and punishment to be enacted against her most dramatically.

Inscribed electronically by today's "infotainment" media and defined in relation to not only prostitution and illegitimate financial dealings, but also Jewishness, drug abuse, and homosexuality, Heidi's story is symptomatic of a crisis of news space where the boundaries of "legitimate," informational journalism and sensationalized, tabloid entertainment are no longer clearly defined and reproduced. I explore here the various ways a rhetoric of contagion is used to define and situate Heidi as a threat to a society whose very semblance of cohesiveness, order, and propriety is constructed through the public narrativizing and imaging of transgression and containment.

Writing (and) the Prostitute: Circulating the Unruly Woman in Narrative and Commerce

As Peter Brooks notes in *Reading for the Plot*, prostitution can be readily connected not only with the exchange of money, but with the evolution of serialized, commercial writing in Western culture. Brooks traces the metaphor of the prostitute in literature back to the nineteenth century with serial novelists such as Eugène Sue, who advanced this new form of narrative by exploiting the figure of prostitute as a conduit into the socially deviant milieu of industrial society's seedy underbelly. As a transgressive and transformative subject who incorporates an idiosyncratic, deviant, and mobile lifestyle that is essentially theatrical and performative, the prostitute embodies what Brooks refers to as a "novelistic destiny":

> The prostitute's plot is by definition a deviance, and in literary terms she is often seen as herself defining an original trajectory through the world, a plot by which her life achieves a new and exemplary style and meaning. . . . The prostitute is not only herself narratable, she provokes the stuff of story in others.[6]

Since, as Brooks so insightfully notes, one encounter with a prostitute produces both accounts and recounts, the processes of circulation, exchange, and repetition found in both storytelling and commerce are initiated and reproduced: "Here, sexuality, money, danger, deviance converge to form a powerful potential for a story."[7]

Unlike the serialized narratives of the nineteenth century whose prostitution stories allowed novelists to explore the feminine sexuality and deviance of only lower-class women, contemporary prostitution narratives such as those of Heidi Fleiss and Sidney Biddle Barrows ("the Mayflower Madam") indicate that often it is a middle-class or upper-class woman who is constructed as a "nice girl gone wrong."[8] Screenwriter Matt Tabak describes how a story like Heidi's initiates such strong intrigue: "How does someone go from being a nice Jewish girl whose father is a doctor to being arrested as an alleged Beverly Hills madam? How does that happen? It's gotta be an amazing story."[9] From her role as the daughter of a prominent Los Angeles pediatrician to her role as a facilitator in the exchange of sex for money, Heidi's public persona as mediated through tabloid journalism brings together the spheres of commerce, labor, ambition, and desire in a somewhat uneasy narrative formation.

Of course, the contradictions of the "nice girl gone wrong" plot complicate each other, for it is through this improper (and seemingly unwarranted) "fall from grace" that the woman as prostitute is able to transgress her class (and/or ethnic, racial, sexual, age, national) identity and move through different social circles, while mingling with members of other groups. Transforming those with whom she comes into contact, the prostitute turns thinking minds into desiring bodies and demonstrates that, with regard to sex at least, the top of the social hierarchy is really no different from its bottom. It is in this regard that the prostitute is often labeled a dangerous transgressor, a woman who, because she operates at the level of the body and performance, is empowered to function in all positions, crossing the social barriers which may normally exclude her.[10]

Although the prostitution trade functions subculturally "underneath" the dominant systems of regulation, exchange, and sexuality, and although those who participate in its rules, language, and codes complicate the borders which separate the private and public spheres (as well as the porous lines which divide social groups), by placing the satisfaction of bodily desire into the domain of commerce, we should not be overoptimistic about its transgressive potential. Since women are rarely able to occupy a stable place within patriarchal society, we are usually left with no choice but to travel *between* places of power and authority. Thus, although the hierarchy of prostitutes may begin with the streetwalker and end with the call girl (or even the "kept" mistress)—a hierarchy which suggests class divisions and the material possessions that come to those at the higher end of the scale—it is important to note that these women rarely possess a place of their own, be it a street corner, a hotel room, or a residence owned by a "sugar daddy." Never allowed to occupy space, they only pass through it. The negative connotations that arise around a woman who stops her movement to stand still and occupy a place—especially if it occurs in public—give evidence to the power structures that keep women not "in their place" but constantly moving.

If woman's place is *no place*, then Heidi's location of her business within her home not only complicates the conventional assumption of affiliation between femininity and domesticity (and, in turn, what it means to be a woman who "works at home"), but also points to a serious transgression of the boundaries of both "legitimate" capitalist commerce (where exchange takes place in the public market) and "proper" sexual relations (where physical intimacy is exchanged freely, not traded as a commodity). As a successful businesswoman who created within her home an extremely lucrative career out of the illegal commodification of sex, Heidi's allegedly "flamboyant" behavior and public self-congratulation was seen by many as indicative of an overly ambitious braggart who most assuredly did not know her place.

Indeed, the stories circulating at the time of her arrest and arraignment demonstrate the various attempts to displace Heidi from her well-entrenched position in the prostitution trade of Los Angeles, as well as the glamorous social circles of Hollywood. For example, much of the discourse surrounding Heidi's arrest and arraignment focused on her (former) house, a $1.6 million mansion in the posh Los Angeles area of Benedict Canyon. The media has made a major point of connecting this house not only to its former owner, actor Michael Douglas (who, ironically, has been recently rehabilitated for "sex addiction"), but to Heidi's father, Dr. Paul Fleiss, who was the owner of the house (as well as the registered owner of Heidi's Corvette) at the time of her arrest.[11] The connections of Heidi's property to these two men, as well as the many repeated references to her former associations with Hungarian film and television director Ivan Nagy as well as Columbia studio executive Michael Nathanson, point to a repetition compulsion which attempts to deny Heidi's business savvy by inscribing that of a man in its place, a strategy which implicates not only Nagy but Heidi's father as her "pimp."[12]

The Los Angeles Police Department, the State of California, and the United States government seemed bothered, then, not by the sexual services Heidi provided, but by her ability to establish and maintain a place for herself in both Los Angeles's illegitimate underground and Hollywood's jet-set milieu. The stories in the press about her lack of property—the house isn't hers, the dress isn't hers, the girls aren't hers—speak therefore of a need to disempower Heidi by displacing her as a successful businesswoman whose roots had been firmly established in Los Angeles by the time of her arrest.[13]

Bodies in Danger: The Containment of Liminal Transgressions

I would like to connect the above discussion of women as mobile, transgressive figures having "no place" with a discussion of liminal individuals as those who are placeless, have an indeterminate social status, and, thus, are able or required to function in the fissures, crevices, and margins of society. Liminal states, functioning ritually as moments of contestation between dominant ideology and alternative ideologies, initiate a temporary loss of boundaries, often through processes of inversion. In spite of such potentially transgressive power, however, liminal rituals are always sanctioned by official culture and thus work to reinstate rather than dismantle dominant social structures and hierarchies.

Advocating an approach which would demonstrate the dialectic nature of liminality, Mary Russo argues that conservative structuralist theories of such states often focus only on their temporal nature at the expense of dismissing their transgressive potential.[14] In turn, I would argue that theorists of space and movement, such as Michel de Certeau, speak optimistically, if not in a utopian manner, of the transgressive, mobile power of the disenfranchised.[15] Rather than promoting such univocal interpretations of transgression, I agree with Russo, who argues for more dialectic approaches which theorize liminality as engaging in the *simultaneous* transgression and reinforcement of existing social structures.[16] In the case of prostitutes, for example, their ability to pass (both literally and figuratively) offers temporary transgression of the social boundaries which are, at the same time, fortified through the definition, regulation, and containment of prostitutes' excessive sexuality, unruly bodies, and deviant behavior.

While Victor Turner argues that liminal cultural formations make possible "the deconstruction of the 'uninteresting' constructions of common sense, the 'meaningfulness of ordinary life' . . . into cultural units which may then be reconstructed in novel ways," he also indicates that some of these are "bizarre to the point of monstrosity."[17] In turn, Mary Douglas, in her brilliant and provocative study of pollution and social order, calls attention to the doubled danger involved in the marginal state of liminality by arguing that "danger lies in transitional states, simply because transition is neither one state nor the next, it is undefinable. The person who must pass from one to another is himself [*sic*] in danger and emanates danger to others."[18] Indeed, it is this notion of excessive "monstrosity" which connects Heidi's mediate position as transgressor to various theories of liminality and liminal subjects as "quintessentially dangerous."[19]

Noting that there are special risks for women and other marginalized individuals in liminal states which put them in danger when their bodies enter the public sphere, Russo argues, "In the everyday indicative world, women and their bodies, certain bodies, in certain public framings, in certain public spaces, are always already transgressive-dangerous, and in danger.[20] While Russo describes the dangers for the public woman because of her gender, the media commenting on Heidi as a scandalous woman foreground the various ways her excessive public behavior (rather than the media's publicization of her arrest as scandal) endangered not only Heidi, her "girls," and her business, but also her family (especially her father), and the various clients whose positive reputations depend on her silence and secrecy.[21]

To understand the power of the mediated discourse surrounding Heidi's case, the conflation of her social position as Jew and madam must be considered in relation to the theorized position of the transgressive, liminal subject who, as someone tenuously between official and unofficial cultures, is always a body in danger. As Douglas argues, the liminal transgressor is often denigrated as a dangerous or monstrous transient, a pollutant or virus that infects and spoils society's sense of order: "The polluter becomes a doubly wicked object of reprobation, first because he [*sic*] crossed the line and second because he [*sic*] endangered others."[22] It is interesting to note, therefore, that Russo uses Jews who were stoned and women who were raped during early European carnivals as examples of liminal "bodies in danger." The connection here of Jews and women is not surprising considering the long history in European culture of attempting to code the male Jew as a feminized Other because of his dress, long hair, or the excessive bodily movements found in Hasidic dancing.[23] Such attempts to emasculate Jewish men are strongly connected to beliefs about Jews as foreign contagion, viral wanderers who threaten to infect non-Semitic society through their transgressions of the official boundaries of nation, religion, and commerce. As Douglas notes, "Belief in their sinister but undefinable advantages in commerce justifie[d] discrimination against them—whereas their real offence [was] always to have been *outside the formal structure* of Christendom."[24]

While in *Vested Interests* Marjorie Garber cites numerous examples of anti-Semitic emasculations of Jewish men (as well as attempts by male Jews to distance themselves from femininity),[25] I would suggest that it is not just the connection of Semitism and femininity that should be emphasized in relation to the mediate narrative of Heidi, but also the connections made between Jews and *prostitutes*, for there exists a profound parallel history of degradation and stigmatization among these two groups of social outcasts.[26] Indeed, prostitutes and Jews were often conflated into a single sumptuary class not only through similar sartorial codes (for example, earrings), but also through deliberate sociopolitical rhetoric that defined them as contagious viruses infecting "legitimate" systems of commerce and society.[27] Tenuously positioned as both necessary for and dangerous to society and commerce, Jews and prostitutes were simultaneously exploitable and regulatable at the whim of those in power.

Heidi's mediated position as a Jewish madam speaks not only to the prevalent stereotype of Jews as "money-hungry" outcasts who pollute "legitimate" systems of commerce, but also to the popular notion of prostitution as a vampiric danger infecting young women (and the victims whom they suck dry) with an insatiable lust that makes the virile viral. What remains latent in the media's descriptions of this "Hollywood madam" is not only the anti-Semitic stereotype of the Jew as an overly ambitious merchant, but that of the spoiled "Jewish-American-Princess," an insatiable vamp(ire) who uses her girlish charm to seduce, exploit, and ruin men. According to the media, it was Heidi's excessive, materialist ambitions which drove her to prostitution in the first place.[28] Although the term "Jewish-American-Princess" was never used in media accounts of Heidi, the numerous descriptions of her being "daddy's little girl" as well as lengthy musings on her proclivity for older, richer father figures (for example, Ivan Nagy, actor James Caan, and jet-set financier Bernie Cornfield) code her as a "JAP," a spoiled "rich little Jewish girl" who can't be happy with just one man and the material possessions he can provide.[29]

Garber's discussions of the narrativization of the "Jewish-American-Princess" by "macho-Jewish writers" such as Norman Mailer are useful here in considering the threat the vampiric "JAP" poses to phallic authority.[30] As she argues, the "Jewish-American-Princess" is often fantasized and narrativized in such texts as a phallic woman who transgresses into the public sphere, a place which has been put into question by the ambivalent status of Jewish men in a predominantly non-Semitic culture. Heidi's position as "the Hollywood madam" points, then, to the uncomfortable and potentially dangerous conflation of conventional gender roles within the Jewish community (where the merchant is always male and the matchmaker for couples—the yenta—is an older female), as well as to the inversion of gender roles within patriarchal ideology where "real men" are involved in business and "real women" stay home. In a somewhat interesting case of inversion, then, Heidi as madam is coded by the media not as outside the law (as in the case of most male "outlaws"), but as *above* it—a phallic woman, a woman on top (as it were).

In light of Garber's discussion of how Jewish men have distanced themselves from stereotypical connections with femininity, it is interesting to note that her analysis fails to problematize how such maneuverings might also function as displacements from the perceived dangers which homosexuality poses to the ideology of regeneration and reproduction found in heterosexual patriarchal society. As Sue Ellen Case comments,

> From the heterosexist perspective, the sexual practice that produced babies was associated with giving life. . . . Queer sexual practice . . . impels one out of the generational production of what has been called "life" and history, and ultimately out of the category of the living. . . . Queer desire punctures the life/death and generative/destructive bipolarities that enclose the heterosexist notion of being.[31]

While prostitution also poses a threat to the ideology and practices of reproduction, one might question how issues of homosexuality relate to Heidi, a woman whose prostitution trade was coded as predominantly heterosexual (due to the media's repeated references to the mysterious "johns" of the Hollywood film industry who used Heidi's services). According to various reports, it would seem that "the Hollywood Madam" has a proclivity not only for rich, older men, but for attractive, younger women. For example, Lynn Hirschberg of *Vanity Fair* reveals that Heidi was "lover" to both Claudia Carnesella (one of her "girls") and a *Penthouse* centerfold model identified only as "Mimi."[32] Hirschberg also hints at Heidi's lesbian relationship with her longtime friend Victoria Sellers (daughter to actor Peter Sellers), but Heidi has denied such a bond, insisting that they were only in bed together when participating in "three-somes" (a response that assumes *ménages à trois* to be heterosexual). *Premiere* magazine's John Richardson also reported a rumor that Heidi supplied call girls "on a massive scale" to the lesbian wives of studio executives (a rumor which calls into question the very nature of the secrets Heidi has kept hidden in her "little black book").[33]

The media's disclosure of Heidi's possible connections to lesbianism (along with repeated references to her illicit ab[use] of drugs), while potentially titillating, further code Heidi as a member of an illegitimate and improper subculture of sexual and ethical deviants. Indeed, the positioning of Heidi as dwelling in LA's underground can be seen in Hirschberg's description of Heidi's lifestyle as "vampiric." While I believe that Hirschberg is drawing on popular connotations of the vampire as nymphomaniac (like the prostitute), her invocation of those predisposed to sexual excess also calls to mind the prevalent homophobic stereotype of the homosexual as a sexually promiscuous individual, who, like the vampire, preys on innocent victims to satiate a libidinous appetite.[34] Coded as a lesbian, drug-abusing madam who operated an extremely lucrative but illegal business based on sexual pleasure rather than reproduction, Heidi has been effectively positioned as a considerable threat to the reproductive and procreative practices of our predominantly heterocentric society. Once defined in this way, her danger to society was more easily contained, regulated, and punished by those who could and would "show Heidi her place."

Tabloids, Unruly Sensationalism, and the Crisis of Legitimate News

If, as Brooks argues, "industrial literature" such as the serialized novel led to a "progressive unveiling of the erotic body," it is interesting to note how the contemporary media not only continue that unveiling but participate in discursive and representational strategies that rely not on rational thought but on emotion, sensation, and affect strategies distinctly connected to the body.[35] To expand Brooks's ideas about the figure of the deviant prostitute in the evolution of commercialized narrative, then, we might consider how unruly women such as Heidi Fleiss function in the media today, especially tabloid journalism, which is known for its reliance on sensationalized representations of scandalous "personalities."

Functioning as "mediated gossip," tabloid journalism entertains us through a subjective, undisciplined, and excessive sensationalism which highlights the transgressions of unruly personalities.[36] With its focus on publicizing scandals, rumors, and secrets, tabloid journalism has transformed modern narrative, favoring not the "legitimate" hermeneutic codes of contemplative decipherment, but the proairetic, performative codes of distraction and attraction firmly based in the body through experience, affect, and sensation.[37] Bearing a strong resemblance to tourism as a mediated form of sightseeing, tabloid journalism promises its readers and viewers access to the secret "back regions" of individual private lives and the deviant and/or marginal regions of society.[38] The circulation and reproduction of private secrets as publicly shared information is significant, therefore, especially when we consider the effects of tabloid journalism as a mediated discourse that appears to depend heavily on the private/public binary while operating in many ways which disrupt and/or deny the possibility of such bifurcated existence.

With its commodification of private gossip, rumors, and secrets for public consumption, as well as its ability to traverse the fine lines between various media (for example, visual and print) and formats (for example, glossy "scandal sheets" and "legitimate" national newspapers), tabloid journalism (and, by extension, its readers and the personalities who appear on its pages and "infotainment" TV programs) is marked as an "illegitimate" transgressor into the more "legitimate" realm of news.[39] In many newspaper reports following on the initial media frenzy set into action by a front-page story of Heidi's scandal in the *Los Angeles Times*, "responsible" news forums describe the rhetorical, visual, and reporting strategies of "flash and trash" tabloid journalism as "leaking over" into "legitimate" journalism. In such instances, tabloid journalism—especially tabloid television—is positioned as a pollutant upsetting and transforming the processes through which newsworthy information is gathered, narrativized, and disturbed.

Since stories about scandalous personalities have functioned for years as the backbone of tabloid journalism but are now beginning to pop up more and more in "legitimate" media forums, it seemed only a matter of time before the media recognized this crisis and began commenting on their actions self-reflexively, if not self-critically. For example, only five days after the first story announcing Heidi's scandal appeared in the *Los Angeles Times*, an article appeared on how "Heidi Copes with Life in Media Fishbowl."[40] In this front-page story, reporter Shawn Hubler turns the eye of the media back upon itself, but lacks any self-critique of his own perpetuation of the media blitz surrounding Heidi.[41] (Hubler is not only one of the journalists who wrote the front-page story publicizing the gossip surrounding Heidi's arrest, but also the reporter who, in December 1992, publicized Heidi's "flamboyant" boast about the success of her prostitution business.) Hubler distances the *Los Angeles Times* in particular and newspapers in general from the media hype by describing how television news helicopters drown conversation inside Heidi's home, how the evening news on television makes her look (in Heidi's words) "sleazy and gross," and how she must run a "gauntlet of tabloid reporters and cameramen" to get from her car into her house (and vice versa).[42]

In another *Los Angeles Times* story which focuses on the hype surrounding Heidi's scandal, all media—from local California television stations to CNN to *Newsweek* and the *London Sun*—are indicted for the tabloidization of Heidi's story and news in general. As the reporters note, "Some of the nation's most respected publications have found themselves sloshing around in the same muck as the supermarket tabloids."[43] Six months later, the *Los Angeles Times* published a front-page analysis of the tabloidization of journalism entitled "Obsessed with Flash and Trash."[44] Again, the tabloids (here specifically, tabloid television) are accused of "de-legitimizing" news space, "responsible" journalism, and narratable information: "The tabloid TV shows compete frantically to be first, often paying people for their exclusive stories—which reputable newspapers don't—and this drives prices up and standards down."[45] In a last-gasp effort to define (and defend) itself as informational, rational, objective, moral, responsible, and disciplined, "legitimate" journalism bolsters its phallogocentric authority by positioning tabloid journalism as both the unruly Other ("yellow journalism") and "feminized entertainment" (that is, entertainment whose focus is on the body, emotion, and affect, as well as entertainment whose consumers are assumed to be women).

Characterized by its excessive rhetorical style, sensational visual displays, and primary focus on scandalous personalities, tabloid journalism ostensibly blurs the boundaries of not only the private and public but also information and entertainment, thus provoking considerable analysis in the field of journalism and among media, literature, and rhetoric scholars.[46] But while tabloid television, magazines, and papers have this transgressive potential, tabloid journalism can be theorized as engaging simultaneously in the strategies of containment, operating through both the repetition and repression of excess and emotion. As Mellencamp suggests, through its coding as feminized, unruly, deviant culture, its mediation of gossip and secrets, and its traveling parade of scandalous bodies and personalities, tabloid journalism might well represent not transgression but negation or denial through the displacement and/or containment of affect, much like the popular serialized novels of the nineteenth century which focused not only on the transgressive deviance of the erotic female body but, perhaps more importantly, on its surveillance and rehabilitation.[47] The publicization of Heidi's arrest and trial (like that of O. J. Simpson's) on the front page of a "respectable" newspaper, as well as the movement of her scandalous narrative through the various sections of the *Los Angeles Times* (that is, "national news," "local news," and "business") and into national magazines and tabloid television, not only signals a profound confusion over where to properly situate Heidi in media space, but indicates a profound crisis in defining "legitimate" journalism and narratable, newsworthy information.

Conclusion (?)

As the media continues its panoptic focus on Heidi's "flamboyance," the hermeneutic hook for those who want to satisfy our epistemophilic desires is her "little black book," which contains the names of those who have also been complicit in traversing into illegitimate sexual and commercial relationships. While Heidi's attorneys have made numerous threats to reveal whatever names are necessary so as to alleviate the burden their client carries for being charged as solely responsible for crimes of prostitution, Heidi seems less willing to disclose the names of her clients and has acknowledged how her revelation of this information could destroy careers, marriages, and families (an ironic statement on the part of a madam whose business functioned in opposition to the ideologies and practices of domesticity, monogamy, and reproduction).[48]

On the one hand, Heidi's refusal to "tell all" seems a grotesque inversion of the typical mediated rape narrative, for here it is the man (as sexual initiator) whose identity is protected from publicity. But perhaps Heidi is correct in her assessment of the danger to patriarchal society involved in *her* revelation of such secrets. By refusing to be complicit in the very system that surveys her body, pathologizes her behavior, and exploits her story, Heidi's refusal to "tell all" acknowledges that it is her confession that is required for the appropriate processes of regulation and punishment to be enacted against her, an acknowledgment that the power rests not with the one who speaks but, as Michel Foucault argues, "in the one who listens and says nothing."[49] Because Heidi refuses to reveal names, she refuses to participate in a system that relies on the confession of the disempowered to signify and situate the power and authority of the law. As her life is endlessly revealed and commodified in the frenzied rush for information which helps secure a liberal notion of heterosexual masculine subjectivity at the expense of exposing a "deviant" female body, Heidi has learned very well who has the power in this mediated game of "show and tell." By revealing nothing about her clientele, she remains the keeper of her secrets, and we, as avid epistemophiliacs, are kept waiting.

Afterword

Two years after Heidi's arrest, I am preparing for yet another surgical operation that will leave me immobile and disempowered within the space I have constructed as both my home and workplace. Once again, my thoughts return to Heidi, a woman imprisoned within the panoptic gaze of the media for two years before the physical incarceration resulting from her convictions for pandering and, possibly, money laundering and tax evasion.[50] Like the unruly tissues that threaten my body, Heidi will be extracted from the place she established for herself within the underground of Los Angeles's prostitution trade and the high-life of Hollywood and put under the watchful eye of prison guards who are sure to continue the gossip circulating around Hollywood's most infamous madam. Whether or not those rumors find their way to print or television is, of course, another story.

Notes

1. Mary Douglas, *Purity and Danger: An Analysis of the Concepts of Pollution and Taboo* (London: Routledge & Kegan Paul, 1966), 4.

2. News of the scandal involving Heidi was first publicized on the front page of the *Los Angeles Times* on August 1, 1993, almost two months after her arrest and eight days prior to her arraignment on charges of pandering and possession of narcotics. See Shawn Hubler and James Bates, "Heidi's Arrest Is the Talk of Tinseltown," *Los Angeles Times*, August 1, 1993.

3. The jury in Heidi's case deadlocked on decisions over two other counts of pandering. In addition, she was found not guilty on one count of trafficking in cocaine. Although Heidi's attorneys filed for a mistrial after being made aware that several of the jurists discussed the case outside the court before reaching their verdicts, a Superior Court judge denied the motion for a new trial. Nora Zamichow, "Judge Rejects Fleiss' Bid for Retrial, Sets Sentencing for May," *Los Angeles Times*, March 25, 1995, B1. Convicted on three counts of pandering, Heidi was sentenced to three years in jail and given a $1,500 fine on May 24, 1995. She remains free on bail pending the appeal of her conviction. Nora Zamichow, "Fleiss Gets 3 Years in Prison for Pandering," *Los Angeles Times*, May 25, 1995, B1.

4. Shawn Hubler, "For Former Madam of Beverly Hills—A Final Indignity," *Los Angeles Times*, December 14, 1992, B1, B8. Heidi is quoted as saying, "What took ['Madam Alex'] years to build, I built in one." We might connect images of Heidi as "flamboyant" taken at the time of her arraignment (and before her arrest) with photographs of Heidi at trial. With the addition of a pair of sunglasses to an outfit that included a wrapdress whose fabric and cut emphasized her feminine figure, Heidi personified the glamorous Hollywood celebrity at her arraignment in August 1993. In an effort to legitimize herself in the court's (and public's) eyes during her trial over a year later, Heidi has opted for more "masculine" (dark, monotone) business suits, turtlenecks, and eyeglasses, which connote white-collar success and the "clean money" that is earned via legitimate business practices.

5. Patricia Mellencamp, *High Anxiety: Catastrophe, Scandal, Age, and Comedy* (Bloomington: Indiana University Press, 1992), 160.

6. Peter Brooks, "The Mark of the Beast: Prostitution, Serialization, and Narrative," in *Reading for the Plot: Design and Intention in Narrative* (New York: Vintage Books, 1985), 156–157, 168. While Brooks uses the feminine gender in relation to prostitution specifically because of the nineteenth-century focus on the erotic female body, I apologize for sexing the prostitute here as female. Unfortunately, the limits of

this paper do not afford me the space to consider male prostitution (either hetero- or homosexual).

7. Ibid., 156, 168–169. In this regard, Heidi was the most on target when she explained the rationale behind the media's frenzied coverage of her case by using the cliché "sex sells."

8. Ibid., 159.

9. Tabak quoted in Hubler and Bates, "Heidi's Arrest Is the Talk of Tinseltown," A37.

10. Brooks implies such danger when he refers to the prostitute jokingly as "the old equalizer." Brooks, "The Mark of the Beast," 156–157.

11. References to these men appeared as early as Hubler and Bates, "Heidi's Arrest Is the Talk of Tinseltown" (A38), including the first reference to Dr. Paul Fleiss's ownership of Heidi's Benedict Canyon home. A more recent article, however, indicates that Heidi's cousin and one of her sisters helped purchase the home. Shawn Hubler, "Did Father Know Best?" *Los Angeles Times Magazine*, April 9, 1995, 32.

12. Despite much evidence against him, the charges of pandering against Nagy were dropped after his arrest on August 4, 1993.

13. Lynn Hirschberg of *Vanity Fair* reported that the Norma Karnali dress worn by Heidi during her arraignment belonged to her friend L'Hua Reid. Hirschberg, "Heidi Does Hollywood," *Vanity Fair* (February 1994): 123. With Hirschberg, several magazines have suggested that Heidi, with the help of Nagy, "stole" her girls from Madam Alex. John H. Richardson, "Lies and Whispers," *Premiere* (October 1993): 76; John Connolly, "Dirty Movies," *Us* (October 1993): 64.

14. Mary Russo, "Female Grotesques: Carnival and Theory," in *Feminist Studies/Critical Studies*, edited by Teresa de Lauretis (Bloomington: Indiana University Press, 1986), 215.

15. Michel de Certeau, *The Practice of Everyday Life*, translated by Steven Randall (Berkeley: University of California Press, 1984), 29–42, 115–130.

16. For example, Natalie Zemon Davis, "Women on Top," in *Society and Culture in Early Modern France* (Stanford, CA: Stanford University Press, 1965), 131.

17. Victor Turner, "Process, System, and Symbol: A New Anthropological Synthesis," *Daedalus* (Summer 1977): 68.

18. Douglas, *Purity and Danger*, 96.

19. Turner, "Process, System, and Symbol," 68.

20. Russo, "Female Grotesques," 217.

21. Paul Fleiss has been constructed in the media in direct opposition to his wayward daughter through rhetoric which describes the "good doctor" as altruistic, trustworthy, caring, and innocent. Heidi, in turn, is positioned as the "wild kid" whose troubled lifestyle has finally damaged her father's reputation.

22. Douglas, *Purity and Danger*, 139. Dick Hebdige, in *Subculture: The Meaning of Style* (London: Routledge, 1979, 92–99), provides another provocative analysis of the process of societal recuperation using Roland Barthes's theory of incorporation of deviance *via* an ideological effect produced by naturalizing the Other and/or transforming it into "meaningless exotica." See Roland Barthes, "Myth on the Right," in *Mythologies*, translated by Annette Lavers (New York: Noonday Press, 1972), 148–156.

23. As Zemon Davis suggests, the politics of inversion found in transgressive cultural formations often come to be centralized in a noncoherent, unruly body, a body that, through such categorization (if not pathologization), is coded by official culture as distinctly "feminine." Zemon Davis, "Women on Top," 124–127.

24. Douglas, *Purity and Danger*, 104 (emphasis added).

25. Marjorie Garber, "Jew, Woman, Homosexual," in *Vested Interests: Cross-Dressing and Cultural Anxiety* (New York: Routledge, 1992), 224–233.

26. Diane Owen Hughes, "Distinguishing Signs: Ear-Rings, Jews, and Franciscan Rhetoric in the Italian Renaissance City," *Past and Present* 112 (August 1986).

27. For example, Adolf Hitler in *Mein Kampf* metaphorically related the stereotype of the "wandering Jew" with that of the vampire, a rhetorical strategy which not only stigmatized Jews as blood-sucking monsters who carried a viral disease that would "bastardize the white race," but also rationalized the regulation, imprisonment, and murder of millions of Jews in Nazi Germany. Quoted in Sue Ellen Case, "Tracking the Vampire," *differences* 3, no. 2 (1991): 6. Most recently, we can see the connection between social outcasts, vampires, and pollutant viruses in the anti-AIDS discourse that fuses male homosexual desire with the contamination of virile (that is, potentially reproductive) bodies.

28. Heidi told Lynn Hirschberg of *Vanity Fair*, "I saw [prostitution] as a way that girls could really take advantage of men. And we did exactly that—every man was taken advantage of." Hirschberg, "Heidi Does Hollywood," 92.

29. Ibid., 92; Connolly, "Dirty Movies," 62.

30. Garber, "Jew, Woman, Homosexual," 229.

31. Case, "Tracking the Vampire," 4.

32. Hirschberg, "Heidi Does Hollywood," 122, 125.

33. Richardson, "Lies and Whispers," 80.

34. Case, "Tracking the Vampire," 6.

35. Brooks, "The Mark of the Beast," 143.

36. Mellencamp, *High Anxiety*, 155.

37. Ibid., 179.

38. The term "back region" was coined by Erving Goffman in *The Presentation of Self in Everyday Life* (Garden City, NY: Doubleday, 1959), 144–145.

39. Mellencamp, *High Anxiety*, 156.

40. Shawn Hubler, "Heidi Copes with Life in Media Fishbowl," *Los Angeles Times*, August 6, 1993, A1, A23.

41. Ibid., A23.

42. Ibid., A1, A23.

43. Faye Fiore and Terry Pristin, "Media Circus: Midsummer Madness," *Los Angeles Times*, August 14, 1993, B1, B8.

44. David Shaw, "Obsessed with Flash and Trash," *Los Angeles Times*, February 16, 1994.

45. Ibid., A13.

46. For an example of this kind of analysis, see Kevin Glynn, "Tabloid Television's Transgressive Aesthetics: *A Current Affair* and the 'Shows That Taste Forgot,'" *Wide Angle* 12, no. 2 (April 1990): 22–44.

47. Mellencamp, *High Anxiety*, 232–233.

48. Her attorneys' willingness to reveal the names of Heidi's "johns" points to the unequal power relations between attorney and client (not to mention man and woman): if Heidi's lawyers reveal these undisclosed names, the taint of feminized gossip is removed by the phallic authority of the law so that truths are revealed, not secrets.

49. Michel Foucault, *The History of Sexuality: An Introduction*, vol. 1, translated by Robert Hurley (New York: Vintage Books, 1990), 62.

50. Sentenced to three years of imprisonment, Heidi remains free on bail pending the appeal of her conviction for pandering. She was indicted with her father in July 1994 on fourteen counts of money laundering and tax evasion. That trial has been tentatively scheduled for late June 1995. If convicted, Heidi could serve an additional four to six years behind bars. [Addendum 2017: While Heidi Fleiss's initial conviction at the state level was overturned in 1996, she eventually served twenty months in federal prison for tax evasion before being released in 1998.]

THIRTEEN

Out on Stage

LGBT Politics of Entertainment Award Shows

RAFFI SARKISSIAN

I HOPE YOU'RE NOT DISAPPOINTED THAT THERE WON'T BE A BIG COMING-OUT SPEECH TONIGHT BECAUSE I ALREADY DID MY COMING OUT ABOUT A THOUSAND YEARS AGO. . . . BUT NOW, APPARENTLY, I'M TOLD THAT EVERY CELEBRITY IS EXPECTED TO HONOR THE DETAILS OF THEIR PRIVATE LIFE WITH A PRESS CONFERENCE, A FRAGRANCE, AND A PRIMETIME REALITY SHOW.

JODIE FOSTER, 2013 GOLDEN GLOBES

When Jodie Foster took the stage to accept the Cecil B. DeMille Lifetime Achievement Award at the 2013 Golden Globes ceremony, she not only unleashed a stream of criticism toward expectations from public figures to make an announcement and spectacle of private matters (in her case, the official disclosure of her sexual orientation), but also made evident the power of the podium to command cultural capital as well as the strong relationship between the award show stage and social politics. Despite Foster's plea for privacy, the chatter and criticism that followed her speech focused more on her muddled and indirect coming-out rhetoric at a time when gay visibility, particularly at these big industry kudos-fests, was at a peak. Thus, it only managed to direct more attention to the way issues like gender and sexuality operate in Hollywood both on and off the screen.

The politics of visibility, ideological motives of the industry, and effects of mass-mediated images, particularly in film and on television, have long been tied to issues of representation. Nowhere has this been clearer than at the public podium, for the open stages at the Oscars and the Emmys have and continue to be cultural symbols of acceptance in various meanings of the term. Concerns for minority representation have been present throughout much of the time we have had a mass entertainment medium, and they show no signs of resolution. For example, a 2012 *Los Angeles Times* investigation made headlines when it reported that Academy of Motion Picture Arts and Sciences voters (Oscar judges) are overwhelmingly white (94 percent), overwhelmingly male (77 percent), and overwhelmingly older, with a high median age of sixty-two (86 percent over fifty).[1] While the implicit critique in these statistics—and the explicit critique in annual articles on representation at the Oscars[2]—refers predominantly to a lack of racial and gender diversity in the nominee pools, this paper will explore the politics of LGBT representation at these award shows.

Seeing as LGBT characters, since their increasing presence in film and television from the 1990s on, often fare better than racial minorities in industry accolades, I examine some of the conditions and implications of awarding LGBT content and artists. I argue that the relative prevalence of LGBT awards attention is often due to Hollywood's politics of limited liberalism—either bestowing upon itself a bloated sense of self-righteous cultural-political influence or maintaining a post-gay rhetoric, depending on which medium you're watching. By observing how the Oscars and the Emmys valuate LGBT diversity through wins and nominations, I argue that the acting categories of these award shows, with their divergent cultural messages regarding sexual minorities, reinforce stereotypes and perpetuate gendered binaries that have ideologically shaped film and television.

While as media scholars we often face an uphill battle to claim relevance and assert the rigor of our work and methodologies, sometimes there is even a hierarchy of value placed on certain research subjects within our respective fields. The lack of scholarship on award shows is perhaps due to their association with low culture and relevance to lived social conditions (much like critiques hurled against reality television), thus making it what Judith Halberstam would call a "silly archive."[3] However, the arguments of this paper are predicated on at least two specific reasons why award shows are fruitful sites of analysis for pop culture. First, award shows serve as a reflection of industry politics and attitudes. In this paper, I focus strictly on the Oscars and Emmys because they represent the golden standard for their respective mediums—an industry-wide evaluation whose judges cover the gamut of all creative and even relevant business departments in that field. While images and narratives of other shows, like the Golden Globes, Broadcast Film Critics Association Critics' Choice Awards, or SAG Awards, may carry comparable weight in cultural capital—as Jodie Foster's speech at the Globes attests—they draw from a specific branch or very small and unrepresentative section of their industry. While I recognize that when it comes to issues of representation (LGBT representation in this case) award shows are not texts to take to task for what are usually deep-rooted industry practices, they are nonetheless excellent texts to study the crystallization of those attitudes and practices. In a sense, they offer a streamlined peek into the back stage of Hollywood politics.

Second, they also convey more explicitly the front stage of the industry—the narrative Hollywood wants to show the world. They are reflections of Hollywood taste and respectability. With hundreds of millions of dollars spent by studios on campaigning every year, the awards circuit is an entire industry unto itself now, and one that also extends into various other businesses like TV reporting, professional blogging, daytime, late-night interviews, festivals and special screenings, pre-parties, and after-parties. Most importantly, running strong through both these back- and front-stage considerations is the immeasurable amount of cultural capital in circulation. By cultural capital I mean values and import that are attributed—by the industry, by the market, and by audiences and participants—to titles ("Academy Award Winner"), statues, and stage presence, all of which contribute to a person's or idea's cultural worth. As James F. English asserts, awards and prizes deal heavily in the economy of cultural prestige.[4] With these considerations in mind, I turn to the specific ideologies that I argue LGBT presence in Oscar and Emmy award celebrations reinforce and perpetuate.

When television was becoming an imminent object of study, there was a strong debate about its "place" in film and media studies (much like most new media forms that gain popular attention). Early logic, as Patrice Petro explicates, consigned television to the realm of the passive, debased, and low culture that due to its focus on consumption, mass appeal, melodramatic content, and even its status as a household appliance or piece of furniture—the realm of the domestic—was often equated with the feminine.[5] This was in stark opposition to film and technology, which carried with them masculine attributes of the active, artistic, and high cultural value. One specific example of this gendered ideology comes from Keir Keightley, who compares television and the simultaneous introduction of hi-fi as furthering this binary, arguing that high fidelity (high-quality sound technology), in contrast to television, was associated with and marketed to masculine sensibilities,[6] while television sets, as Lynn Spigel documents, were seen more in women's magazine ads.[7] As Lynn Joyrich further explores the gender dynamic by assessing the growing influence of melodrama on television content,[8] it comes as no surprise that the turn to "quality" programming in the 1990s has coincided with a remasculinization of the medium not only in content but also in production (with an increased focus on high definition and a cinematic aesthetic in cinematography, editing, and score) and talent (borrowing producer-directors like Steven Spielberg and Martin Scorsese and established film actors like Dustin Hoffman, Jeff Daniels, and Jeremy Irons).[9] While this sexist paradigm might now seem outdated, I argue that the way LGBT content operates at award shows plays into and reinforces these gender binaries.

The basic premise for this paper came from my observations throughout the years of not only the different roles for gay characters and gay actors in film versus on television, but also of how they were valuated through industry accolades. When thinking of film and the Oscars, for example, I found that, typically, very established actors—established whether in their career, their public heterosexuality, or often both—play very sympathetic gay characters. These actors are lauded for being able to make gay characters likable and relatable (or at least pitiable), or in other words, sellable to a mainstream ticket-buying audience. These mostly leading and wholly dramatic roles hold many similar characteristics, perhaps not coincidentally, to classic compensatory moral codes that regulated Hollywood film content for decades.[10] The most notable trope is death. Four of the five actors who have won the Oscar for playing gay—leading actors William Hurt (*Kiss of the Spider Woman*), Tom Hanks (*Philadelphia*), and Sean Penn (*Milk*) and supporting actor Christopher Plummer (*Beginners*)—all portrayed characters who died by the end of the film. The only one who did not bite the dust was Philip Seymour Hoffman's Truman Capote, though the melancholic ending state of his character falls into a variation on the trope of the "sad young man."[11] If we add all three female actresses who have won for portraying lesbian, bisexual, or trans characters—Hilary Swank (*Boys Don't Cry*), Nicole Kidman (*The Hours*), and Charlize Theron (*Monster*)—then the count goes up to seven out of eight, as all the winning characters portrayed by female actresses died at the end of their films. A majority of the nominated male performances also fit the mold: Colin Firth (*A Single Man*), Jake Gyllenhaal and Heath Ledger (*Brokeback Mountain*), Ed Harris (*The Hours*), Javier Bardem (*Before Night Falls*), and Ian McKellen (*Gods and Monsters*)—on this list, the only openly gay actor to portray a major gay character. The other nominated female roles fared a little better—Annette Bening (*The Kids Are All Right*), Cher (*Silkwood*), Felicity Huffman (*Transamerica*), Judi Dench (*Notes on a Scandal*), and Julianne Moore (*The Hours*) all survived, though often not without tremendous cost.

In striking contrast, the roles for gay characters and actors on television disproportionately fall into the comedy sitcom genre and are predominantly nominated in supporting categories.[12] However, there is more variety as far as an assortment of gay actors playing gay characters, gay actors playing straight characters, and straight actors playing gay characters. In the drama categories, there have only been four LGBT roles that have earned nominations: David (Michael C. Hall) in *Six Feet Under*, Dr. Weaver (Laura Innes) in *ER*, Kalinda (Archie Panjabi) in *The Good Wife*, and Ray Fiske (Zeljko Ivanek) in *Damages*. (As the only gay male role to win in a drama category, and arguably a "quality" drama at that, Fiske falls in line with filmic conventions of killing off the queer.) Ellen DeGeneres became and remains the only actress to be nominated in a lead comedy category as either an out lesbian actress or a lesbian character (in her case, both), though she only ever won for writing.[13] All four principal actors in *Will & Grace* took home Emmys throughout its eight-year run, including Eric McCormack (straight playing gay), Sean Hayes (closeted playing gay), and Megan Mullally (straight playing generally queer). The show was also awarded the Emmy for Best Comedy Series in 2000. *Glee* earned nominations for both its gay and lesbian actors, and *Modern Family* has cleaned up the top comedy prize for three years running, with Eric Stonestreet (straight actor portraying gay character Cam) winning twice so far. There is also the curious phenomenon of gay actors playing straight characters who get nominated only after they come out of the closet. Both Neil Patrick Harris and T. R. Knight played existing straight characters on their shows, *How I Met Your Mother* and *Grey's Anatomy*, on air for one and two seasons, respectively, before being outed in the fall of 2006. During the following Emmy cycle, they were both nominated in supporting roles for their portrayal of straight characters, almost serving as a congratulatory or compensatory pat on the back from their peers.

In assessing the meaning these patterns convey, genre distinction is the most easily discernible point of difference, followed by gender, star power, and level of effeminate behavior. The scale is undoubtedly tipped more toward gay male roles than any other sexual minority, especially on television, where the roles are allowed to be more flamboyant and stereotypically "queeny" (Will, Jack, Mitch, Cam, Kurt, etc.). This brings into question television's linking of more identifiably (stereotypically effeminate) gay depictions with its underlying commercial imperative. As the prominence of the gay market has largely been based on the stereotype of the cultured gay man with more disposable income than his straight counterpart (dual-income, no kids household),[14] this linking of consumption by evoking the effeminate gay man reinscribes its ties with the feminine as the target audience of television. And what is more powerful in perpetuating the images associated with either television or film than the actors who take the stage at these awards and the ensuing press that circulates that capital?

It should be stressed, however, that these are not claims against the various voting bodies of the awards shows, but rather, how they actually reflect a crystallization of industry beliefs and practices, which can be traced to various media and cultural trends that emerged in the 1990s. For example, as tolerance for and incorporation of LGBT content was on the rise, the materialization of the gay market[15] coincided with the emergence of independent and queer cinema, perhaps curbing Hollywood's inclusion of explicitly gay content and talent into their more mainstream fare. While cable would eventually do the same for television, the prevalence of LGBT content on commercial broadcast TV pointed to the pressures to offer edgier content to a more sophisticated, "slumpy" (socially liberal, urban-minded professionals) demographic in order to compete with (the more masculine) cable content.[16] The trade-off, however, created a lose-lose situation, in which the broadcast content was either neutered or highly stereotypical and the "quality" cable content was more groundbreaking but ultimately either too fringe or too threatening to the overtly masculine and heteronormative logic that shaped many of the top award-winning shows. This is why series like *The Sopranos*, *Mad Men*, and *Breaking Bad* have received disproportionately more awards and nominations, and thus mainstream prestige, than more disrupting programs like *Six Feet Under*, *The Wire*, *Queer as Folk*, *Oz*, and *The L Word*. Thus, much like how queer and independent cinema largely segmented LGBT films away from the mainstream, which typically also distanced it from awards potential, "quality" cable programming did the same for gay content on television, with lesbian and trans representation largely ignored (stemming from the systemic "problem" of marketability of/to these groups).[17] The few awards that are spared typify the traditional gendered binary of either the revered artistic, high-culture value of film or the consuming, inoffensive (least common denominator) characteristics of television.

Finally, and most notably, is the rhetoric of Oscar and Emmy speeches that further reinforces the active/passive binary, particularly how one plays down politics whereas the other privileges it. With film, the nominations and especially wins are treated as political statements, as evidenced through their acceptance speeches. One need only listen to Tom Hanks's achingly poetic, bleeding heart, and undoubtedly rehearsed speech for *Philadelphia* or Sean Penn's condemnation of the timely passing of Proposition 8 during his speech for *Milk* to get a taste of this rhetoric.[18] Oscar speeches are made out to be important steps in a linear progress narrative of the gay rights movement. Speeches made at the Emmys for winning LGBT performances or prominently gay-themed shows, on the other hand, are lacking in asserting almost any cultural-political significance. The gay nature of the content is usually not as important, these speeches indicate, as is being able to entertain and get laughs (or get you to keep watching and not offend you). This is best seen in Steven Levitan's 2011 Emmy acceptance speech for Best Comedy Series, *Modern Family*:

> A gay couple came up to us and said, "You know, you're not just making people laugh, you're making them more tolerant." [*Applause*] And I thought to myself, they're right; we are showing the world that there is absolutely nothing wrong with a loving, committed relationship between an old man and a hot, young woman. And looking around this room tonight, I see many of you agree.[19]

This undoubtedly again feeds into the commercial nature of much of the comedy series that get Emmy attention; they do not want to overpoliticize the content so as to maintain as many viewers as possible and not scare away advertisers. And when they do bring it up, as in the above quote, it is coyly bypassed for a joke or mentioned in an off-the-cuff manner, like when Max Mutchnick stated, "This award really indicates a whole new meaning to the phrase, 'acceptance speech'" at the tail end of his speech for *Will & Grace*'s Best Comedy Series win in 2000. Both examples insinuate that they have arrived at a certain point at which the gay content is not political anymore because some kind of goal has been achieved (acceptance), conveniently suggesting a post-gay order. Thus, film, once again, by exhibiting a more passionate and proactive position (through its mostly straight affirmation of gay progress), is seen as more masculine and valued in cultural-political effect than the indifferent politics that perpetuates television's ideological place and practice as driven by consumption.

While the focus of this paper has centered on a particular ideology as fueled by industry beliefs and practices, I do not claim this assessment to be wholly intentional or all-encompassing, but rather, an opening point in a larger discussion about gender, media, technology, and how sexual orientation might now be complicating or contributing to such existing relationships and theories. As I discuss patterns in specific events, I do not profess my data pool to be exhaustive; I hope others will join me in continually expanding the scope of analysis when it comes to these large media events. Finally, as I make assertions of meaning tied to decisions made by people in the industry, I also contend that there are varying other considerations (some that I am limited from including, and others that are admittedly unknowable) that contribute to the outcomes of these awards. But, in the end, it is that outcome—what's written in that envelope, how the prize is claimed, and how it is delivered to the masses—that carries so much weight. Consequently, I hope this paper furthers dialogue on the operation of the type of capital that is at work—won, earned, traded, and circulated—in the cultural economy of pop culture and award shows.

Notes

1. John Horn, Nicole Sperling, and Doug Smith, "Oscar Voters Overwhelmingly White, Male," *Los Angeles Times*, February 19, 2012.

2. Articles either decrying the lack of diversity (see Dodai Stewart, "Will This Really Be 'The Whitest Oscars in 10 Years'?" *Jezebel*, October 1, 2010, accessed July 17, 2013, http://jezebel.com/5653216/will-this-really-be-the-whitest-oscars-in-10-years) or the newsworthiness of the prospect of more diversity (Kyle Buchanan, "Could Harvey Weinstein Make History with Three Black Best Actor Oscar Candidates?" *Vulture*, May 17, 2013, accessed July 19, 2013, http://www.vulture.com/2013/05/could-2013-see-three-black-best-actor-nominees.html).

3. In *The Queer Art of Failure* (Durham, NC: Duke University Press, 2011), Judith Halberstam uses this term in describing the search "for low theory and counter-knowledge in the realm of popular culture" (19).

4. James F. English, *The Economy of Prestige: Prizes, Awards, and the Circulation of Cultural Value* (Cambridge, MA: Harvard University Press, 2005).

5. Patrice Petro, "Mass Culture and the Feminine: The 'Place' of Television in Film Studies," *Cinema Journal* 25, no. 3 (1986), 5–21.

6. Keir Keightley, "Low Television, High Fidelity: Taste and the Gendering of Home Entertainment Technologies," *Journal of Broadcasting and Electronic Media*, 47, no. 2 (2003): 236–259.

7. Lynn Spigel, *Make Room for TV: Television and the Family Ideal in Postwar America* (Chicago: University of Chicago Press, 1992).

8. Lynne Joyrich, "All That Television Allows: TV Melodrama, Postmodernism, and Consumer Culture," *Cinema Obscura* 16, no. 1 (1988).

9. For an overview of this phenomenon, see Anikó Imre, "Gender and Quality Television: A Transcultural Feminist Project," *Feminist Media Studies* 9, no. 4 (2009); and Michael Kackman, "Quality Television, Melodrama, and Cultural Complexity," *Flow* 9, no. 1 (2008), accessed July 17, 2013, http://flowtv.org/archives/volume-9/901/.

10. For more on the history of queer representation in film, see Vito Russo, *The Celluloid Closet: Homosexuality in the Movies* (New York: Harper & Row, 1987), and Harry M. Benshoff and Sean Griffin, *Queer Images: A History of Gay and Lesbian Film in America* (New York: Rowman & Littlefield Publishers, 2006).

11. See Richard Dyer, *The Matter of Images: Essays on Representation* (London: Routledge, 1993), 40–42.

12. Due to the scope of this article, I am focusing only on the categories that reflect the distinguishing nature of TV (as a serial medium). Consequently, for purposes here, this excludes guest acting categories as well as categories for short-lived programs like TV movies and miniseries.

13. Toni Collette in *The United States of Tara* would be a slight exception here, as she has won Best Actress in a Comedy for playing a character with multiple personalities, one of whom is a man.

14. Katherine Sender, *Business, Not Politics: The Making of the Gay Market* (New York: Columbia University Press, 2004), 144–154.

15. For a detailed account of the making of the gay market, see ibid.

16. Ron Becker, *Gay TV and Straight America* (New Brunswick, NJ: Rutgers University Press, 2006).

17. See chap. 6, "Neither Fish nor Fowl," in Sender, *Business, Not Politics*.

18. See "Tom Hanks Winning an Oscar for 'Philadelphia,'" http://www.youtube.com/watch?v=bBuDMEpUc8k; and "Sean Penn Winning Best Actor for 'Milk,'" http://www.youtube.com/watch?v=9HFRjamyuao.

19. "*Modern Family*: Outstanding Comedy Series," producer, Mark Burnett, 63rd Annual Golden Globes, September 18, 2011, accessed July 17, 2013, at http://www.youtube.com/watch?v=DG54KZMWKz4.

FOURTEEN

Lesbian Cop, Queer Killer

Leveraging Black Queer Women's Sexuality on HBO's *The Wire*

JENNIFER DECLUE

HBO's drama series *The Wire* has been the subject of at least one academic conference, an online academic journal, numerous college courses, and several scholarly articles, and as of this writing, there are rumors of a forthcoming book on the series. Although much has been written and probably even more has been spoken about *The Wire*, concerns have primarily been with the realistic manner in which institutionalized racism, political corruption, and impoverished communities are depicted. I find it startling that fewer discussions have been concerned with the representation of racialized genders and sexualities given that a host of black queer characters populate this HBO series.

The five seasons of the controversial and provocative series (2002–2008) expose the inner workings of the Baltimore Police Department through ongoing police investigations that utilize wiretapping (hence the title) to break codes of communication used by local crime rings. The show's fictional narratives address contemporary social and political issues specific to Baltimore. In doing so, the show cast local talent as well as professional actors, and incorporated actual neighborhood businesses into its narratives. This combination of real life and fiction creates diegetic complexity and an atmosphere of authenticity. As a result, *The Wire*'s strengths lie in the narrative deconstruction and critique of systems of power that conspire through racialized violence, failed education, nefarious politicians, and law enforcement to subjugate marginalized communities in the United States. Nearly every major character in *The Wire* has a rich emotional interior that provides an entryway into the complexities of life in Baltimore. *The Wire*'s creator, David Simon, prides himself on linguistic accuracy achieved through immersing his cast and crew in a city's rhythms and sounds during production.[1] The rich realism with which Simon treats his characters is attributed to his long career as a crime reporter with the *Baltimore Sun*; through a mix of veracity and fiction, this HBO drama is habitually credited with being the "real thing."[2]

During what Ron Becker calls the gay nineties, prime-time television programs included gay characters who were predominantly white, save Carter, a black gay character on *Spin City*.[3] Becker critiques these representations of gay and lesbian characters on prime-time television for not depicting the "lived experiences of thousands of gay and lesbian people" who experience poverty, racial discrimination, and social oppression.[4] He says:

> The problem, of course, as with nearly all television representations, is that they do embody stereotypes. Instead of images of nelly queens or motorcycle dykes we are presented with images of white, affluent, trend-setting, Perrier-drinking, frequent flyer using, PhD-holding consumer citizens with more income to spend than they know what to do with.[5]

Since the so-called "gay nineties," there has been an increase, albeit a small one, in representations of queer characters of color on TV shows, including *Greek*, *Ugly Betty*, *Noah's Arc*, *The L Word*, *Six Feet Under*, and *RuPaul's Drag Race*. *The Wire* also rectifies this disparity with the inclusion of several black queer characters that present a range of genders, sexualities, income levels, and ethics. The black queer characters on *The Wire* expand the representation of blackness on television beyond the lone black gay character like Carter or past the parameters of an explicitly black gay show like Logo's *Noah's Arc*. Furthermore, *The Wire* also stands apart from other television representations for its incorporation of black queer female characters; along with *The L Word* and *Pretty Little Liars*, *The Wire* is among the first fictional TV programs in the US to depict black queer women. *The Wire* creates a dystopic landscape in which black queer women navigate their surroundings without their sexualities or genders inhibiting their movements or causing their premature deaths.[6] An impeccable attention to detail in writing, direction, and production creates never-before-seen black queer women that we love and despise.

While the presence of these characters on television expands representations of black sexualities in popular culture, I argue this expansion is tempered by the use of black sexual taboo to produce an aesthetic of quality TV.[7] With media representations of marginalized groups come expectations that lived experiences are taken into account; in my discussion of quality TV, I consider the manner in which visual representations of blackness have been mired in the rhetoric of authenticity. Specifically, I interrogate the ways that the fraught history of black women's sexuality in the US is leveraged in the production of *The Wire*'s black queer women characters.[8] I contend that *The Wire* both complicates and exploits black queer sexuality in order to produce provocative quality television.

My analysis of *The Wire* hones in on the narrative treatment of two of the black queer characters, Detective Shakima "Kima" Greggs, a sexy lesbian cop, and Felicia "Snoop" Pearson, a hypermasculine ruthless criminal. I attend to the representations of Kima's and Snoop's sexuality and gender by examining the production of black queer women's sexuality in the context of quality TV, wherein race and gender have played a key role in the elevation of television through complex, sophisticated narratives. In this context, I question the manner in which *The Wire* both expands the parameters of quality television and concomitantly situates itself solidly within this genre by utilizing black queer sexuality to refine aesthetic values and intensify narrative arcs. I am concerned with the ways in which quality TV programming creates a demand for black queer characters but then delimits the depth with which these characters can be written into existence.

Quality TV and *The Wire*

Quality TV has been troubled by its value-laden moniker because "quality" inherently distinguishes that which falls within its parameters from television programs that are presumably lacking in quality.[9] Robert J. Thompson asserts that "quality TV is best defined as what it is not. It is not 'regular' TV."[10] This distinction between quality TV and "regular TV" is reminiscent of the distinction made between art and mass culture, which placed television solidly within the purview of the latter. Thompson characterizes quality TV as having a "quality pedigree" and asserts that quality TV writing is complex enough to handle multiple plots woven among a large ensemble cast. He argues that the audience is from a "blue chip" demographic of "upscale, well educated, urban dwelling young viewers."[11] Quality TV, according to Thompson, tends both toward controversial subject matter as well as realism.[12] "'Quality TV' is then simply television's version of 'art film.'"[13]

Janet McCabe and Kim Akass address the manner in which HBO exhibits "the best of American TV" through "misogynistic violence" and the pleasure derived from pushing moral boundaries.[14] They write:

> Contentious subject matter and edgy scripts containing adult themes are predicated on risk-taking that strains broadcasting limits. . . . Pushing limits of respectability, of daring to say/do what cannot be said/done elsewhere on the networks, is entwined with being esoteric, groundbreaking and risk-taking.[15]

This discussion of HBO's edgy, quality television programming that at once promotes diversity while taking advantage of gender, race, and class differences informs my analysis. *The Wire* secures its quality TV status, in part, by foregrounding the marginalized sexualities of black queer female characters. While many characters marginalized by race, class, gender, and sexuality do appear in *The Wire*, Kima and Snoop, in particular, produce quality television narratives that push moral boundaries and showcase diverse representations.

While *The Wire* boldly makes black queer women characters visible, the series does not escape reproducing stereotypes either. Rather, representations of black queer women on *The Wire* reinforce and resist stereotypes. In addressing these complex characters, I begin by contextualizing the pathologization of black women's sexuality in the US as a way to reflect on the history in which Kima and Snoop are situated. I turn toward this history in order to discuss the secrecy and taboo that are implicit in the provocative nature of black lesbian sexuality that is utilized in the production of quality TV.

Black Women, Gender, Sexuality, and Quality TV

Historically, black sexuality has been constructed as existing outside of heteronormativity yet perpetually perceived as heterosexual. Roderick Ferguson offers insight into this paradox: "As figures of nonheteronormative perversions, straight African Americans were reproductive rather than *productive*, heterosexual but never *heteronormative*."[16] Heterosexual blackness not only exists outside of heteronormativity, but queer sexuality has been conceived of as inauthentic to blackness. Patricia Hill Collins discusses a twist in logic that renders blackness inescapably heterosexual:

> Either Black people could not be homosexual or those Blacks who were homosexual were not "authentically" Black. Black people were allegedly not threatened by homosexuality because they were protected by their "natural" heterosexuality.[17]

If blackness is constructed as diametrically opposed to homosexuality, then being black means being heterosexual. This understanding of authentic blackness as naturally heterosexual but not heteronormative situates black queerness as inevitably aberrant. The denial of black homosexuality is linked to black women's sexuality that historically has been produced as insatiable, wanton, and perpetually available to sexual domination and violence.[18]

Black women in the Victorian-era uplift movement designed and enforced a politics of respectability that was initially meant to protect black women from being stigmatized as lascivious and immoral, a pathology that was rooted in chattel slavery. During this period of time, respectable black women upheld strict codes of silence and dissemblance around their own experiences of sexuality and desire in an effort to elevate black women from the status of property to human.[19] This culture of impeccable morality and sexual secrecy, however, further effaced black women's desire.[20] From the black women's club movement to the civil rights movement, discussions of sexuality were silenced in order for black people to attain equal rights of citizenship.[21] Given the contentious sexual landscape in which black women are sexualized into depravity and racialized outside of heteronormativity, Kima's and Snoop's sexualities in *The Wire* are inescapably imbricated in these fraught conceptions of black womanhood.

Along with sexuality, black women's gender has been pathologized as overly aggressive and the catalyst for the demise of the black family. In 1965, sociologist turned senator Daniel Patrick Moynihan published *The Negro Family: The Case for National Action*, which accused the female-headed household of being the fundamental problem with the Negro family:[22] "As a familial formation that 'retards progress' because of its nonheteronormative conformity, the female-headed household impedes the march of civil rights."[23] The Moynihan Report shifted the blame off of racism, capitalism, and patriarchy and onto the backs of black women:

> The problems facing communities of color no longer stem primarily from discrimination but from the characteristics of these communities themselves, from unrestrained sexual behavior and childbirths out of wedlock,

> crime, welfare dependency, and a perverse sense of group identity and group entitlement.[24]

The Wire's representation of Kima's and Snoop's genders and sexualities relies on this type of pathology of black womanhood to produce quality television. Simon's realistic approach calls upon familiar and damaging *knowledge* about black womanhood that has circulated in politics and culture since the time of chattel slavery. The reproduction of stereotypical knowledge of black women's nonheteronormativity through Simon's verisimilitude allows the edge of quality television to be produced through forbidden black sexuality and suspect gender identity. While Kima's and Snoop's sexualities are handled differently because of their gender presentation, both of these characters' queer masculinities tread on taboo ground in the production of scintillating quality television. Kima's masculinity places her in a traditional, dominant, homonormative role in the relationship with her girlfriend Cheryl and also grants her entry into the Baltimore Police Department's old boys' club. Snoop's gender presentation, on the other hand, fits solidly within the realm of masculinity. When characters in the show refer to Snoop as "she," a dissonance occurs that forces Snoop's masculinity out of a presumably male body into a gender-ambiguous one. Snoop's masculinity obscures her legibility as a woman or a man, a reality that makes her sexuality impossible for the show to represent.

In *Female Masculinity*, Jack Halberstam discusses the indelible ties between white maleness, masculinity, legitimacy, and privilege. Halberstam asserts: "Masculinity . . . becomes legible as masculinity where and when it leaves the white male middle-class body."[25] Kima's and Snoop's respective masculinities embody the disaggregation of masculinity and male bodies, exposing the construction of masculinity as an ideological source of power and domination that remains the property of middle-class white men.[26] Kima's masculinity, however, is less effective than Snoop's in upsetting the ideological connections between middle-class white males and masculinity. Kima's black female masculinity retains enough femininity that her womanhood is never called into question and as such does not threaten to displace men from masculinity. By contrast, Snoop's black female masculinity wrests masculinity from male bodies. While Snoop's masculinity does make black female masculinity legible in culture, the show's refusal to depict black female masculine sexuality mars this representation. Snoop's possession of masculinity forecloses the possibility of her having a love life because her gender ambiguity blurs the line between woman and man. Snoop snatches masculinity from the possession of white male bodies but does not deposit it into an easily identifiable woman's body. The dissonance that this ambiguity produces twists Snoop's gender into her sexuality and withholds her black female masculine love life from viewers.[27]

Kima: Lesbian Cop

At the police station, the cops treat Kima like one of the guys. Her lesbian identity, rather than ostracizing her, situates her as a member of the old boys' club in the Baltimore Police Department. Kima's sexy masculinity is commanding yet disarming. She is tough and no-nonsense on the streets and in the squad room. As a detective, she wears pants suits on the job or loose-fitting denim and sweaters. She has long wavy hair that is usually underneath a ball cap or pulled back away from her face. As with many police officers, Kima has to negotiate her love of police work with her partner's desire for her to quit the force for safer, more intellectual endeavors.

Kima proves her allegiance through police work routine to the streets of Baltimore's west side. For example, on a typical day at the towers, one of the housing projects in Baltimore, the midlevel drug dealers manage the yard of young drug dealers and crackheads. When narcotics officers descend, Kima included, drug dealers and drug addicts scatter. Bodie, a midlevel drug dealer, is caught by a narcotics officer who works him over. Kima runs toward Bodie, presumably to rescue him from police brutality. Instead, she joins in the fight, kicking and cursing Bodie as he cradles his body trying to shield himself from the blows.

At home, Kima's lesbian sexuality is made clear by the relationship she has with her girlfriend, Cheryl. There are several sex scenes between Kima and Cheryl in which Kima takes the lead. In the season one episode "Old Cases," Kima and Cheryl lie on the couch in their pajamas. Kima wears a white A-line tank-top and cotton boxer shorts and Cheryl wears a nightgown. As they kiss, Kima moves on top of Cheryl. Kima's lesbian love life with Cheryl and her dominant role in the relationship produce a queer female masculinity that reinforces her position as "one of the guys" on the detective squad. Even though Kima possesses a female masculinity, her gender identity remains clearly within womanhood. Kima is masculine enough to make her inclusion within the old boys' club believable and

Figure 14.1. *The Wire* (2002–2008)

feminine enough that she remains alluring when climbing on top of her girlfriend.

Snoop: Queer Killer

Snoop's character stands in stark contrast to Kima's. Whereas Kima is played by Sonja Sohn, an established Hollywood actor, Snoop is a native of Baltimore's inner city and is not a trained actor; Snoop was cast as part of the show's authentic Baltimore flair. In addition, her character is a member of Marlo Stanfield's drug crew that appears as the younger, wicked rival to the established Barksdale crew, which controls the drug trade in west Baltimore. Because Snoop first appears in several scenes without speaking, it is difficult to decipher her gender; she has masculine body language and wears baggy jeans, jerseys, and T-shirts. While her face is pretty, everything else about Snoop is hardened and masculine. Snoop's initiation into Marlo's crew includes dressing up in an emasculating disguise complete with pink bows in her hair, a pick satin jacket, and denim pedal pushers. In this costume, Snoop rides on the back of a motorcycle and guns down members of the rival Barksdale crew.

Although characters easily refer to Snoop as a woman, her gender identity is ambiguous if not simply accepted as masculine, and even as hypermasculine. The show conflates Snoop's gender and her sexuality; because Snoop is gender-ambiguous and hypermasculine, the narrative expects us to assume that she is lesbian; yet, the only hint about Snoop's sexual desire is a scene in which Snoop and her male partner in crime, Chris, are handcuffed and sitting on the curb after being pulled over by Kima and her partner Bunk. Bunk stands in front of Snoop and Chris, smoking his cigar:

> **Snoop**: Think you all that for hasslin' niggas and shit.
> **Bunk**: I know I'm all that. I'm thinking about some pussy.
> **Snoop**: Yeah me too.

These three words are the only utterances of Snoop's sexuality. Masculine womanhood, however, does not necessarily correlate to lesbian identification. Gender identity and sexuality are distinct as well as overlapping expressions; yet the conflation of gender and sexuality in Snoop's character obscures the complexities of both of them.[28] Snoop's gender ambiguity is constructed to stand in for her lesbian sexuality, which is almost never discussed. Arguably, the absence of Snoop's love life and home life makes the character more menacing and constructs her as the scariest of all bad guys in *The Wire*; her lust for killing is insatiable and remorseless.[29] Snoop's ability to kill concretizes her masculinity and makes the sight of her as ominous as the grim reaper itself.

The tropes of gender-deviant women, cross-dressing men, and transgender characters have been used in the creation of villains throughout American film history: John Huston's 1941 film *The Maltese Falcon*; the

Figure 14.2. *The Wire* (2002–2008)

1950 film *All About Eve*, directed by Joseph L. Mankiewicz; Alfred Hitchcock's 1940 *Rebecca* and his 1960 film *Psycho*; and Jonathan Demme's 1991 film *The Silence of the Lambs*, to name just a few. The horror of villainous characters is intensified by their gender transgression; this device reinforces a presumed oddity of gender deviance and transgender identities. Snoop's ambiguous gender serves to make her character more monstrous and less human. While it may have been a conscious choice to omit any allusions to Snoop's family or a love life, these omissions ultimately avoid depicting the sexuality of a gender queer black character.

Halberstam's concept of transgender butch, "a form of gender transitivity that could be crucial to many butches' sense of embodiment, sexual subjectivity, and even gender legitimacy," offers a way to think through the imbrication of gender and sexuality of queer masculine women like Snoop.[30] Black womanhood complicates Halberstam's notion of transgender butch; crucial to black female masculinity is the struggle black women have faced, both historically and contemporarily, to be considered women.[31] Black transgender butchness produces a tension between retaining contested black womanhood and occupying a gender-ambiguous female masculinity. Black female masculinity as embodied by Snoop tears apart masculinity and white maleness while it evokes the pathological aggressiveness that has historically been attributed to black women's gender identity. That Snoop's gender eclipses her sexuality is indicative of the blurred lines between gender and sexuality as well as of masculinity's ties to white male bodies. Snoop's black gender-ambiguity throws masculinity into disarray, thus contributing to the impossibility of portraying Snoop's sexuality.

Discourse of Reality

In almost every discussion I have had about *The Wire*, whether at a conference or in a casual conversation, people consistently refer to the show as depicting "reality." To the production team's credit, their collective research, writing, and production efforts have masterfully constructed a convincing depiction of Baltimore that resonates as authentic to natives of Baltimore as well as those who may only know the city through this mediated representation.[32] *The Wire* is captivating, provocative, and unnerving because the narrative content combines nodes of real Baltimore street life. This program's focus on a privileged, corrupt few that wield power over an impoverished multitude that is, wittingly or unwittingly, embroiled in perilous drug warfare can stimulate introspection and a renewed sense of community engagement as it simultaneously reproduces stereotypical conceptions of blackness.

This discourse of reality emanates from the "water cooler" and from the set. In a 2007 interview with Brian Lehrer, Felicia "Snoop" Pearson discusses the manner in which David Simon's narrative treatment of Baltimore's crime and corruption is not unlike the reality of surviving Baltimore's perilous street life. Pearson states that "*The Wire* is all reality, they just put it out there that this is what's going on in the world. Either it's in Baltimore, New York, Chicago, wherever, it's going on."[33] Lehrer then interjects, "It's a scripted drama but it's more like a reality show than *American Idol*."[34] Pearson emphatically agrees with Lehrer on this point.[35] Because Pearson was born and raised on the streets from which Simon draws his inspiration, it is difficult to contest her assertion. Pearson's claim that *The Wire* is a portrait of reality is understandable given that few representations of blackness on television detail the complexities of racist systems of oppression with such conviction and depth.

Writing about *The Sopranos*, Dana Polan raises important concerns about scholarly research on the HBO drama series that can be applied to discussions of *The Wire*. He says, "They read past form to imagine that the show enables one to peek into real-life situations and raises moral or philosophical issues that come from the narrative's placing of characters in thematically resonant situations."[36] Polan's concern reveals a problem that is not particular to HBO, quality TV, or *The Wire*: underrepresented communities that are depicted in popular culture, especially in television and film, are often expected to reflect the lived experiences of the communities that they represent. *The Wire* thus serves as a form of entertainment that catches an audience's attention by depicting abhorrent racialized violence and taboo sexual lives of black queer men and women but not without consequences; the social complexity, sexual deviance, and atmosphere of authenticity produces specific knowledge about blackness.

Black cultural production has been plagued by a problematic need to reflect reality. In her discussion of the discourse of reality that frames Spike Lee's films, Wahneema Lubiano examines the expectation of authenticity in African-American cultural representation: "Realism used uncritically as a mode for African-American art implies that our lives can be captured by the presentation of enough documentary evidence or by insistence on another truth."[37] The quest for truth in cultural representations of African-American people derives from a response to generations of Euro-American distortion of African-American people in culture. A mission of African-American cultural producers during the Harlem Renaissance was righting racialized wrongs, a tradition that set the foundation for a black aesthetic dedicated to producing narratives that counter racist depictions of black life.[38] Lubiano identifies a fundamental problem with truth claims: "Realism establishes a claim to truth, but it also presents the ground for its own destruction—somebody else's truth."[39] While the desire to depict the truth has become a facet of black aesthetics, representing black sexuality beyond the scope of eternal heterosexuality is more productive than attempting to divine the truth from narratives of black life. Indeed, the presence of Kima's and Snoop's respective genders and sexualities on *The Wire* not only counters the impossibility of black homosexuality, but the specificities of their genders and sexualities make visible a range of queer possibilities.

The black queer characters on *The Wire* resist heterosexual representations of blackness and contribute to the multiplicity of black sexuality present in popular culture, filling a deficit left by the slew of gay nineties prime-time programs.[40] Yet these black queer characters do not represent the reality of lived experiences of queer black people, following Stuart Hall's insight that popular culture is not where black subjects go to find out who we really are but rather is "a theater of popular desires" in which "we discover and play with the identifications of ourselves, where we are imagined, where we are represented, not only to the audiences out there who don't get the message but to ourselves for the first time."[41] Because of the scarcity of black queer characters written with depth and complexity, an expectation of veracity and a desire for authenticity looms in these characters' shadows. The distinction between enjoying a representation of blackness that expands the scope of black theatricality and visuality and determining that a fictionalized narrative represents reality is crucial in that the former preserves the field of play and the latter runs the risk of collapsing a fruitful and vital expansion of blackness.

Conclusion

Historic constructions of black women's sexual desire and tropes of monstrosity are exploited in order to produce complex narratives that push social and political boundaries to generate edgy, quality television programming through the bodies of Kima and Snoop.[42] *The Wire* expands the confines of quality television as it positions itself squarely within this genre by leveraging black queer female masculinity in the production of sensational narratives and cinematic textures. The presence of a black lesbian Baltimore police detective, and a black, arguably transgender, butch killer for hire in *The Wire* produces, responds to, and complicates the presence of racialized queer characters on quality TV.

As is the case with black women's sexuality, Kima's lesbian sexuality and Snoop's genderqueer identity are encumbered by a history of sexual violence, monstrosity, subhumanity, and sexual depravity. The history of black women's sexuality in the US makes representing black queer women characters a precarious venture, one that treads on the discourse of reality that is imbricated in black cultural production. By making black queer women characters visible, *The Wire* counters misguided notions of blackness being inescapably heterosexual while it also reinscribes the indelibility of masculinity within white male bodies by refusing to represent black female masculine sexuality in culture.

Entering into the terrain of black sexuality ensures that the presence of black queer women in *The Wire* at once achieves racialized sexual diversity in popular culture while it also draws heavily upon the historic abject sexuality of black womanhood in the production of quality television. Story lines that feature Kima and Snoop push the boundaries of television, thus making the narratives more complex and sophisticated, as quality TV demands. The discourse of reality that shrouds representations of marginalized communities, specifically black people, appears as a threshold that must be crossed before it can be set aside. In order to appreciate the "theater of desires" at work in representations of black queer sexuality, blackness must be represented without being representative of a totalizing blackness and without producing knowledge through visceral encounters with sexy, captivating, black queer women characters.

Notes

1. J. C. Freñán, "Interview: David Simon," *Slant*, May 7, 2010, http://www.slantmagazine.com/tv/feature/interview-david-simon/225 (accessed January 17, 2011).

2. "2010 MacArthur Fellows, David Simon: Author, Screenwriter, Producer," MacArthur Foundation, September 28, 2010, http://www.macfound.org/site/c.lkLXJ8MQKrH/b.6241271/k.8712/David_Simon.htm (accessed January 17, 2011).

3. Ron Becker, "Prime-Time Television in The Gay Nineties: Network Television, Quality Audiences, and Gay Politics," *The Velvet Light Trap* 42 (1998): 43.

4. Ibid., 44.

5. Ibid.

6. Ruth Wilson Gilmore, *Golden Gulag: Prisons, Surplus, Crisis, and Opposition in Globalizing California* (Berkeley: University of California Press, 2007), 28. Gilmore defines racism as "the state-sanctioned or extralegal production and exploitation of group-differentiated vulnerability to premature death."

7. While my paper is chiefly concerned with Kima's and Snoop's black queer sexuality, it is important to acknowledge the strides made with the character Omar, an out and proud black gay man. Omar is afforded a love life and respect on the street; he does not hide his sexuality and is allowed to be black, gay, and maintain his masculinity.

8. Although this paper focuses on black queer women and does not attend to the host of castrating black mother characters, I do recognize that the depiction of most of the black mothers in HBO's *The Wire* is problematic, especially in light of the truth claims made about the series.

9. In her article "Is Quality Television Any Good? Gender Distinctions, Evaluations, and the Troubling Matter of Critical Judgment" (in *Quality TV: Contemporary American Television and Beyond*, edited by Janet McCabe and Kim Akass [London: I. B. Tauris, 2007]), Sarah Cardwell contends that a fundamental problem with quality TV is the value judgment implicit in the moniker. Cardwell suggests that quality TV is not synonymous with good TV but rather denotes a set of traits consistent with this kind of programming.

10. Robert J. Thompson, *Television's Golden Age: From* Hill Street Blues *to* ER (New York: Continuum, 1997), 13.

11. Ibid., 14–15.

12. Ibid.

13. Ibid., 16.

14. Janet McCabe and Kim Akass, "Debating Quality," in McCabe and Akass, *Quality TV*, 63, 66.

15. Ibid, 67.

16. Roderick Ferguson, *Aberrations in Black: Toward a Queer of Color Critique* (Minneapolis: University of Minnesota Press, 2004), 87.

17. Patricia Hill Collins, *Black Sexual Politics: African Americans, Gender, and the New Racism* (New York: Routledge, 2005), 105–106.

18. Sojourner Truth's famous "Ain't I a Woman" speech, delivered in 1851 at the Women's Convention in Ohio, addresses the manner in which blackness excludes black women from being considered women. Ferguson's *Aberrations in Black* discusses the manner in which black families exist outside of heteronormativity because of the stigmatized conceptions of blackness that were disseminated in studies like Daniel Patrick Moynihan's 1965 *The Negro Family: The Case for National Action*. The Moynihan Report ultimately blamed black women for the demise of the black family. Patricia Hill Collins's *Black Feminist Thought: Knowledge, Consciousness, and the Politics of Empowerment* (New York: Routledge, 2000) delineates the manner in which black womanhood is constructed as overly aggressive, hypersexual, docile, and caretaking of whiteness. Saidiya V. Hartman's *Scenes of Subjection: Terror, Slavery, and Self-Making in Nineteenth-Century America* (New York: Oxford University Press, 1997) addresses the precarious

position enslaved black women occupied in which they were inherently unrapable during chattel slavery because of being considered property and not human.

19. In *Hine Sight: Black Women and the Re-Construction of American History* (Bloomington: Indiana University Press, 1994), Darlene Clark Hine discusses the manner in which black women's sexuality was forced into concealment during the late nineteenth century and early twentieth century because of Victorian-era codes of womanhood and the legacy of chattel slavery that constructed black womanhood as wanton and lacking morality.

20. Evelynn Hammonds, "Black (W)holes and the Geometry of Black Female Sexuality," *Differences: A Journal of Feminist Cultural Studies* 6, nos. 2–3 (1994): 5.

21. Claudette Colvin, a teenager in 1955, refused to give up her seat on a bus to a white person in Montgomery, Alabama, nine months before Rosa Parks refused to give up her seat on a bus in that same city. After Colvin's arrest, she became pregnant and was considered not to be an appropriate representation for the bus boycott. This account is detailed in Phillip Hoose's *Claudette Colvin: Twice Toward Justice* (New York: Farrar Straus Giroux, 2009) and is the subject of an NPR story by Margot Adler. In his biography of Bayard Rustin (*Lost Prophet: The Life and Times of Bayard Rustin* [New York: Free Press, 2003]), John D'Emilio chronicles the consequences of Rustin's sexuality as it impacted his role in the civil rights movement. For example, after an arrest for sodomy, rather than be exposed as a homosexual, Rustin stepped down from his role as leader of the Southern Christian Leadership Conference.

22. Cited in Ferguson, *Aberrations in Black*, 119.

23. Quoted in ibid., 122.

24. Ibid., 123.

25. Judith Halberstam, *Female Masculinity* (Durham, NC: Duke University Press, 1998), 2.

26. Ibid.

27. For more about black female masculinity in the context of television programming, refer to Kara Keeling, "'We Got Next': The WNBA Advertising Campaign's Negotiations with Femininity," in *Sexual Rhetoric: Media Perspectives on Sexuality, Gender, and Identity*, edited by Meta Carstarphen and Susan Zavoina (Westport, CT: Greenwood Press, 1999), 199–207.

28. In his article "Are Lesbians Women" (*Hypatia* 11, no. 2 [Spring 1996]: 94–121), Jake Hale addresses the cultural and regional specificity that informs gender identity and the manner in which people are gendered through sexuality but that encourages us to attend more carefully to variations of gender identity, as they are not interchangeable or consistent from person to person.

29. I am using the pronoun "she," but I do recognize that "she" does not address Snoop's gender complexity. I am not attempting to simplify Snoop's gender by addressing the character with "she" or "her." If Snoop were written as trans, I would use the pronoun the character uses, but as written the character uses "she," and I will address Snoop with this pronoun throughout the paper. This usage of "she" or "her" does not minimize Snoop's trans identity, and pronoun usage is not the only way to signal trans identity; gender presentation is also a factor.

30. Halberstam, *Female Masculinity*, 144.

31. See Deborah Gray White's *Ar'n't I a Woman? Female Slaves in the Plantation South* (New York: W. W. Norton, 1985) and bell hooks's *Ain't I a Woman: Black Women and Feminism* (Boston: South End Press, 2007) for in-depth discussions of black women's struggles to be recognized as women.

32. See Tim Goodman, "Yes, HBO's 'Wire' Is Challenging. It's Also a Masterpiece," SFGate.com, September 6, 2006, http://articles.sfgate.com/2006-09-06/entertainment/17312122_1_wire-storytelling-desperate-housewives (accessed January 19, 2011); Rick Kushman, "A Fond Farewell to HBO's 'The Wire,'" *Miami Herald*, March 7, 2008, http://www.miamiherald.com/2008/03/07/447957/a-fond-farewell-to-hbos-the-wire.html (accessed January 19, 2001).

33. "Felicia 'Snoop' Pearson: My Life Is Like 'The Wire,'" YouTube, 00:02:40, wync-radio, December 17, 2007, http://www.youtube.com/watch?v=GvVLJIJIOJw (accessed January 17, 2011).

34. Ibid.

35. Ibid.

36. Dana Polan, "Cable Watching: HBO, *The Sopranos*, and Discourses of Distinction," in *Cable Visions: Television Beyond Broadcasting*, edited by Sarah Banet-Weiser, Cynthia Chris, and Anthony Freitas (New York: New York University Press, 2007), 268.

37. Wahneema Lubiano, "But Compared to What?: Reading Realism, Representation, and Essentialism in *School Daze*, *Do the Right Thing*, and the Spike Lee Discourse," *Black American Literature Forum* 25, no. 2 (1991): 263.

38. Ibid.

39. Ibid.

40. Becker, "Prime-Time Television in The Gay Nineties," 43.

41. Stuart Hall, "What Is This Black in Black Popular Culture," in *Black Popular Culture*, edited by Gina Dent and Michelle Wallace (New York: New Press, 1983), 32.

42. Thompson, *Television's Golden Age*, 14–15.

PART V Fandom and Transmedia

FIFTEEN

Resurrection of the Vampire and the Creation of Alternative Life

An Introduction to *Dark Shadows* Fan Culture

HARRY M. BENSHOFF

In recent years, the examination of fan culture has become an increasingly important aspect of popular culture studies. Previous work done on fan culture situates and privileges fan activity as a model of active spectatorship. As Henry Jenkins has noted:

> One becomes a "fan" not by being a regular viewer of a particular program but by *translating that viewing into some kind of cultural activity*, by sharing feelings and thoughts about the program content with friends, by joining a "community" of other fans who share common interests.[1]

In attempting to counter monolithic models of popular culture that descend from the Frankfurt School's hypodermic injection model, recent studies in popular culture have drawn on the work of a wide array of theorists, including Antonio Gramsci, Roland Barthes, and Michel de Certeau. What these studies have suggested is that the rereading, rewriting, and reappropriation of specific mass media texts exemplifies a dynamic two-way model of popular culture, one in which viewers are more empowered than has hitherto been thought. As one self-professed fan has noted: "Some nay-sayers may claim that people have no imagination or creativity anymore. Fans by nature deny that opinion."[2]

There are those who still might question the validity of academic investigation into popular culture artifacts such as soap operas. Besides dem-

Figure 15.1. *Dark Shadows* (1966–1971)

onstrating an elitist bias against mass-produced artifacts, the opponents of such a study might argue (à la Theodor Adorno) that the culture industry cannot help but produce artifacts which reinscribe dominant ideology, leaving no room for individualized response or subversive readings. For example, Tania Modleski has pointed out how the television soap opera may simultaneously speak to some women in ways that may empower them as viewers, yet ultimately functions to keep them firmly situated within the home.[3] In contrast, this essay draws upon concepts of Gramscian hegemony and post-Althusserian ideology for its conceptual framework. It views popular culture as an arena wherein different ideas and ideologies may circulate, coexist, and even conflict. According to this position, it is the nature of the cultural hegemony to negotiate with subaltern groups, rather than merely absorb or obliterate them. Although the sites of these intersections are frequently confused and contradictory, they nonetheless demonstrate active struggle within the culture over topics such as traditional gender roles, sexuality, community, and history.

Dark Shadows fan culture serves as an exemplary model for such processes of hegemonic negotiation. This essay is based on ethnographic data collected over a period of two years, including interviews and correspondence with fans, and a look at other available fan productions such as fanzines and videotapes. In addition, I have drawn heavily on approximately fifty detailed survey response questionnaires, which I recently circulated through *DS* fandom via one of its leading fanzines. Responses came back to me from all over the world, and almost all participants were very willing to talk at length about their interest in *Dark Shadows*. Note: this methodology is in no way meant to endorse a simple belief in empiricism or objectivity. The ethnographic "ideal" of an outside objective interpreter (which I reject outright as mythic) is further subverted by the fact that I too consider myself to be a *DS* fan. Rather than invalidate my observations on *DS* fandom, however, I feel that this stance openly rejects the pretense of objectivity, while simultaneously allowing my readers to benefit from an "insider's" perspective. My observations thus partake actively of fan culture but also hopefully maintain a certain theoretical distanciation. In so doing I hope to provide a richer and more detailed description of the phenomenon under question.

The Text(s)

Dark Shadows was perhaps the world's first (and only?) daily serial to feature vampires, werewolves, witches, and warlocks as leading characters. The show also dabbled in time travel and parallel universes, frequently creating a televisual analog to the literary historical romance. The thirty-minute show ran on ABC-TV on weekday afternoons from 1966 to 1971, a total of 1,225 episodes. The series inspired two feature films, *House of Dark Shadows* (1970) and *Night of Dark Shadows* (1971). It was also marketed vigorously as a series of thirty-two paperback novels by Marilyn Ross, not to mention the merchandising of *Dark Shadows* games, comic books, (hit) records, wristwatches, posters, postcards, magazines, masks, models, music boxes, puzzles, Viewmasters, chewing gum, and even a *Dark Shadows* cookbook. Most recently, as nineties pop culture becomes ever more infused with a postmodernist sensibility, *Dark Shadows* was resurrected in yet another incarnation: an hour-long, prime-time, weekly television series on NBC, newly repackaged by original producer Dan Curtis.[4] MPI Video has also begun to market videotapes of the original daytime soap opera; if all the original episodes are released, there will be over 200 two-hour tapes available.

Immediately one can see that the idea of a single, static, original "text" is undercut by the fact that *Dark Shadows* exists as a plethora of mass-produced tie-ins and spin-offs. (The very nature of daily serial television also undercuts the classical notion of textuality: this is a format which constantly denies any form of narrative closure.) Added to this multiplicity is the presence of *Dark Shadows* fan culture itself: today, over twenty years since the original show was canceled, *DS* "fandom" is still thriving, not as a monolithic spectator community based around a daily viewing event, but as an active and loose coalition of individuals and organizations across the United States. Many *DS* fans produce newsletters or fictional "fanzines" based upon the show and its characters. Others contribute stories, drawings, and songs to fanzines, form fan clubs, or produce amateur theatricals and videotapes. As this essay will demonstrate, this creative fan output varies a great deal. What *DS* fandom does provide for all of its members is an open forum wherein fans may share their ideas about the show and communicate with like-minded individuals on similar topics.

DS Fans and the Appeal of *DS*

Obviously, *DS* fans come in all shapes and sizes, ages, sexes, classes, colors, and sexualities. The singular appeal of the show, however, remains elusive. Obviously, there is a whole constellation of factors to which the fans respond. Many report enjoying the blend of Gothicism with the soap opera format, often citing the suspense generated by the show's use of daily cliffhangers. Another fan "really like[s] the show because it . . . always explored the occult in such a serious way: Egyptian mythology, I-ching, time travel." It is not uncommon to find fans who are interested in alternate religions, witchcraft, and/or vampirism in their "real" lives, while others value *DS* for its depiction of "a pure and complete fantasy world."[5] The great majority report that they are attracted to vampirism as a central theme, and many cite Anne Rice's vampire novels as among their favorite books.[6] These books make vampirism a romantic and/or explicitly erotic physical condition. And while the latent/blatant sexuality of the *DS* characters holds a special appeal for many viewers, there were those who (during the show's initial run) championed it precisely because it was "not like all the other [soaps] during the day, with all the sex, abortion, and illegal pregnancies."[7]

Perhaps most interestingly, many fans today cite a complex interplay of character, actor, diegesis, and extradiegetic pleasure as the chief appeal of *DS*. Cassandra Amesley, in her work on *Star Trek*, observes that its fans are able to respond to the diegetic world of *Star Trek* while simultaneously engaging in a meta-critical discourse regarding the show's stars, production values, plot mechanisms, etc.[8] *DS* fans also seem to engage in this sort of "double viewing." While many fans (even today) still find the show's chief appeal to be straightforward and diegetically centered ("A beautiful romantic gothic horror fantasy"), others celebrate its campy strained seriousness and technical shortcomings. Results such as these obviously problematize theories of popular culture which posit a universal subject constructed by the text. One fan summed up both appeals in one well-worded response: *DS* is an "excellent combination of campy soap opera and classic gothic horror." Likewise: "Now I appreciate the show's campiness and (strangely at the same time) the emotional depth and pathos of some of its characters and stories." Thus it appears that even individual subjects may relate to the show in seemingly contradictory ways.

The majority of *DS* fans that I surveyed fell into an age group of approximately twenty-five to forty years, people who had grown up watching the show during its initial run. Besides the expected soap opera audience of housewives (and to a lesser extent college students), *DS* was also watched by children of all ages.[9] Many *DS* fans told me that while growing up they felt like outsiders and that *DS* afforded them a place of comfort and/or a fantasy of power.[10] The following statements reflect the perceived need of the fans to find an alternative society, and their gratefulness in finding a home at Collinwood:

> "Life seemed less complex when we were able to visit there."
> "It was moody and gothic and the characters became my friends."
> "I longed for supernatural powers 'cause I hated my body perhaps."
> "Collinwood was my home. I remember it with *great* fondness."
> "Probably one of the most important programs of my formative years."

A nostalgic yearning for an accepting community must thus be figured as yet another appeal of the text. Perhaps the continuing interest in the show is somewhat dependent upon the reimagining of Collingwood as a place/state of happy childhood.[11]

As might be suspected from these findings, *DS* also holds a special appeal for gay and lesbian individuals. One fan noted, "I could probably predict that there is a higher percentage of gays and lesbians in *DS* fandom than the average population. And that would probably be attributable to the fact that [gay] people have more of an aesthetic interest than the general population." Although this comment reflects an essentialist (and certainly arguable) notion of what might be involved in the description of a gay sensibility, it nevertheless raises issues of how social marginalization bears on fan status and how these issues are read by the popular culture at large.[12] Henry Jenkins has asserted that:

> Fandom is a vehicle for marginalized subcultural groups (women, the young, gays, and so on) to pry open space for their cultural concerns within dominant representations; fandom is a way of appropriating media texts and rereading them in a fashion that serves different interests, a way of transforming mass culture into popular culture.[13]

Jenkins argues that the negative mass media stereotyping of fans is the result of a complex negotiation between marginalized societal groups and the dominant hegemonic mass culture. "That our stereotype of the fan is often either an overweight weepy woman or a nerdy and undersexed man speaks to the links within popular discourse between textual proximity and misogynistic conceptions of 'femininity.'"[14] The surveys compiled for this essay suggest the accuracy of these statements: for some people, the word "fan" has become demonized. One respondent balked at the word, which she clearly felt had pejorative connotations: "I'm *not* a *fanatic*. I try to keep levelheaded." However, this same viewer also noted that she would "give my right arm to have the new show back" and characterizes her present *DS* viewing habits as "Watch, think, rewind, rewatch." Her statements make her sound like a "fanatic" even if she denies the term. She seems to partake of the overriding cultural condemnation of fandom even as she embraces its practices.

DS Fan Clubs and Conventions

Many *DS* fans have sought and found alternative communities in the "real" world (as well as on TV) by participating in *DS* fan clubs.[15] Certainly *DS* fan clubs existed during the show's initial run; according to oral fan history, there has never been a period of time when there was no organized fan activity surrounding the show. Precursors of present-day fan clubs appeared in 1971, immediately following the cancellation of the series. As of this writing, "The World of *Dark Shadows*" fanzine lists about twenty different *DS* fan clubs in existence across the United States.[16]

Just how does one go about creating a fan club? One such individual decided to form a fan club after attending a *DS* convention in 1986. He had noticed that there were many single men and women at the convention. He admits to an ulterior motive behind his efforts: to provide an alternative to bars and nightclubs wherein he might bring together and meet people with common interests. He ran newspaper and TV ads and began to attract *DS* fans to meetings and parties at his home. Soon there were too many people to accommodate at home and outside space had to be obtained for the meetings. For this individual, running the *DS* fan club was "a labor of love." Despite the social nature of these groups, there is frequently an aversion to manifest politicking: "I tend to shy away from being opinionated or having a political interest in the whole fandom." The rewards of *DS* fandom may thus be tied into idealized feelings of community and dreams of social utopia. "Our fan club has been really great—it's gay and straight, there's married couples and kids, and everybody seems to accept everybody very well and get along. It's really nice to see everybody integrated and sort of a community instead of having to have separate this and separate that."

Fan conventions might be likened to extended fan club meetings. They have become a national affair, with Los Angeles and New York City (as well as Newark, New Jersey) serving as the recent sites of two- to three-day *DS* conventions throughout the 1980s. At most conventions, one can find dealers in *DS* memorabilia, costume contests, screenings of *DS* episodes and the two *DS* movies, blooper reels, skits, and trivia contests. However, the highlights of the conventions are usually the extended reminiscence/question-and-answer sessions with *DS* actors and technicians. The *DS* cast has, as a whole, been quite faithful to the fan following; almost all who are still living regularly appear at fan conventions. They seem to be tireless in recounting old memories, signing autographs, and answering questions. Often the conventions are videotaped and distributed in that format. As do local fan club meetings, national conventions provide a chance for the fans to meet face to face, as opposed to the mail-based networking that fanzines afford.

DS Fanzines

Fanzines can range from a few Xeroxed sheets announcing a fan club meeting to a slickly produced and desktop-published *DS* novel. Most fall somewhere in between and usually feature both fan productions (such as fiction, drawings, and poems[17]) as well as reproduced news items about cast members, convention reports, upcoming events, etc. The most highly processed fanzine that I have encountered, *The World of Dark Shadows*, is published by Kathleen Resch of Temple City, California. Due to the current revival of interest in *DS*, *The World of Dark Shadows* has recently begun publishing double issues, making each issue almost 200 pages long. There are regular question-and-answer columns, recurrent "Bloopers" sections, letters columns, and unique features such as "The Collinsport Debating Society," a "what if . . . ?" type column wherein fans discuss alternative meanings and possible narratives that arise from their ideas about the text(s). Fans are now almost as likely to comment on fan-produced material as they are likely to discuss the original text(s).[18]

Henry Jenkins has noted the many different ways fans can choose to rewrite their original text(s), including eroticization, personalization (the dreaded "Mary Sue" stories), recontextualization, and genre shifting.[19] Analysis of the short stories included in two recent issues of *The World of Dark Shadows* reveals an interest in certain recurring themes familiar to the original text(s): vampirism, time travel, romance, and love as a force capable of transcending time and history. Barnabas Collins (or vampirism) figures prominently in most of these stories. Most are written in an omniscient narrative style, although a few experiment with first-person narration, one even attempting the distinctive broken vocal inflections of (*DS* character) Willie Loomis. The majority of the stories are serious in tone and are written by women; conversely, most of the stories with a comedic edge are written by men, although there are certainly exceptions to all of these generalizations. Many of the stories describe vampirism in erotic terms. This excerpt is from a first-person story, written by a man, entitled "To Serve Her" (the vampiric Angelique):

> She stroked my head as she held it and I knew that her mind was further entering mine. I could feel her inside me becoming part of me more and more. It was terrifying and yet I was uncontrollably excited by it and even satiated in a primal, emotional way. . . . Once more I held onto her as I licked the running blood up her body and buried my face between her breasts. She in turn coiled her arms around me and began stroking my back with her hands while making low groaning sounds. I sucked her blood ravenously.[20]

In an interesting blur of gender, in this story it is the man who is penetrated by a female vampire. Other stories soften the vampire's animalistic magnetism into romantic longing. Generally speaking, the stories by women seem to be less sexually explicit than those by men, although one novella by two women entitled *Are Old Acquaintances Best Forgotten?* is self-described as "an adult fanzine [that] will not be knowingly sold to anyone under twenty-one years of age." It too contains many of the requisite thematic elements: time travel, and a focus on Barnabas and his newest reincarnated love. However, the novella seems hardly more "adult" than the above story excerpt.

As is typical of many *DS* fans, the author of *Are Old Acquaintances Best Forgotten?* seems almost apologetic about her work, reluctant to offend:

> Adult writing is often a matter of opinion, and what is "fluff" to one person is "smut" to another. I don't know how you'd classify the sexual situations in my 'zine. I tried to be as tasteful as possible. The 'zine was read by three high school students (without my knowledge until it was too late) who thought that the scenes were no worse than things they had seen on afternoon soap opera. On the other hand, I had a friend tell me it was "filthy."[21]

It seems that different fandoms cater to specific tastes; some are more adult in nature, other remaining resolutely "PG-13." Reportedly, the fandom surrounding the recent television version of *Beauty and the Beast* has given rise to a lot of erotic fanzine activity, but there seems to be less adult material produced in *DS* fandom. Slashzines based on *DS* characters (if they exist) are hard to find. "Slashzines" are fan-produced fictions that posit a homosexual relationship between the two male leads on a particular television show: in the case of *Star Trek*, K/S slashzines depict a love affair between Kirk and Spock. Constance Penley, in her groundbreaking research, has reported that these stories are produced mostly by and for heterosexual female fans, arguing that they reconfigure heterosexual masculinity through a homosexual matrix.[22] Many *DS* fans interviewed for this essay had not heard of slashzines.

Slashzine or fanzine, however, *DS* fan fiction often does explore and expand ideas otherwise latent within the original text. One such story, entitled "The Challenge of Her Destiny," deals with reincarnation and the ability of love to transcend time.[23] It negotiates many issues surrounding sexuality, gender roles, and historical progress. Primarily, the story is a dialogue set in Heaven in 1839 between the spirit of Julia Hoffman and the angel Gabriel. Julia's spirit is concerned with being reincarnated so that she may return to Earth with her soul mate, who has been reincarnated as the vampire Barnabas Collins. Gabriel hits upon a plan to send Julia back to Earth in the twentieth century where she might train to be a doctor and thus cure Barnabas of his "blood disease."

> "I . . . I see," she said, slowly. "But . . . there are no doctors who are women. Are you suggesting that I change my—"
>
> "No dear lady, I am not," he chuckled, amused. "I must tell you that the time is coming when there will be many changes on Earth. Women will begin to do things that they have never been allowed to do before."[24]

The possibility of homosexuality is raised but dismissed with an amused chuckle. More interesting is the postulation of history as a model of progressive change: Julia must wait until the twentieth century to be reincarnated as a doctor, because the idea is unthinkable in 1839.

However, Gabriel acknowledges the sexism inherent in even the twentieth-century medical institution: "You will have to make up your mind to be a doctor, in a time when it is not quite yet very widely accepted. There will be scorn, ridicule, and opposition, from friends and family as well as teachers and co-workers. They will tell you that it is a woman's place to be a nurse, not a doctor. They will say that a woman cannot handle being a doctor."[25]

Gabriel tells Julia that she may have to "become cold, and hard . . . a bossy unpleasant woman" just to get through the ordeal of medical training. He warns her that this might have an adverse effect on Barnabas: "a strong, argumentative woman would bring much of his fear to the surface, and excite his anger." Interestingly, in another example of the blurring of essentialist gender roles, Barnabas is somewhat feminized in this particular story: following his portrayal on the show, he is a creature of whims and moods, natural cycles, with a tendency towards "over-romanticizing everything." Julia acknowledges his weaknesses, especially those inherent in his "Josette fixation," but insists on being strong for both of them.

Ultimately, Julia accepts "The Challenge of Her Destiny," and the story ends with a coda set in 1942 in which the teenage Julia tells her family that she wants to become a doctor. This story does address the nature of sexism within society, but also posits a historical cure for it: in time, things will get better. Julia is shown to be a strong and determined woman of means. Yet, somewhat problematically perhaps, the only reason offered by the author for Julia's future interest in medicine is her "superhuman love" for Barnabas: she wants to study medicine in order to cure him and facilitate a happy ending through idealized romantic coupling.[26] Like Janice Radway's romance readers, readers of "The Challenge of Her Destiny" may find issues of history, gender roles, and sexuality being addressed, but ultimately they may be more or less trapped within the fortress of patriarchal ideology.[27]

Other *DS* Fan Productions

Like other fan cultures, *DS* fandom has its share of creative fan productions besides those of fiction, poetry, and artwork.[28] Most of these have been made possible in recent years by the development of home video and audio technologies. Filksongs, for example, are the musical equivalent of fan fiction.[29] *DS* filksongs feature lyrics based on *DS* characters set to original music or preexisting tunes. The lyrics to one such tune were recently printed in *The World of Dark Shadows*: they recount the future fate of Collinwood in 1995 to the tune of "Creeque Alley."[30] Filksongs can be purchased on cassettes at conventions or by mail, or they can be sold as song sheets. One ad states: "These filksong books, first published about ten years ago, feature serious and humorous words to all types of music: folk/traditional, show tunes, holiday, popular, C/W, and special interest songs—even children's tunes and nursery rhymes."[31]

Music videos are another type of fan production. Basically, these are videos created by laboriously splicing together favorite scenes from the show with a new extradiegetic selection of music. For example, a compendium of action scenes may be edited briskly and set to "Ghostbusters" or "The Theme from *Miami Vice*," or scenes of Angelique may be cut together and accompanied by The Cars' "Tonight She Comes."[32] One can also buy "near exact replicas" of wooden signs that say THE BLUE WHALE or COLLINSPORT INN, personal stationery with "Collins Enterprises" letterhead, bumper stickers, and three-inch acrylic photo ornaments "suitable for Christmas trees or use as key chains." Amateur theatricals are another popular form of fan production. Often fans will perform favorite scenes at conventions or fan club meetings. This phenomenon reportedly led to an off-off-Broadway production of *Dark Shadows* a few years ago.

Still other fans turn to videotape to record their theatricals. One of the most charming and unique of these, "Baby *Dark Shadows*," was made by Richard Halpern, a Los Angeles–based fan. With the aid of his young niece and nephews, Halpern staged and videotaped favorite scenes from the show. The effect of "Baby *Dark Shadows*" is one of gentle parody. Frequently Halpern himself gets into the act by playing Grayson Hall as Dr. Julia Hoffman, as well as her 1795 incarnation, the Countess DuPres. Other fan videos can be even more elaborate. *A Doctor Remembers* is a twenty-minute faux-documentary made in 1985 by Tom Soderberg and Owen Robertson. In it, Dr. Julia Hoffman (played by Soderberg) reminisces about her years spent in Collinwood.

Both of these videos demonstrate the strong appeal that Grayson Hall held and still holds for many of her fans. The fact that male fans have taken to impersonating her raises yet again more questions surrounding gender roles and sexuality in *DS* fandom. Grayson Hall's strong, independent female characters (both on and off the series) and her broadly mannered acting style have made her a figure ripe for much camp reappropriation. Her gender-bending appeal is often cited in fan fiction: Dr. Hoffman's "voice was softly husky, deeper than most women's, but not at all masculine. . . . She was a lady, in the proper sense of the word."[33] Doubtless her Academy Award–nominated appearance in 1964's *Night of the Iguana* as a lesbian schoolteacher adds yet another level of intertextual appeal to her persona.

A Doctor Remembers works in ways similar to a drag cabaret act for those in the know. The tape is full of witty (inter)textual references. Julia mentions that she is up for a part in Aaron Spelling's newest TV show, *Dark Mansions*, and an alleged photo of her father, "Judge Herman Hoffman," shows *DS* cast member Louis Edmonds as he was then appearing on another soap opera. Julia tells us that Vicky has run off with a millionaire who supposedly murdered his wife.[34] Soderberg-as-Hoffman satirizes many of the show's more outlandish credibility gaps in a deadpan style of delivery. Standing in the woods between Collinwood and the Old House, Julia remembers how she used to go from "one house to the other, one house to the other, one house to the other . . . at the end of a busy night I'd go to bed quite dizzy." The sign for Julia's Hospital, Wyndcliffe Sanitarium, reads A NICE PLACE TO GO INSANE. Julia also discusses her ability to wear so many different hats: "You see, besides being an MD, blood specialist, biologist, and family historian, I'm also a licensed psychologist." Ultimately, Julia confesses to the camera and comes to "realize and confront the truth, that yes, I had a love-jones" (for Barnabas).

Despite its camp tone, *A Doctor Remembers* raises many of the same issues as did the short story "The Challenge of Her Destiny." Both productions focus on Julia, her difficulty in overcoming patriarchal oppression in becoming a professional woman, and her unrequited love for Barnabas. The two works are interesting to compare because *A Doctor Remembers* ostensibly represents a (gay?) male POV while the story "The Challenge of Her Destiny" is written by a (straight?) female. Whereas the written story posits a transcendent love affair between Barnabas and Julia as the necessary force behind her choice of medical career, the video Julia becomes a doctor because she wants to be one, not because she has any prescient plan to save Barnabas from the curse of vampirism. Thus, on the level of narrative, the video version of Julia Hoffman appears to be less trapped within the patriarchal hegemony. On the other hand, a feminist argument against the male drag of *A Doctor Remembers* might also be invoked: here we see men performing as women in order to (1) allegedly make fun of them, and (2) show them the proper way to be "independent" (as in Sydney Pollack's *Tootsie* [1982]). There *is* an element of cruelty in Soderberg's satire of Grayson Hall, yet at the same time the tape is dedicated "In Loving Memory of Grayson." Like many points of cultural negotiation, the artifacts themselves are frequently overdetermined and contradictory.

There is another difference between the taped (male) Julia and the written (female) Julia. Although both Julias are resigned to Barnabas's preference for young ingénues, the written Julia continues to fight for her man against all odds, even against Heaven and Earth. The taped Julia is less overtly romantic. Indeed, the overall camp tone of *A Doctor Remembers* quite effectively deflates the overweening romanticism of "The Challenge of Her Destiny." The taped Julia finds nonromantic relationships to be equally meaningful: "I was always there for [Barnabas], even after Vicky left, and he found other Josette substitutes. But I really didn't mind. He could be so kind and gentle sometimes, and we were always the best of friends." The tape concludes with the lines: "Memory and old friends . . . I can't think of a better prescription." The sentiment echoes those of other fans quoted above, those who also find memory and friendship to be among the most pleasurable aspects of both *DS* and *DS* fandom.

Conclusion

Throughout this essay, I have tried to let the fans speak for themselves whenever possible. Often their lived experiences are far more eloquent and revealing than any amount of academic theorizing, or my own highly subjective musings based upon a fraction of the total evidence. There exists a multitude of very different *DS* fans, and I do not want to be mistaken for trying to argue that any one perspective on *DS* fandom is somehow more "true" or more correct than any other. That would be foolish and overreaching in light of the highly individualized nature of most fan productions.

Hopefully, what I have demonstrated is that for many of its participants, *DS* fandom functions as an alternative community—one that exists primarily on paper, or on video, or in fan clubs, or in shared thoughts. It is a community cherished by many of its members as a refuge from a larger society of which they often feel less enamored. This alternative community might be understood as a communication network through which people rewrite and respeak *Dark Shadows* in order to manifestly negotiate issues (such as but not limited to historical progress, sexuality, or feminism) that were inherent but latent within the original text(s). Concomitantly, the endless play of the *DS* signifiers that fandom celebrates affords a very definite pleasure to the fans. Like a set of building blocks or a deck of cards, *DS* characters, stories, and themes are endlessly transmutable: each recombination affords new pleasure while simultaneously recalling memories of past pleasure. And while fans may be acutely aware of the opprobrium heaped upon them by mass culture at large, they seem to hold faith in a utopian concept of community based upon shared common interests. *DS* fandom is a place where a forty-three-year-old "married, conservative" man from Texas, identifying with (*DS* character) "Joe Haskell—[the] clean cut boy next door [and his] wholesome romance with Maggie Evans," can find common ground with a lesbian fan who disdains the "too normal and adamant about it" characters in favor of the "vulnerable, obsessed, tormented, peculiar, hiding something—in other words interesting" characters. Perhaps the creation of that privileged common ground is ultimately the most important thing that *DS* fandom can and does provide.

Notes

1. Henry Jenkins, "*Star Trek* Rerun, Reread, Rewritten: Fan Writing as Textual Poaching," in *Close Encounter: Film, Feminism, and Science Fiction*, edited by Constance Penley, Liz Lyon, Lynn Spigel, and Janet Bergstrom (Minneapolis: University of Minnesota Press, 1991), 175 (emphasis added).

2. Kathleen Resch, ed., *The World of Dark Shadows* (fanzine published in Temple City, CA) nos. 59–60 (June 1991): 142.

3. Tania Modleski, *Loving with a Vengeance* (New York: Routledge, 1982), 85–109.

4. The show lasted only twelve episodes. See Jim Pierson, *Dark Shadows Resurrected* (Los Angeles: Pomegranate Press, Ltd., 1992), for a discussion of how fans were instrumental in bringing the show back to network television and, once there, trying to keep it on the air.

5. The *Dark Shadows* Fan Club of Southern California has a member who professes to be a vampire.

6. As of this writing [1993], Anne Rice's vampire books include *Interview with the Vampire* (1976), *The Vampire Lestat* (1985), *Queen of the Damned* (1988), and *The Tale of the Body Thief* (1992).

7. Quoted in Joan Barthel, "Out in Detergent Land: A Hard Day's Fright," *New York Times*, July 30, 1967.

8. For a more in-depth analysis of double viewing, see Cassandra Amesley, "How to Watch Star Trek," *Cultural Studies* 3, no. 3 (October 1989): 323–339.

9. This was a fact the network producers were not unaware of during the initial run of the show: *DS* was always scheduled in the late afternoon to allow children the opportunity to watch the show after returning home from school.

10. Previously I have discussed the appeal of *DS* in psychoanalytic terms: I argue that its monstrous characters serve as displacement figures that provide a power fantasy wish fulfillment for otherwise disempowered viewers.

11. Interestingly, *Dark Shadows* wasn't the only show that provided this sort of haven for television viewers seeking alternative communities. One fan reported: "I think *The Munsters* and *The Addams Family* were wonderful examples of happily functioning families. They always got along and were very loving towards themselves and the community. Being gay myself, I feel different as a minority functioning in the world. I think these families were positive role models for me: here's something different functioning in the real world and enjoying it and dealing with it, and it gave me hope that I could be different and live in the general world too." Thus, while some critics may argue that shows such as these merely replicate dominant ideology, it seems apparent that some viewers found within them viable models for celebrating oppositional ideologies.

12. Gay and lesbian participation in fan cultures is a well-documented phenomenon. For example, there is a national science fiction club known as the "Gaylactic Network," which produces its own texts dealing with homosexuality in a science fiction setting.

13. Jenkins, "*Star Trek* Rerun, Reread, Rewritten," 174.

14. Henry Jenkins, "'If I Could Speak with Your Sound': Fan Music, Textual Proximity, and Liminal Identification," *Camera Obscura* 23 (May 1991): 169.

15. This is obviously easier for some fans than others. Several respondents reported that even during the show's initial run, they used it as a springboard for social activities: "I would talk to a guy at school about it—a little fellow was he." Others still lament their status of being on "the outside": "Where are all the fans, clubs, conventions I hear about? I don't know anyone to watch it with or talk about it with except him." Despite their popularity, fan clubs and fanzines are still something of an underground culture: they would doubtless lose some of their appeal if they appeared too mainstream.

16. The majority of these fan clubs are regional clubs ("The Dark Shadows Fan Club of St. Louis"), although there are also clubs devoted to specific actors associated with the show ("The David Selby Fan Club").

17. There is a high degree of intertextuality in the stories and cartoons produced by the fans. *Doctor Who* seems to be a text that recurs in much fan discourse; both *Doctor Who* and *DS* share the subject of time travel. Both shows configure history as something that can be changed for the better when the right person goes back in time to "fix" it. (*Twin Peaks* has also been incorporated into several cartoons.)

18. *The World of Dark Shadows* features a wide array of advertisements for other fan-produced writing: more fanzines such as *Shadowgram*, *Wyndcliffe Watch*, *Shadows of the*

Night, and *Echoes . . . From the Past*; "*DS* Concordances" (which synopsize the plot of the show episode by episode and are illustrated with fan drawings); and novels such as *Beginnings: The Island of Ghosts*. Many of these writings are produced by editor Kathleen Resch, who by this point must surely be considered a cottage industry in and of herself. In 1990, Resch and fellow fans Melody Clark and Marcy Robin (who edits *Shadowgram*) crossed the fan/professional authorship boundary when their article "The *Dark Shadows* History" appeared in Pomegranate Press's gift book *The Dark Shadows Companion: 25th Anniversary Collection*.

19. Henry Jenkins, *Textual Poachers* (New York: Routledge, 1992). Jenkins also lists expanding the original texts' timelines, refocalization, moral realignment, crossovers, character dislocation, and emotional intensification as other tropes of fan writing.

20. Rob Haycock, "To Serve Her," *The World of Dark Shadows*, nos. 57–58 (1991): 138–139.

21. Personal communication, fall 1991.

22. Constance Penley, "Brownian Motion: Women, Tactics, and Technology," in *Techno-Culture*, edited by Constance Penley and Andrew Ross (Minneapolis: University of Minnesota Press, 1991), 135–162. See also Constance Penley, "Feminism, Psychoanalysis, and the Study of Popular Culture," in *Cultural Studies*, edited by Lawrence Grossberg, Cary Nelson, and Paula Treichler (New York: Routledge, 1992), 479–500.

23. May Sutherland, "The Challenge of Her Destiny," *The World of Dark Shadows*, nos. 59–60 (June 1991): 103–114.

24. Ibid., 110.

25. Ibid.

26. Here we can clearly see how *DS* taps into the appeal of the literary romance genre as outlined by Janice Radway in her book *Reading the Romance*. Like the novels that Radway examines, *DS* also features an ever-deepening romantic relationship between hero and heroine (Barnabas and Julia, or perhaps Barnabas and Angelique), though of course the happy closure of either of these relationships is denied by the openness of the soap opera form. See Janice Radway, *Reading the Romance* (Chapel Hill: University of North Carolina Press, 1984), especially chapter 4, "The Ideal Romance: The Promise of Patriarchy," 119–156.

27. Janice Radway, "Interpretive Communities and Variable Literacies: The Functions of Romance Reading," *Daedalus* 113, no. 3 (Summer 1984).

28. Plus there are many instances of less tangible ways in which the *DS* text(s) influences people's lives. One fan named his pet lizards after Quentin Collins and Count Petofi. Another designed a dollhouse modeled on Rose Cottage. Still others create period apparel based upon costumes from the show.

29. According to oral history, the name "Filk" arose from a typographical error with the word "Folk." The fans seemed to like the neologism, and it has remained in the discourse ever since. Jenkins, "If I Could Speak with Your Sound . . . ," note 7.

30. Resch, ed. *The World of Dark Shadows*, 128.

31. Ibid., 161.

32. Again, there seems to be less impulse in *DS* fandom than in science-fiction fandom towards editing clips together in order to de-repress the homoerotic impulse

of the show's male-bonded couples. See Jenkins, *Textual Poachers*, especially chap. 7, "'Layers of Meaning': Fan Music Video and the Poetics of Poaching," 223–249.

33. Sutherland, "The Challenge of Her Destiny," 105.

34. Actress Alexandra Moltke [Isles], who played governess Vicky Walters, was the alleged "other woman" in the Claus von Bülow trial. This fact is common knowledge among *DS* fans; some even have the footage of "Vicky" at the von Bülow trial, recorded from television's *A Current Affair* show. *A Doctor Remembers* plays on this fact as well as the *DS* diegesis when it reports that "Vicky was never good at trials." Vicky had been on trial for witchcraft in the 1795 flashback sequence.

SIXTEEN

The Rumors Are True!

Gossip Girl and the Cooptation of the Cult Fan

ELENA BONOMO

In September of 2007, when discussing *Gossip Girl* (2007–2012), the newest television show on the burgeoning network The CW, executive vice president for marketing and brand strategy Rick Haskins explained: "We're starting to cross-pollinate different mediums. . . . We're trying to make all mediums work together."[1] In other words, the producers of *Gossip Girl*—like those of *Dawson's Creek* (1998–2003), *Lost* (2004–2010), and *Heroes* (2006–2010), among others—have embraced convergence. They have created a transmedia story. One that, as in the words of Henry Jenkins, "unfolds across multiple media platforms, with each new text making a distinctive and valuable contribution to the whole."[2] The distinctive and valuable texts of *Gossip Girl* include: (1) a serial novel, conceptualized by the "book packager" 17th Street Productions (now called Alloy Entertainment) as a transmedia story and accredited to Cecily von Ziegesar; (2) the television show, aired on The CW television network, streamed on The CW website, and sold on iTunes; (3) additional web content, including (a) a fictional blog, penned in the voice of the show's anonymous narrator "Gossip Girl" and featuring in-depth episode recaps, character background information, and additional narratives, interactive maps, still photos, and space for viewer/user comments; (b) music downloads of songs featured on the show; (c) message boards; (d) links to "The Upper East Side," the *Gossip Girl* Second Life property; (e) space for viewer/users to make their own blogs; and (f) additional streaming content, including video interviews with cast members and producers and "behind-the-scenes featurettes"; and (4) mobile content (specifically for users of Verizon Wireless), including downloadable ringtones, videos, character interviews, episode recaps, episode previews, character biographies, and wallpapers, as well as text message alerts from characters on the show.

Accordingly, the content of *Gossip Girl* flows across several media platforms—from serial novel, to television screen, to computer screen, to mobile device—and thus incorporates multiple media industries, while anticipating and demanding a more active media audience. Here, I will discuss how *Gossip Girl* not only appropriates fan practices once described as "cult" into the "mainstream," but also distinguishes itself from other texts in this "age of media convergence" by embedding convergence culture into the narrative itself.

In his explanation of transmedia storytelling, Jenkins notes not only a shift in how stories are told but also a shift in the nature of the stories themselves: "More and more, storytelling has become the art of world building, as artists create compelling environments that cannot be fully explored or exhausted within a single work or even a single medium."[3] While Jenkins sees potential for both artists and audiences alike in "world building," he also aligns such practices with how cult texts—including *Star Trek*, *Star Wars*, and *Buffy the Vampire Slayer*, among many others—have generated similar forms of audience engagement. Still, Jenkins claims that "the Web has made visible the hidden compromises that enabled participatory culture and commercial culture to coexist throughout much of the twentieth century."[4] As commercial culture addresses these specialized, participatory audiences, Matt Hills's fears of media producers co-opting cult TV seem to have been realized.

Accordingly, *Gossip Girl* fits almost perfectly into the mold that Hills constructs of "how one would go about designing a cult show."[5] He begins: "A good start would be to use key production personnel who have worked in the past on shows included in fans' 'intertextual network' of cult shows."[6] Appropriately, *Gossip Girl* executive producers Josh Schwartz and Stephanie Savage were made famous through their work on *The O.C.*, another teen show certainly included in the "intertextual network" of shows that blur the distinctions between "cult" and "mainstream." Hills continues: "One might also cast a mixture of unknown actors/actresses as well as one or two that have appeared in previous cult shows."[7] Among

Figure 16.1. *Gossip Girl* (2007–2012)

the cast of *Gossip Girl*, Blake Lively (who plays Serena van der Woodsen) garnered initial fan appreciation through her role as Bridget in *Sisterhood of the Traveling Pants*, another Alloy Entertainment transmedia success.

While *Gossip Girl* is not based on the typical "science-fiction/fantasy/horror" premise of shows like *Buffy the Vampire Slayer* or *The X-Files*, as Hills suggests, the world of *Gossip Girl* is still undeniably a fantasy. For most viewers, the lifestyle of these wealthy high school students—a life of extravagant parties, underage drinking, drug use, and casual sex—is completely foreign, but made "familiar to fans" through the ongoing narration of the character Gossip Girl and through audience identification with other characters outside of this community (characters who must also learn the lifestyle).[8] While the narrative of *Gossip Girl* revolves around a "mystery or narrative puzzle that will never be answered"—who is Gossip Girl?—several characters (including Blair and Chuck and Lily and Rufus) are "narratively blocked from consummating their love or attraction."[9] As a manufactured cult text, *Gossip Girl* once again aligns itself with the show *Dawson's Creek* and with what Hills, in another article, dubs as the "mainstream cult."[10]

In his definitive essay "*Star Trek* Rerun, Reread, Rewritten: Fan Writing as Textual Poaching," Jenkins describes "fandom" as "a vehicle for marginalized subcultural groups . . . to pry open space for their cultural concerns within dominant representations" and as "a way of appropriating media texts and rereading them in a fashion that serves different interests."[11] Yet, fans of these mainstream cults, including *Gossip Girl*, need not "pry open space for their cultural concerns within dominant representations" because the dominant representations—the shows and their producers—have provided and thereby co-opted that space. In The CW-generated polls on the *Gossip Girl* message boards, fans not only have the opportunity to voice their opinions, but those opinions also can then be used by The CW for its commercial advantage. Thus, in this age of media convergence, catering to the "migratory behavior of media audiences who will go almost anywhere in search of the kinds of entertainment experiences they want" is not without commercial imperatives. Convergence is the attempt to co-opt the cult fan and the cult text.

While *Gossip Girl*, as a transmedia, mainstream cult text, has precursors in other television shows like *Dawson's Creek*, *Lost*, and *Heroes*, *Gossip Girl* distinguishes itself from these precursors by featuring notions of convergence as part of the narrative itself. More specifically, the narrator Gossip Girl and the other characters in the show use multiple media platforms to circulate narratives—or the gossip upon which the show is based—to their peers, "who will go almost anywhere in search of the kinds of entertainment experiences they want." Though every episode features the characters using multiple media platforms to share and to learn about the most current gossip in the world of the show, the episode "All About My Brother" serves as a particularly appropriate case study of how *Gossip Girl* promotes convergence culture as crucial to the lives of teenagers, though uncontrollable by those who do not understand it.

At the start of the episode, Gossip Girl (Kristen Bell) announces, in voice-over as always, the outrageous rumors circulating about the dueling protagonists, Blair Waldorf (Leighton Meester) and Jenny Humphrey (Taylor Momsen). As Blair (known on the blogs as "The Queen B") and Jenny (known as "Little J") and their respective entourages scale the steps outside the Metropolitan Museum of Art, Gossip Girl resolves: "It looks like the battle between 'The Queen B' and 'Little J' has moved from the streets to the blogs." In this world, mediated rumors are equally as destructive as face-to-face slander or physical abuse.

Meanwhile, Jenny's interactions with her father Rufus Humphrey (Matthew Settle) show how transmedia stories, though pervasive, are difficult to control, especially for adults. Though Rufus acknowledges the importance of media, he still does not know how to harness their power. After Jenny lies about going to choir practice (when she is going to a party at her boyfriend Asher's house), Rufus visits his friend and former lover Lily van der Woodsen (Kelly Rutherford) for a "mother's advice." As Lily tries on wedding dresses (in preparation for her imminent nuptials to Bart Bass), Rufus explains his dilemma: "I tell [Jenny] she can't see Asher; she calls him. I take away her phone; they are on iChat. How can you keep them from growing up when they can have a full relationship from the confines of their own bedrooms?" Lily responds: "The answer is you can't. She's going to grow up no matter what!" In this exchange, the adults not only blur the distinctions between virtual and "full" or physical relationships, but also acknowledge that the communicative properties of new media are unstoppable. The parents must simply trust that their children know how to use them appropriately.

Rufus then admits that raising his son Dan was "so much easier." While Lily attributes this discrepancy in child-rearing to the differences between boys and girls in general, perhaps raising Dan was easier for Rufus because Dan is professedly an outsider to this media-consuming teen community. Though Dan uses a cell phone, Dan does not read "Gossip Girl"; thereby Rufus can understand and control Dan more easily.

Furthermore, Dan's removal from this community also prohibits him from effectively communicating with his sister. When Dan (Penn Badgley) spies Jenny's boyfriend Asher (Jesse Swenson) kissing another boy, Dan attempts to tell his sister in person. Yet, Jenny will not listen. Thus, Dan seeks help from Blair and his girlfriend Serena, both of whom understand the power of transmedia storytelling. Blair ruthlessly explains, "All that matters to someone like Jenny right now are the four Gs—Guys, Girlfriends, and Gossip Girl." Serena kindly attests, "It's true. Don't feel bad. Unless it's coming from one of them, she's not going to hear it." Following their advice, Dan decides to text his knowledge of Asher anonymously to Gossip Girl, hoping that Jenny will finally listen to him. Yet, Dan is ineffective once again. Gossip Girl and her readers doubt Dan's claim. Though Dan physically saw Asher, he has no "proof"—he does not have a picture. Unlike Dan, masters of these transmedia stories understand that multiple media platforms—for example, phone and camera—are necessary for the most successful communicative experiences.

In the end of the episode, Blair, "The Queen B," proves herself as one of these masters; she fully understands the power of stories that move through multiple mediums. In a final effort to sabotage her opponent Jenny, Blair steals Asher's cell phone. When her friends ask what she will do with it, she elusively explains: "It was once said that a person's eyes are the windows to their soul—that was before people had cell phones!" At the same time, the viewer sees Blair forwarding the texts in Asher's inbox to the email account on Blair's computer. While Asher's cell phone may hold incriminating evidence about him (and Jenny, by association), Blair knows that the stories will only gain power when moving through media. At the conclusion of the episode, when Blair triumphantly reads Gossip Girl's blog report of Jenny's tragic fall from grace, the viewer understands the complete transmedia progression of this story. Blair earns her status as high school "royalty" by employing the full potential of each media platform to share her knowledge. Accordingly, through viewer identification with these characters, *Gossip Girl* thereby encourages such media use to its audience, who can narrativize their own lives by reading the *Gossip Girl* blog and by using Verizon Wireless phones.

Ultimately, *Gossip Girl*—the book, the television show, the website—is a transmedia story that promotes transmedia stories. While Jenkins envisions the creative potential in such texts, one cannot deny the glaringly obvious commercial incentives for transmedia storytellers. Still, the promise of these incentives has yet to be fully realized—*Gossip Girl* struggles in maintaining enough viewers to solidify its place on the weekly television schedule. Do audiences truly want these multimedia entertainment experiences? Or have the conglomerate media industries become so engrossed in moving "content" across media, to achieve total economic potential, that they have overlooked the audience's desires? The future of *Gossip Girl* will certainly provide an interesting answer.

Notes

1. Chad Gervich, "Networks Struggle with Web Marketing," *Variety*, September 11, 2007, http://www.variety.com/article/VR1117971809.html?categoryid=1060&cs=1.

2. Henry Jenkins, *Convergence Culture: Where Old and New Media Collide* (New York: New York University Press, 2006), 95–96.

3. Ibid., 114.

4. Ibid., 137.

5. Matt Hills, "Defining Cult TV: Texts, Inter-texts, and Fan Audiences," in *The Television Studies Reader*, edited by Robert C. Allen and Annette Hill (London: Routledge, 2004), 520.

6. Ibid., 520.

7. Ibid.

8. Ibid.

9. Ibid.

10. Matt Hills, "*Dawson's Creek*: 'Quality Teen TV' and 'Mainstream Cult,'" in *Teen*

TV: Genre, Consumption, and Identity, edited by Glyn Davis and Kay Dickinson (London: BFI, 2004), 55–67.

11. Henry Jenkins, "*Star Trek* Rerun, Reread, Rewritten: Fan Writing as Textual Poaching," in *Television: The Critical View*, edited by Horace Newcomb, 5th ed. (New York: Oxford University Press, 1994), 450.

SEVENTEEN

The Trouble with Transmediation

Fandom's Negotiation of Transmedia Storytelling Systems

SUZANNE SCOTT

Transmedia storytelling, defined by Henry Jenkins in *Convergence Culture: Where Old and New Media Collide* as a narrative that "unfolds across multiple media platforms, with each new text making a distinct and valuable contribution to the whole," has been rapidly adopted as a content model and cross-promotional device for media properties with fannish appeal.[1] Jenkins, accordingly, makes a compelling argument for why transmedia storytelling systems hold allure and creative potential for fans. Invoking Pierre Lévy's definition of texts that function as cultural attractors, creating a circuit of expression where the activity of creators and interpreters mutually sustains each other, Jenkins extends Lévy's terminology to discuss how transmedia texts are both cultural attractors and "cultural activator[s], setting into motion their decipherment, speculation and elaboration."[2] This desire to decipher, speculate, and expand has always been affiliated with fans' textual play and production, filling in narrative gaps and exploring textual excesses through the creation of fanfiction, fanart, vids, and role-playing games (RPGs). Consequently, we can argue that a text doesn't need to be conceptualized as a transmedia story to function as a cultural activator, as fans have been unofficially unfolding narratives across multiple media platforms for generations.

What does distinguish commercial transmedia narratives from their unofficial, fan-created counterparts is their implicit promise to decentralize authorship and promote collaboration, both between creators in different mediums and creators and fans. While Jenkins stresses the decentralized or collaborative model of authorship these systems foster,[3] he offers an important qualification that "the most successful transmedia franchises have emerged when a single creator or creative unit maintains control,"[4] thus problematizing a reading of these systems as democratizing creative ownership. Borrowing Roberta Pearson's language, this is "the Jekyll and Hyde of transmedia storytelling."[5] For all of the rich encyclopedic and elaborative narrative potential that transmedia stories offer creators and fans, the commercial imperative that underlies their creation and the consumptive demands and creative strictures they place on fans have received little scholarly attention. This has resulted in a conflict between those who claim that transmedia storytelling systems offer fans sophisticated webs of content to explore and enhance, and those who see these webs as precisely that: a mode of confining and regulating fannish analysis and textual production.

The goal of this project is to momentarily abandon the utopian readings of transmedia storytelling as "Jekyll" and begin to articulate a number of reasons that audiences and fans could construct transmedia storytelling as "Hyde." Specifically, I'm interested in how emerging transmedia storytelling systems and "authorized" or "official" ancillary content such as podcasts and webisodes reinforce the textual authority of a limited few, even as the text itself expands. This concurrent narrative expansion and constriction of textual authority leads to what Roberta Pearson identifies as the central paradox of transmedia storytelling and convergence culture at large: "that the very digital media that have been hailed as blurring lines between producers and consumers and creating a more participatory culture instead reinforce cultural hierarchies."[6] These hierarchies are, unsurprisingly, strictly gendered, an issue I point to briefly below but one that deserves further analysis.

This critique adopts Pearson's Jekyll/Hyde dichotomy precisely because I don't view transmedia storytelling, its proponents, or the commercial nature of these systems as inherently nefarious. That said, deeply embedded within transmedia storytelling's creative potential is a presumed consumption and comprehension of all of the cross-media narrative elements, a fannish mastery of an ever-expanding canon. It is the time and labor that goes into mediating the various flows of a transmedia story, and how those flows in turn mediate fan consumption and production, that is of central concern to me.

The creative constraints transmedia storytelling systems place on fans come in a series of interrelated forms: First, there is the temporal control of intensified consumption that transmedia narratives encourage. For example, a fan of *Heroes* in any given week could be consuming a television episode, print comic books, and webcomics, rewatching episodes online alongside commentary with the creators and cast, exploring a choose-your-own adventure-style branching narrative steeped in the show's mythology, reading a tie-in novel, poring over the official *Heroes* wiki, exploring websites for the fictional Pinehearst Company or Primatech Paper (among others), creating a character to be potentially featured in *Heroes* webisodes, and so on.[7] Thus, while a narrative nugget of information dispatched in any of these forms could prove inspirational for fans, the creative window of opportunity for them to play within the ever-evolving transmedia narrative has shrunk considerably. Fans who wish to explore the narrative gaps in the canon through the creation of their own fan texts find them either already filled in by the show's creators or difficult to develop before another piece of the transmedia narrative overwrites or negates it.

We can read this shrinking window of time for fans to textually engage with an unfolding canonical narrative as an exacerbated form of what Matt Hills calls "just-in-time fandom."[8] Placing Hills's claim that "practices of fandom have become increasingly enmeshed within the rhythms and temporalities of broadcasting,"[9] in a convergence context, I share Hills's anxiety that a simplistic reading of this trend as "a techno-evolution towards fuller 'interactivity' neglects the extent to which this eradication of the [analog fanzine] 'time lag' works ever more insistently to discipline and regulate the opportunities for temporally-licensed 'feedback,' and the very horizons of the fan experience."[10] Transmedia storytelling strives to eradicate these time lags altogether, formulating a new "just-in-time fandom" that is defined by an increased rate of consumption and canonical mastery, rather than fannish analysis and textual production.

Consequently, we might view this adoption of transmedia storytelling techniques and ancillary content models as a two-pronged industrial attack on the current drive towards time shifting. While we can assume that fannish rhythms of reception[11] ensure that a new installment of a text will be consumed on (or shortly after) its original airdate or release date, positioning a series within a web of transmedia content that has direct bearing on the unfolding serial narrative offers fans incentives to eradicate time shifting, thus maximizing ratings and downloads. Moreover, this ancillary content is routinely located on the series' official website, offering alternative revenue streams for the network as they concurrently promote the show and make strides towards upgrading television's failing commercial model.

Moving beyond the temporal demands transmedia models potentially place on fans, we arrive at a second issue: in transmedia's efforts to create a "unified and coordinated entertainment experience,"[12] a unification of interpretive meaning is frequently a by-product. This unifier of meaning, tasked with keeping the fictional world that is being built in order, is frequently a male author-god. Jenkins uses *The Matrix*'s Wachowski siblings for his test case,[13] but contemporary examples of transmedia fanboy author-gods abound: George Lucas, Ron Moore, Joss Whedon, Eric Kripke, Josh Schwartz, J. J. Abrams, Tim Kring, and the list goes on. These masculine voices of authority, referred to as "The Powers That Be" (or TPTB) in fan communities, are implicitly invoked in their role as continuity watchdogs, and vocally and visibly confirmed as the creative authority over the text through acknowledgments and interviews.

For example, Ron Moore is positioned as *Battlestar Galactica*'s transmedia figurehead through a number of channels: first and foremost, as the show's creator, but also through his weekly episodic podcasts (where he serves as a mouthpiece and interpreter of the text on behalf of the property's entire creative team), and in multiple interviews with other authors under *Battlestar Galactica*'s transmedia umbrella. The writers of the various *Battlestar Galactica* comic book series (*Zarek*, *Season Zero*, etc.) are particularly quick to stress the canonic ties of their transmedia contributions, assuring fans that "every aspect of the comic universe is run directly through Ron Moore's office."[14] Thus, for every example of *Battlestar Galactica* allowing other authors to help construct their transmedia story, Moore is perpetually reinforced as textual foreman and his interpretation becomes the one definitive, "correct" reading of textual events.

The result, according to fan and scholar Kristina Busse, is that "certain groups of fans can become legit if and only if they follow certain ideas, don't become too rebellious, too pornographic, don't read too much against the grain."[15] The "certain groups of fans" Busse is referring to, those too "pornographic," those who "read too much against the grain," are likely the writers and readers of slash fiction, the creators and consumers of slash art and vids. Historically celebrated in the first wave of fan studies in the early 1990s for their subversive reading of heteronormative popular culture texts, slash as a form of fan production has been dominated by female authors and readers. Consequently, while Busse's concerns might be directed towards slash fans specifically, they're directed generally at female fans, their reading practices, and their gradual exclusion as "legitimate fans" in this convergence model.

This concern is compounded by the fact that transmedia stories present an opportunity to push queer readings or queer characters to the periphery of the narrative, allowing for a concurrent acknowledgment of the homoerotic subtext that inspires slash fiction and a ghettoization of such readings, isolating them from the primary commercial text the fandom revolves around. Two recent examples[16] would be Buffy's lesbian experimentation in issue 12 of the *Buffy the Vampire Slayer Season 8* comic book series and the outing of Lieutenant Felix Gaeta and Lieutenant Hoshi as lovers in *Battlestar Galactica*'s second set of webisodes, entitled "The Face of the Enemy."

As Jenkins divides convergence-era creators into "prohibitionist" and "collaborationist" camps with regard to fan production,[17] it forces us to interrogate the prohibitionist tactics of transmedia storytelling systems' "collaborationist" objectives. To some degree, we could see transmedia narratives as a more covert form of cease-and-desist letters, creatively (rather than legally) prohibiting fans from certain interpretations of or elaborations on the text. As transmedia storytelling reinforces the boundaries between "official" and "unofficial" narrative expansion, often resulting in a celebration of authorial intent and establishing the fanboy auteur as a key player in how convergence culture is shaped, it has also appropriated fan labor for its own promotional gain. Theoretically, the acknowledgment and distribution of fantexts by a show's creative and corporate overseers could be read as a decisive break from prohibitionist tactics, but these instances of collaborationist fan outreach are fraught with legal and promotional ties, and gendered implications.

One example is the *Battlestar Galactica* Videomaker Toolkit, which launched in 2007. In exchange for offering vidders and fan filmmakers raw material from the television series in the form of audio and video files, fans would turn over the rights to their finished vid to SciFi and attach a promotional tag for the show to the end of their clip. Thus, fans traded ownership over their finished product in exchange for heightened visibility and an aura of professional validation. Importantly, the raw material offered to fans was primarily comprised of clips of gun battles, Centurian robots, and ships careening through space, fodder that would prove most inspirational to action or science fiction narratives, and certainly targeted male fan filmmakers over vidders. Vidding, a fan practice dominated by women, relies on popular music and footage of characters to create relationship-centric music videos. The fact that there was no footage of characters from the show made available to fans, and that the Videomaker Toolkit rules strictly forbade use of copyrighted material outside of that offered on the site, severely limited the types of fantexts that could be produced.

We also need to distinguish between the overtly commercial components of transmedia stories (e.g., novels, video games, comic books, etc.) and the supposedly "free" ancillary content offered through official websites that often have just as much bearing on the unfolding transmedia narrative as their overtly commercial counterparts. Fandom, and to some degree the Internet at large, operates as a gift economy. Lewis Hyde, in *The Gift: Imagination and the Erotic Life of Property*, distinguishes gift economies from commodity culture in their ability to establish a relationship between the person giving the gift and the person receiving,[18] creating a communal bond founded on a sense of obligation and reciprocity.[19]

While it's easy to critique transmedia storytelling's motives on purely economic terms, ancillary content models such as those adopted by *Heroes* and *Battlestar Galactica* exist somewhere in between commodity culture and a gift economy. Taking on the guise of a gift economy by offering fans transmedia tokens, these systems strive to build relationships with fans and integrate themselves into fan communities while simultaneously establishing a series of tolls and fees in the form of ads, and commercials, and allowing fans to reciprocate only within a strict set of legal and ideological parameters. Gift economies have routinely been theorized as "feminine" economic systems that are most clearly evident in female fan communities, and attempts to professionalize and monetize fan practices by men outside those communities, such as the case with FanLib, have been swiftly and vocally rejected. Ancillary content models, I would argue, could be seen as something of a regifting economy.[20] Their liminal placement between the commercial culture of transmedia narratives and fandom's gift economy leaves fan-oriented web content striving to regift fan culture and fan narratives back to fandom, with promotional strings attached.

Fittingly, since I began by addressing transmedia storytelling within a Jekyll/Hyde framework, I'd like to return to this construct to close by pointing towards one of transmedia's greatest potential threats: its ability to fracture fandom and studies of fandom into two gendered camps, instead of focusing on its intersections and questioning binary assumptions about how fans consume and produce. Male fans, essentialized through their affiliation with canonical mastery, collection, and a presumed desire to "go pro" or develop a close relationship with creators, are arguably those being catered to by transmedia narratives and ancillary content models. In turn, they become fandom's Jekyll, held up as pure consumers, "proper" fans. Female fans, then, become Hyde: outside of transmedia's control by choice, and thus textually and legally threatening. Jenkins acknowledges that the "current configuration of the entertainment industry makes transmedia expansion an economic imperative," and notes that only "the most gifted transmedia artists [can] surf these market pressures to create a more expansive and immersive story."[21] I would contend that a greater challenge is posed to fans surfing and mediating the narrative flow of transmedia stories to remain artists in their own right.

Notes

1. Henry Jenkins, *Convergence Culture: Where Old and New Media Collide* (New York: New York University Press, 2006), 95–96.

2. Ibid., 95.

3. Ibid., 96.

4. Ibid., 106.

5. Roberta Pearson, "Participation or Totalization: Fans and Transmedia Storytelling," paper presented at the "Television and the Digital Public Sphere" conference, Université Paris II, October 23, 2008.

6. Ibid.

7. The bulk of the aforementioned transmedia content is accessed through NBC's official *Heroes* website (http://www.nbc.com/Heroes/).

8. Matt Hills, *Fan Cultures* (New York: Routledge, 2002), 178–179.

9. Ibid., 178.

10. Ibid., 179.

11. Reworking Tania Modleski's turn of phrase from her 1983 essay "The Rhythms of Reception: Daytime Television and Women's Work," my construction of fans' rhythms of reception inverts the presumptions about the daytime audience/housewife's mode of distracted viewership.

12. Henry Jenkins, "Transmedia Storytelling 101," Confessions of an Aca-Fan: The Official Weblog of Henry Jenkins, March 22, 2007, http://henryjenkins.org/2007/03/transmedia_storytelling_101.html (accessed March 24, 2007).

13. Jenkins, *Convergence Culture*, 93–130.

14. William McCarty, "Brandon Jerwa on New *Battlestar Galactica: Season Zero*," Newsarama.com, http://forum.newsarama.com/showthread.php?t=113605 [Addendum 2017: URL no longer active].

15. Kristina Busse, "Podcasts and the Fan Experience of Disseminated Media Com-

mentary," October 2006, available at Ephemeral Traces, May 1, 2007, https://kbusse.wordpress.com/2007/05/01/my-presentation-for-flow-2006/.

16. Notably, both of these shows have featured homosexual characters. In the case of Buffy, it is her precarious feminine/feminist positioning that makes her queering especially controversial. In the case of *Battlestar Galactica*, lesbianism is alternately framed as heterosexist fantasy (Gaius's ménage à trois with Six and D'Anna), or devolving into violence/abuse (as with another transmedia example, from the TV movie *Razor*, which explores the relationship between Admiral Cain and Gina). Both of these transmedia flirtations with homosexuality are tempered by the fact that Gaeta is revealed to be bisexual (perhaps as a direct result of his tryst with the Eight on New Caprica that is revealed in the webisodes), and Buffy's experimentation is dubbed a "one-time thing" by the character and creators alike.

17. Jenkins, *Convergence Culture*, 134.

18. Lewis Hyde, *The Gift: Imagination and the Erotic Life of Property* (New York: Vintage, 1983), xx.

19. Ibid., 86.

20. I expand on the term "regifting economy" in "Repackaging Fan Culture: The Regifting Economy of Ancillary Content Models," *Transformative Works and Cultures* 3 (Fall 2009), doi:10.3983/twc.2009.0150.

21. Jenkins, "Transmedia Storytelling 101."

Contributors

About the Editors

Roxanne Samer is Visiting Faculty in Visual and Media Arts at Grand Valley State University. In 2016–2017, she served as Postdoctoral Scholar/Teaching Fellow in Cinema and Media Studies at the University of Southern California. She was the editor of *Spectator* 37, no. 2 (Fall 2017), a special issue dedicated to the study of transgender media, and she has published peer-reviewed essays in *Jump Cut*, *Feminist Media Histories*, and *Ada: A Journal of Gender, New Media, and Technology*.

William Whittington is the Assistant Chair of Cinema and Media Studies at the University of Southern California. In the School of Cinematic Arts, he has served as the managing editor for USC's film and television journal *Spectator* since 2002 and was formerly the curator of the USC Warner Bros. Archives. Dr. Whittington is the author of *Sound Design and Science Fiction* (University of Texas Press, 2007), and he is working on a new book entitled *Sound Design and Horror*.

About the Contributors

Harry M. Benshoff is Professor of Media Arts at the University of North Texas. Dr. Benshoff is the author of *Monsters in the Closet: Homosexuality and the Horror Film* (Manchester University Press, 1997) and *Dark Shadows* (Wayne State University Press, 2011); most recently he edited *A Companion to the Horror Film* (Wiley/Blackwell, 2014). With Sean Griffin, he co-authored *America on Film: Representing Race, Class, Gender, and Sexuality at the Movies* (Blackwell, 2009 [2004]), and *Queer Images: A History of Gay and Lesbian Film in America* (Rowman & Littlefield, 2006). He was also the co-editor of *Queer Cinema: The Film Reader* (Routledge, 2004). His numerous essays and book chapters cover topics such as blaxploitation horror films, Hollywood LSD films, *The Talented Mr. Ripley* (1999), *Brokeback Mountain* (2005), *Milk* (2008), and *Twilight* (2008).

Elena Bonomo received her PhD in Critical Studies at the University of Southern California's School of Cinematic Arts, with a dissertation entitled "Channeling Shirley MacLaine: Stardom, Travel, Politics, and Beyond." She received her MA in English with a concentration in film studies from the University of Exeter. She works at the Skirball Cultural Center in Los Angeles.

Jennifer DeClue is Assistant Professor in the Program for the Study of Women and Gender at Smith College. Prof. DeClue's research focuses on queer studies, black feminism, and visual culture. Her analysis of Dee Rees's *Pariah* is forthcoming in *Sisters in the Life: 25 Years of Out African American Lesbian Media-Making (1986–2011)*. Her discussion of black queer erotica appears in *No Tea No Shade: New Writings in Black Queer Studies*. In addition to her academic work, Prof. DeClue has worked as a film programmer for the Outfest Los Angeles LGBT Film Festival.

Anna Everett is Professor of Film, Television, and New Media Studies at the University of California, Santa Barbara. Her many publications include *Returning the Gaze: A Genealogy of Black Film Criticism, 1909–1949* (Duke University Press, 2001); *Learning Race and Ethnicity: Youth and Digital Media* (MIT Press, 2008), for the MacArthur Foundation's Digital Media, Youth, and Learning Program; her award-winning book *Digital Diaspora: A Race for Cyberspace* (State University of New York Press, 2009); and the edited volume *Pretty People* (Rutgers University Press, 2012), among others.

Eric Freedman is Dean of the School of Media Arts at Columbia College Chicago. He is the author of *Transient Images: Personal Media in Public Frameworks* (Temple University Press, 2011).

Hollis Griffin is Assistant Professor in Queer Studies and Media Studies in the Department of Communication at Denison University. He is the author of the book *Feeling Normal: Sexuality and Media Criticism in the Digital Age* (Indiana University Press, 2017). He has also had research published in *Cinema Journal*, *Popular Communication*, *Television and New Media*, *Velvet Light Trap*, *Journal of Popular Film and Television*, *Quarterly Review of Film and Video*, and the anthologies *Film and Sexual Politics* (Cambridge Scholars Press, 2006) and *The Companion to Reality Television* (Wiley, 2014).

Sean Griffin is Professor in the Division of Film and Media Arts at Southern Methodist University Meadows School of the Arts. He received his PhD from the University of Southern California in 1997, and his dissertation became the book *Tinker Belles and Evil Queens: The Walt Disney Company from the Inside Out* (New York University Press, 2000). He is also the author of *Free and Easy: A Defining History of the American Musical Film* (Wiley/Blackwell, 2017) and coauthor of *America on Film: Race, Class, Gender, and Sexuality at the Movies* (Wiley/Blackwell, 2009) and *Queer Images: A History of Lesbian and Gay Film in America* (Rowman & Littlefield, 2005).

Mary Celeste Kearney is Director of Gender Studies and Associate Professor of Film, Television, and Theater at the University of Notre Dame. She is completing work on "Power Chords and Groupie Chicks: Gender and Rock Culture," forthcoming from Oxford University Press, and "Making Their Debut: Teenage Girlhood and the Teen-Girl Entertainment Market, 1938–1966," forthcoming from the University of Texas Press. She is the editor of the Routledge Research in Gender, Sexuality, and Media book series and a member of the executive board of Console-ing Passions.

Marsha Kinder is University Professor Emerita and Professor Emerita of Critical Studies at the University of Southern California. She is the author of more than one hundred published essays and ten books. Her website can be found at www.marshakinder.com.

Amy Lawrence is Professor of Film and Media Studies, and the Parents Distinguished Research Chair in the Humanities at Dartmouth College. Her most recent book is *The Passion of Montgomery Clift* (University of California Press, 2010).

Christie Milliken is Associate Professor and Chair of the Department of Communication, Popular Culture, and Film at Brock University in Ontario, Canada. She is the author of numerous book chapters and journal articles on a range of subjects, including sex education film and video, 1960s film and film culture, environmental documentary, and gender and cinema. She sits on the editorial board of the *Canadian Journal of Film Studies* and is coediting, with Steve Anderson, an anthology entitled "Rethinking Popular Documentary."

Scott D. Paulin is Lecturer in Musicology at Northwestern University's Bienen School of Music. His articles on topics related to music and film have appeared in the volumes *Music and Cinema* (Wesleyan University Press, 2000) and *Wagner and Cinema* (Indiana University Press, 2010) and in the journals *American Music*, *Music and the Moving Image*, and *Opera Quarterly*, among others.

Raffi Sarkissian is a PhD candidate at the Annenberg School for Communication and Journalism at the University of Southern California. His research covers new modes of representation and participation, from traditional to digital media. His dissertation analyzes the intersection of the popular and political in contemporary LGBT movements and media cultures. He has published a book chapter on the queer conventions of TV's *Glee* in *Queer Youth and Media Cultures* (edited by Christopher Pullen, Palgrave Macmillan, 2014).

Suzanne Scott is Assistant Film Professor in the Department of Radio-Television-Film at the University of Texas, Austin.

Gaylyn Studlar is David May Distinguished University Professor in the Humanities at Washington University in St. Louis, where she directs the Program in Film and Media Studies. Her most recent books are *Have Gun—Will Travel* (Wayne State University Press, 2015) and *Precocious Charms: Stars Performing Girlhood in Classical Hollywood Cinema* (University of California Press, 2013).

Stephen Tropiano is Associate Professor of Screen Studies at the Ithaca College Los Angeles Program and editor of the *Journal of Film and Video*.

Melissa Williams received her PhD in American Studies at the University of Minnesota in 2009. Her dissertation, "Excuse the Mess, but We Live Here: Class, Gender, and Identity in the Post–Cold War Working-Class Family Sitcom," expands on the themes initially explored in her 2005 article on Roseanne Barr reprinted here. She continues to work in higher education as an instructional designer.

Index